# ADVANCE PRAISE FOR

## AT PLAY IN THE LIONS' DE[N]
### A Biography and Memoir of Daniel [Berrigan]

"As Jim Forest's biography demonstrates, Daniel Berrigan's life was a full measure of grace that soared up and flowed out of all those times and places that witnessed his unyielding personal commitment in word and deed to peace and social justice, his deep compassion and disarming humor, and the consistently heroic levels of his nonviolent resistance that took our breath away and renewed the face of the earth."
—Martin Sheen

"Jim Forest's account of Dan Berrigan's life summons intense interest in how Dan became a lifelong follower of Jesus. The memoir opens the door for younger generations to encounter a challenging, enormously talented Jesuit who simply wouldn't tolerate war."
—Kathy Kelly, Co-coordinator,
Voices for Creative Nonviolence

"As a young activist, who had been kicked out of my home church over the issues of race and war, Daniel Berrigan was the first Christian I heard of who was against the war in Vietnam. So thank you Dan, for keeping my hope of faith in Christ alive. You were among the biblical prophets who showed us the way. And thank you, Jim Forest, for this superlative spiritual writing."
—Jim Wallis, *Sojourners*

"'If you want to follow Jesus, you better look good on wood!' Daniel Berrigan coined that phrase. In this extraordinary biography and memoir, Jim Forest, who knew Berrigan intimately, shows us that Daniel Berrigan looked every bit the good prophet on wood. This is a first-rate story that needs to be read. Highly recommended."
—Ronald Rolheiser, O.M.I., Oblate School of Theology, San Antonio, TX

"Resurrection!! Daniel Berrigan's vim and vision and vitality crackle out of the pages of Jim Forest's book. My uncle is alive in this book: in the stories and remembrances Forest collects, in the author's sharing of his own long friendship with Dan, and in his savvy situating of Dan's life within the life of the Jesuit Order, the Catholic Church, and war and peace and countless movements for justice. Dan Berrigan, Presente!"
—Frida Berrigan

"Thanks to Jim Forest's faithful, joyful portrait of Dan Berrigan's transforming life, here is Dan in our face and hearts all over again—challenging us, loving us, pushing us to give up war and every form of violence. Jim takes us on a walk with Dan and Jesus into that community of communities where everyone on earth is together, 'laughing, drinking beer, and listening to rain battering the windows.' Thank you, Daniel. And thank you, Jim."

—Jim Douglass, author, *JFK and the Unspeakable*

"*At Play in the Lions' Den* takes us into the heart of this very human prophet on his journey where Jesus seems to tell him, as he told Peter, 'You will stretch out your hands and somebody else will put a belt round you and take you where you would rather not go.' (John 21:18) And we know Dan kept his joyful smile, even as he ended up in a difficult place, as prophets generally do. Jim Forest's life has been deeply touched by Dan Berrigan and after reading his memoir, you will know another dedicated and prophetic follower of Jesus."

—Bishop Thomas J. Gumbleton, Detroit

"This beautiful, arresting book about Daniel Berrigan is an introduction into the many lives of a brilliant, holy genius who used all of his gifts for God, and so invites us all to follow his loving example."

—Fr. William Hart McNichols, Painter and Iconographer

"There is no better general introduction to the life of Dan Berrigan, one of the greatest Christians of our age, of any age, than this deeply researched, highly personal, beautifully written biography by his friend Jim Forest. He has captured Dan the poet, the prophet, and the priest. And what a poet! What a prophet! What a priest!"

—James Martin, S.J., author, *The Jesuit Guide to Almost Everything*

"Who better than a literate peacemaker like Jim Forest to tell the story of dear Dan Berrigan and all his commitments to nonviolence. And tell it so well."

—Colman McCarthy, author, *I'd Rather Teach Peace*

"It is hard to deny that God prepares and then uses certain people for very special tasks. As you will see, that is eminently the case with Daniel Berrigan—but also for Jim Forest who seems to always know who is worth writing about, and how to do the writing. Read, and enter into a much larger world."

—Richard Rohr, O.F.M., Center for Action and Contemplation

# AT PLAY IN THE LIONS' DEN

**A Biography and Memoir of Daniel Berrigan**

# AT PLAY IN THE LIONS' DEN

## A Biography and Memoir of Daniel Berrigan

JIM FOREST

ORBIS BOOKS
Maryknoll, New York 10545

ORBIS ✪ BOOKS
**Maryknoll, New York 10545**

**Fathers and Brothers**
**MARYKNOLL**™

Second Printing, June 2018

Founded in 1970, Orbis Books endeavors to publish works that enlighten the mind, nourish the spirit, and challenge the conscience. The publishing arm of the Maryknoll Fathers and Brothers, Orbis seeks to explore the global dimensions of the Christian faith and mission, to invite dialogue with diverse cultures and religious traditions, and to serve the cause of reconciliation and peace. The books published reflect the views of their authors and do not represent the official position of the Maryknoll Society. To learn more about Maryknoll and Orbis Books, please visit our website at www.maryknollsociety.org.

*Design: Roberta Savage*

Names: Forest, Jim (James H.), author.
Title: At play in the lions' den : a biography and memoir of Daniel Berrigan
 / by Jim Forest.
Description: Maryknoll, NY : Orbis Books, 2017. | Includes bibliographical
 references and index.
Identifiers: LCCN 2017017350 (print) | LCCN 2017022768 (ebook) | ISBN
 9781608337132 (e-book) | ISBN 9781626982482 (pbk.)
Subjects: LCSH: Berrigan, Daniel. | Catholic Church—United
 States—Clergy—Biography. | Priests—United States—Biography. |
 Pacifists—United States—Biography.
Classification: LCC BX4705.B3845 (ebook) | LCC BX4705.B3845 F67 2017 (print)
 | DDC 282.092 [B]—dc23
LC record available at https://lccn.loc.gov/2017017350

*"If you want to follow Jesus you had better look good on wood."*

—*Daniel Berrigan*

For my son Daniel,
who has done much that his namesake Dan Berrigan would value,
and for all the tribe,
Ben, Wendy, Cait, Thom, and Anne,
plus their partners and progeny,
in whom I have so many reasons to rejoice.

# Contents

# Prologue: Peacemaking Is Hard

    hard almost as war.
The difference being one
we can stake life upon
and limb and thought and love.

I stake this poem out
dead man to a dead stick
to tempt an Easter chance—
if faith may be
truth, our evil chance
penultimate at last,

not last. We are not lost.

When these lines gathered
of no resource at all
serenity and strength,
it dawned on me

a man stood on his nails

## AT PLAY IN THE LIONS' DEN

an ash like dew, a sweat
smelling of death and life.
our evil Friday fled,
the blind face gently turned
another way. Toward life

A man walks in his shroud.
— *Daniel Berrigan*[1]

# Unindicted Co-conspirators

This book has been a communal endeavor. My heartfelt thanks to all those who assisted me in my research and took time to read, correct, and comment on portions of the manuscript as it evolved, as well as to share stories of Dan, especially John Bach, Michael Baxter, Paul Begheyn, S.J., Jerry Berrigan (son of Phil, a nephew of Dan), Tom Cornell, Joseph Cosgrove (Dan's lawyer for thirty-five years), Carol Crossed, Earl Crow, David Eberhardt, James Gould, S.J., Luke Hansen, S.J., Addison Hart, Steve Kelly, S.J., Anne Klejment, James Martin, S.J., Daniel Mauk, Maureen McCafferty, William Hart McNichols, Fred Ojile, Gordon Oyer, Judy Peluso, Joseph Roccasalvo, Tim Schilling, Carl Siciliano, Thomas Slon, S.J., Gerald Twomey, Mobi Warren, John Williams, and Bill Wylie-Kellermann. My collaborators have greatly enriched these pages.

I owe a particular debt to John Dear, one of Dan's closest friends and coworkers for nearly four decades, as well as executor of Dan's literary estate and editor of several collections of Dan's writings. John devoted countless hours to helping with this project from spark to blaze. Thank you, John. Words are not adequate.

Let me also single out Jim O'Grady and Murray Polner, authors of *Disarmed and Dangerous*,[2] an outstanding dual biography of Dan and Phil that was published in 1997. Apart from Dan's own writings, their book helped me more than any other.

This biography would not exist had it not been for my friend and publisher Robert Ellsberg, who envisioned it, coaxed me into writing it, and who midwifed it week by week as it was taking shape. A word of thanks also goes to all those at Orbis who helped in various ways, especially the production manager, Maria Angelini, and the art director, Roberta Savage, for the layout and design.

Finally, gratitude to my wife, Nancy, who cheered me along and helped greatly as both attentive listener and skilled editor, not to mention font of wisdom.

Halos to one and all! I take credit only for the book's faults, errors, and awkward sentences.

# Introduction:
# In the Lions' Den

Detail from the basilica of Vézely by Jim Forest

*The king commanded and Daniel was brought and cast into the den of lions. The king said to Daniel, "May your God deliver you!" And a stone was brought and laid upon the mouth of the den, and the king sealed it. . . . Then, at break of day, the king arose and went in haste to the den of lions. When he came near to the den where Daniel was, he cried out in a tone of anguish and said to Daniel, "O Daniel, servant of the living God, has your God, whom you serve continually, been able to deliver you from the lions?" Then Daniel said to the king, "My God sent his angel and shut the lions' mouths, and they have not hurt me, because I was found blameless before him."*

—Daniel 6:16–17, 19–22

Daniel in the lions' den was a popular scene in Romanesque stone carving, a visual anticipation of Christ's death and resurrection. In one of the capitals in the basilica of the French town of Vézelay, Daniel is shown as if he were resting on a bed of leaves within an almond-shaped *mandorla* of divine protection. He is no more threatened by the lions on either side of him than I am threatened by Beckett, our household cat. (As I write, I have to confess I have a cat scratch on my right wrist, but Beckett meant no harm—only obliged to leave a token of protest for being unjustly moved.)

Dan Berrigan spent much of his life in various lions' dens—at home as a child when his father was in a rage, in paddy wagons and prisons, in demonstrations that were targets of violent attack, in a city under bombardment, in urban areas police would describe as hazardous—yet remarkably he lived to be ninety-four, dying peacefully in bed, though he bore many invisible scars and scratches.

Like the biblical Daniel, Dan Berrigan was a man of prayer, both private and public. I never knew anyone gladder to celebrate the Eucharist. But, unlike the biblical Daniel, Dan was also a man of play, at play as much in courtrooms and jails as in his apartment assembling a meal for whoever happened to be his guests that night.

I recall him saying, "The worst thing is an omnivorous solemnity." Dan was rarely solemn. I remember one night he and two other friends helped me push my decrepit VW Beetle down a rain-soaked East Harlem street, trying to bring the engine to life, all of us laughing till our bellies ached while Dan told a joke about a nearsighted, sex-starved elephant who mistook a VW for a female elephant that wanted to mate.

For many years Dan lived with a Jesuit community in a building at 220 West 98th Street in Manhattan. Dan had apartment 11L. Once through the door, the many people who were welcomed there found themselves in what might be described as the set for a small Off-Broadway play. Posters and banners, flags and photos were decoratively placed here and there, but what I found most striking was a canticlelike quotation from the great Irish abbess, St. Brigid of Kildare, that Dan had inscribed on one wall, the calligraphy done in black Magic Marker, the text wrapping around his refrigerator:

I should like a great lake of beer for the King of Kings.
I should like the angels of Heaven to be drinking it through time eternal.
I should like excellent meats of belief and pure piety.
I should like flails of penance at my house.
I should like the men of heaven at my house;
I should like barrels of peace at their disposal;
I should like vessels of charity for distribution;
I should like for them cellars of mercy.
I should like cheerfulness to be in their drinking.
I should like Jesus to be there among them.
I should like the three Marys of illustrious renown to be with us.
I should like the people of heaven, the poor, to be gathered around us from all parts.

Barrels of peace, cellars of mercy, meats of belief, flails of penance, the good company of the poor, an assembly brought together from far and near, all gathered with the King of Kings and the three Marys around a great lake of beer. . . . One could shape one's life around so magnetic a vision, so joyful a prophecy, so great an expectation—as compelling a glimpse of heaven as any I have heard. How suitable to discover these holy words in Dan Berrigan's home, a Grand Central Station of hospitality whose countless guests included many who were en route to prison or dying of AIDS.

Inventive man that he was, Dan helped, with his brother Phil, to develop more theatrical forms of protest, civil disobedience, and resistance, and then, as a writer, to transform prosaic events into poetry and theater, as he did in converting the courtroom drama of the trial of the Catonsville Nine into the often-performed play of the same name.

And what could be more theatrical than slipping away, costumed as a giant apostle, from a crowd of FBI agents poised to arrest and handcuff him, thus beginning four months playing hide-and-seek as an underground priest?

Dan was a performer and artist, but his art was rarely art for art's sake. His was a life of lived-out translations of such biblical commandments as "Thou shalt not kill" and "Love one another." How sadly rare it is to find a person—Dan was one of the exceptions—who regards in such a straightforward mandate an obligation to protect life rather than destroy it, even if that requires saying a costly no.

Perhaps Dan's most notable quality was his immense compassion, which guided him one way or another on a daily basis, even late in life when it was a challenge just getting out of bed in the Jesuit infirmary at Fordham University that had become his last home.

I recall Dan using the phrase "outraged love." Many people are driven by rage, which rarely does them or anyone much good and often makes things worse. But outraged love is mainly about love. Dan loved his imperfect church, his not always agreeable Jesuit community, he even loved America—but there was much in all three zones that was outrageous, and Dan was never able to be silent or passive about our betrayals. This could have made him a ranter, but the artist side of Dan always found ways to channel his outrage into one or another form of creativity, whether via poetry or a wide variety of acts of witness. He became one of the most consistent voices of his generation for nonviolent approaches to change and conflict resolution—in that dimension of his life, a spiritual child of Catholic Worker founder Dorothy Day. His commitment to life excluded no one, from a child in the womb to a condemned murderer on death row.

Dan remarked of Dorothy Day, "She lived as if the Gospel were true." The same could be said of Dan. He once said, "If you want to follow Jesus, you had better look good on wood." He didn't mean a Christian had to be a martyr, in the sense of dying for one's faith, but a martyr in the literal meaning of the Greek word *mártys*: a witness. Part of that witness, Dan insisted, is refusing to use death as a means of improving the world, still less creating the kingdom of God.

For the Christian, peacemaking is any action that bears witness to the risen Christ. As Dan said in a talk given at the Abbey of Gethsemani, "To be witnesses of the resurrection is to be contemplative and public all at once."

Dan had countless friends. I was fortunate to be one of them. May this book become an occasion of friendship for those new to his name as we gather around the great lake of beer at which the King of Kings presides and where lions and lambs lie side by side.

*Alkmaar, Holland*
*February 27, 2017*

# Seven Men, Two Women, and Two Wastebaskets of Paper

The Berrigan name is forever linked with Vietnam. The first US military advisers had arrived in Saigon in 1950 when France was fighting a losing battle to retain its colonies in Indochina. France gave up in 1954, following defeat in the Battle of Dien Bien Phu, after which Vietnam was divided, a Communist regime based in Hanoi to the north, a US-backed regime based in Saigon to the south. A national election to bring about unification was supposed to happen, but never did, as it seemed certain to Saigon's sponsors that Hanoi would be the winner. Civil war soon followed.

The slow march into the swamp of a disastrous US-directed war picked up speed as the sixties began, with American troop levels rising year by year to more than half-a-million in 1968. The vast majority of soldiers were draftees who, prior to being sent there, could not have found Vietnam on a world map even if offered a fifty-dollar reward or written fifty words explaining what the war was all about. Few would have gone as volunteers; it had never been a popular war. Opposition grew. By the mid-sixties, for the first time in American history, a large segment of the nation's own population was actively protesting a war in progress. Hundreds of thousands of people had taken part in peace marches, yet the war kept expanding.

By 1968, acts of antiwar protest were increasingly

*"Our apologies, good friends, for the fracture of good order, the burning of paper instead of children, the angering of the orderlies in the front parlor of the charnel house. We could not, so help us God, do otherwise."*
—The Trial of the Catonsville Nine

Phil Berrigan seizing draft files.

*"We say: killing is disorder, life and gentleness and community and unselfishness is the only order we recognize. For the sake of that order we risk our liberty, our good name. The time is past when good men may be silent."*
—The Trial of the Catonsville Nine

becoming acts of resistance. One of the most significant took place in a quiet suburb of Baltimore, Maryland.

May 17, 1968, was proving to be a warm and sunny day in Catonsville when three cars pulled into the parking lot. It was half past noon. The sign in front identified the building as Knights of Columbus Hall, a Catholic organization that took pride in the religious identity of the Italian navigator who had "discovered" America. A casual passerby wouldn't have imagined a draft board was located on the upper floor of the clapboard structure. From this office, letters (Phil Berrigan called them "death certificates") were regularly sent to local young men ordering them to report for physical inspection and, should they be found able-bodied, involuntary induction into the armed forces.

Nine passengers emerged from the cars, two women and seven men, one of whom was wearing a Roman collar—nothing strange about them, though what would have struck an observer as odd were the two wire-mesh wastebaskets they carried with them.

While one of the group, David Darst, stayed below as lookout, the other eight entered the building, ascended the stairs, and walked into the draft board office where three clerks were at work on their typewriters. Tom Lewis, who had visited the office not long before, announced an action against war was about to occur, but he spoke quietly and was ignored by the office staff. Phil Berrigan, the man with the Roman collar, led the way to the file cabinets, and the group began filling their wastebaskets. "My files, my files!" shouted Mary Murphy, one of the clerks, as she fought to take charge of one wastebasket. There was a tussle, but Phil Berrigan easily won the battle. Hoping a passerby might intervene, another clerk, Phyllis Morseberger, threw a telephone out the window, breaking a pane of glass.

In a few minutes the wastebaskets were full—378 files, according to testimony given at the trial—and the group returned to the parking lot. Two bottles of homemade napalm (a flammable liquid widely used in Vietnam that sticks to the skin and causes death or severe burns) were poured on the files.³ A match was lit, and a roar of flame engulfed the paper. Then each of the remaining eight struck a match and added it to the blaze, a token to signify that none of them was merely an onlooker.

Several reporters, a photographer, and a TV cameraman watched it all. They had been tipped off that "a remarkable news event" would occur at Knights of Columbus Hall shortly after noon that day. Exactly what was to happen, they had no idea.

Dan and Phil strike a match.

It would have been a news event no matter who had taken part, but the involvement of two Catholic priests, Daniel and Philip Berrigan, made the headlines even bigger. Phil Berrigan was a familiar face locally; just a few months earlier he had been one of four people who had poured blood on draft files in Baltimore, as had Tom Lewis. At Phil's side was his brother Dan—no Roman collar in his case, but even so, looking clerical in black.

As the fire burned the files, the nine, standing side by side, recited the Our Father.

"We hope," said Dan, "that our action will make it more difficult for men to kill one another."

Reporters were given a press packet that included a statement whose key sentence was the declaration that "some property has no right to exist."

While the files were still burning, the police arrived and took down names and other details. Then several FBI agents arrived and did the same.

It's unlikely that these policemen had ever arrested any

The Catonsville Nine burning draft files with homemade napalm. Baltimore Sun

outlaws more willing to claim responsibility for breaking the law. The nine were as eager as medal-winning athletes that their names be known and to explain what had led them to this obscure parking lot. These were not the sort of people who got in trouble with the law. They were

- Daniel Berrigan, priest of the Society of Jesus, poet, writer, university chaplain, and teacher.
- Philip Berrigan, priest of the Society of Saint Joseph and onetime infantry officer, a man long active in efforts to overcome racism and war.
- David Darst, a Christian Brother, then teaching religion at a Christian Brothers high school that served young black students in Kansas City.
- John Hogan, until recently a Maryknoll Brother who had spent seven years doing mission work in Guatemala.

- Tom Lewis, an artist living in Baltimore.
- Marjorie Bradford Melville, a former Maryknoll nun who had been a teacher in Guatemala, now married to Tom Melville.
- Thomas Melville, former Maryknoll priest, who, in addition to parish duties, had helped found credit and land cooperatives in rural Guatemala, now married to Marjorie Melville.
- George Mische, who previously had worked for the US Agency for International Development in Central America and the Dominican Republic.
- Mary Moylan, a registered nurse and midwife who had worked with nuns in Uganda.

"A full account of the lives of all of the Catonsville Nine," Shawn Francis Peters remarks in his book-length study of the action and its consequences, "represents more than simply a group biography of some quirky radical activists who briefly captured public attention and then faded back into obscurity. It demonstrates how, in perilous times, profound religious and political beliefs can coalesce and motivate sincere individuals to risk their personal freedom in order to resist state policies they deem both illegal and immoral."[4]

Soon the nine, all handcuffed, were in a van bound for processing and arraignment.

Dan Berrigan had written a statement about the event. It quickly gained wide circulation as a manifesto of resistance to the Vietnam War, and became, after that war was long over, a modern classic of dissident literature:

> Our apologies, good friends, for the fracture of good order, the burning of paper instead of children, the angering of the orderlies in the front parlor of the charnel house. We could not, so help us God, do otherwise. For we are sick at heart. Our hearts give us no rest for thinking of the Land of Burning Children and for thinking of that other Child of whom

**Phil and Dan under arrest.** Cornell University, Division of Rare and Manuscript Collections

*"In a time of death some men, the resisters, those who work hardily for social change, those who preach and embrace the truth, such men overcome death, their lives are bathed in the light of the resurrection, the truth has set them free."*
—The Trial of the Catonsville Nine

the poet Luke speaks. The infant was taken up in the arms of an old man whose tongue grew resonant and vatic at the touch of that beauty.

Small consolation, a child born to make trouble and to die for it—the First Jew (not the last) to be subject of a "definitive solution." . . .

All of us who act against the law turn to the poor of the world, to the Vietnamese, to the victims, to the soldiers who kill and die for the wrong reasons, or for no reason at all, because they were so ordered by the authorities of that public order which is in effect a massive institutionalized disorder. We say: Killing is disorder. Life and gentleness and community and unselfishness are the only order we recognize.

For the sake of that order we risk our liberty, our good name. The time is past when good men may be silent, when obedience can segregate men from public risk, when the poor can die without defense. How many indeed must die before our voices are heard? How many must be tortured, dislocated, starved, maddened? How long must the world's resources be raped in the service of legalized murder? When at what point will you say no to this war? We have chosen to say, with the gift of our liberty, if necessary our lives: the violence stops here, the death stops here, the suppression of the truth stops here, this war stops here.

Redeem the times! The times are inexpressibly evil. Christians pay conscious, indeed religious tribute, to Caesar and Mars, by the approval of overkill tactics, by brinkmanship, by nuclear liturgies, by racism, by support of genocide. They embrace their society with all their heart and abandon the cross. They pay lip service to Christ and military service to the powers of death. . . .[5]

# Wolves Howling in the Night

A blue-eyed baby named Daniel Joseph Berrigan was born at home on May 9, 1921, near the town of Virginia in northern Minnesota, a part of the state renowned for its iron mines, lakes, and forests. His first name was chosen by his father in honor of the Irish radical Daniel O'Connell, known as "the Great Emancipator," who, in the first half of the nineteenth century, campaigned for Catholic emancipation, including the right for Catholics to sit in Parliament at Westminster.[6] The biblical meaning of the name Daniel, as he sometimes reminded judges when he stood before them in court later in life, is "God is my judge."

Dan's mother, Frida, born in 1886 in Germany's Black Forest, was four when her father, Wilhelm Fromhart, took ship to America and became a homesteader in a Minnesota that was still largely frontier. After building a log cabin and an outhouse on his forty acres, he dug a well and cleared land for a garden. Wood, nails, tools, and glass cost cash, so he found work in the iron mines. Frida was five when she and her mother, Louise, arrived at Castle Garden at the southern tip of Manhattan and boarded the first of several westbound trains and boats that reunited them with Wilhelm.

Dan's father, Thomas Berrigan, was born in America in 1879. In the early 1850s his father had escaped the social devastation left by the Irish potato famine, crossing the

Dan and older brother Jerry.
Courtesy Berrigan family

Dan at the center, resting his arm on his mother Frida; Grandma Fromhart on the far right. Courtesy Berrigan family

Atlantic from County Tipperary, first settling in Canada, then wandering south into the United States. He was a man with a Paul Bunyan physique. By 1910, when he met twenty-five-year-old Frida, he was driving steam locomotives carrying iron ore and, when not on the rails, running a small farm. Frida later recalled that her friends regarded Tom as "a great catch." They married the following June at Saint Anthony's Church in Ely, Minnesota, a town without paved streets and with a population of nineteen hundred people, the bulk of whom were Swedes, Finns, and Norwegians.

Within twelve years they had six children, all sons. The parade began with Tom Junior, followed by John, James, and Jerry. Dan was the fifth. Philip, the last offspring, was born October 5, 1923, an event that inspired his proud father to buy a windup record player and a stack of Enrico Caruso arias—Phil had an operatic launching. (Early on, Dan developed a special affection for his younger brother: "I remember him . . . as the kid who had no mean streak in him. He was very peaceable, lovable, beautiful."[7])

The Berrigan boys were robust, with the exception of John (strong but afflicted with asthma) and Dan, who had to wear eyeglasses and special shoes that reinforced his weak ankles with whalebone. From his father's point of view, Dan was "the runt of the litter," a "mama's boy" ill equipped for survival in a harsh, unforgiving world.

Dan took his first steps when he was four, an event that would have been further delayed had it not been for the attentive care not only of Frida but of Grandmother Fromhart, who lived with them and who had paid out of her savings for costly custom-made shoes. Every day she massaged her grandson's feet, holding them in sunlight when the sky cooperated. On occasion, when her son-in-law dared to complain about Dan's frailties, she was quick to say, in her half-German English, "Tom, you do a *sindt* [sin]!"[8]

While seeing both mother and grandmother as models of goodness and sanctity, even late in his life Dan was hard-pressed to utter a sympathetic word for his short-fused, sharp-tongued, sometimes abusive, occasionally violent, hypercritical, and often-absent father: "With him," wrote Dan in his autobiography, "my game was survival, my trick, hideaway. Life was hide-and-seek. I wanted only to be off his retina."[9] In a poem about his father written many years later, Dan confessed:

> I wonder if I ever loved him
> if he ever loved us
> if he ever loved me.[10]

Dan saw his father as "an incendiary without a cause" who might strike at any moment. Phil recalled living in constant dread: "When will he erupt again? When will the next battle royale happen? When will he hit [Frida] and possibly kill her? Well, with fear like that to be taken at meal time with your grits, it makes of one a creature of fear."[11]

Yet there were mitigating factors for Thomas Berrigan's grave defects. Dan was aware his paternal grandfather had died of tuberculosis (or "immigrant's lung," as it was often called at the time) when his son was only five, and from childhood on, Thomas had lived a life of unremitting hard labor. Yet he grew up to be a good provider for his family, a man serious about his Catholic faith, a poet (though unpublished), a union member. He was a founder of the local chapter of the Catholic Interracial Council.[12] Thomas Berrigan had an independent mind; he distrusted crowds and didn't mind being a minority of one. One family story reports that Berrigan, as an act of objection to World War I, once refused to blow the whistle on a troop train he was driving. Not of minor significance was the fact that the Berrigan boys grew up in a home whose father subscribed to the *Catholic Worker*, an eight-page monthly tabloid edited by Dorothy Day that focused on social issues and

*"It occurred to me long after my mother's death . . . that such a woman might safely have been entrusted with the fate of the world. . . . Whatever substance has accrued to our lives— whatever goodness, must be laid at our mother's feet. Tardily, with an aching sense of the lateness of the gift and of her loss, I lay it there."* —Portraits

Dan and Phil with mother, Frida Berrigan. Courtesy Berrigan family

9

the creation of a society "in which it would be easier for people to be good." In a more sympathetic treatment of his father, in *Lights on in the House of the Dead*, Dan recalls walking with him to Mass when they had no car or even trolley fare. He "was capable of a sense of mystery. He was honest and generous and hardworking. . . . Perhaps just his irascible, stubborn anger will keep us afloat."[13]

If Tom Berrigan was a dark presence in Dan's childhood, his mother, Frida, was an uncanonized saint, a person who "could be entrusted with the world." She was "providential, foreseeing, compassionate, a woman who . . . had a weather eye for virtually all weathers. And modest."[14] She was also a fearless protector, standing like a stone wall in defense of Dan or any of her sons who had become the target of her husband's dangerous temper. And she was the parent Dan physically resembled. When Dan introduced me to her, I realized that her face was an older, feminine version of Dan's.

Life was a constant struggle for the Berrigan family. Dan was born in the only house his parents ever owned. Soon after his birth the family was forced to move to Babbit, where they shared a miner's barrack with another family. Then in 1923—Tom now the proud owner of a Model-T Ford—they relocated in Winton, a logging center where lumber mills were in need of able-bodied men. Dan remembered helping his mother gather snow and use it to cook the family clothing clean in a copper laundry boiler placed on the stove. The wilderness was still wild, with wolves howling in the night.

"There were wolves aplenty in the world of my childhood," Dan remembered. "We heard them across the lake on whose shore we eked out for a time our parlous existence. . . . [As winter set in] wolves tried the ice of the lake, edged closer under the moon. They could be heard whining and baying; their menacing chorus mingled with the wakefulness of a child, bundled like a papoose against the night rigors."[15]

Dan with his parents, Frida and Tom.
Cornell University, Division of Rare and Manuscript Collections

As a grim joke that afterward haunted his nightmares, one of the older brothers thrust Dan's young face into the frozen muzzle of a green-eyed timber wolf hanging dead and frozen in the barn.

There were other terrors as well. Tom Jr., who had a newspaper route, one day had to outrun a bear. On another day, like a scene from a western, brother Jim came upon the body of a man shot dead the night before following a dispute over a game of poker.[16] But side by side with danger and death were encounters with paradise, as when autumn blueberries weighed down their branches and the brothers ate their fill while keeping alert for bears.

The brothers had a winter game of their own invention: fox and geese. A large circle was drawn in the snow, the center marked and wheel spokes drawn connecting hub to rim. One brother, the fox, stood in the center, the others at the edge. As the fox attacked, the geese raced in concert to new positions, sometimes escaping the fox, sometimes not. "So we ran and yelled and argued and fell laughing, were captured or escaped. But in any case raced about more or less in unison, center to periphery, around the rim of that gelid world."[17]

In 1927 the elder Berrigan ("Dado" to his children) decided he had had enough of Minnesota with its eight-month winters and ever-shifting jobs. When his brothers and sisters suggested joining them in Syracuse, New York, Tom said yes. It was a hard move for Frida, who had spent all but the first five years of her life in the iron country. She was leaving behind her own much-loved family to be closer to the Berrigans, an unwelcoming clan annoyed that Tom had married a German.

Once in Syracuse, Tom got work as a steam boiler operator and handyman at Saint Mary's Maternity Hospital plus use of a rent-free three-story farmhouse, formerly an orphanage, complete with cupola and a view of Lake Onondaga. It was set on ten acres of land in Liverpool Township, to the city's northwest, and in sight

The Berrigan brothers, Dan front center. Courtesy Berrigan family

Dan and Phil with parents, Frida and Tom Berrigan. Courtesy Berrigan family

*"How did I see him? A missing part; a hole perhaps in the heart, or a hole where a heart should have been. An essential lack; something could not be ' cosmetically correct.'"* —Portraits

of a trolley stop. Solid structure though it was, it lacked interior plumbing and central heating, and the rooms dwarfed the family furniture once it arrived. It became familiar but never felt homey to Dan.

The family lived near the city but led a rural life, farming and raising livestock. The annual selection and slaughter of a pig, "screaming, terrified for its life," as Dado prepared to cut its throat was, for Dan, "terrible for a child to behold."[18]

Thomas Berrigan saw himself as king of the castle, his word the last word. "We were brought up," Jerry Berrigan notes of his father, "to totally accept church rules and school rules and, most of all, his rules."[19] Frida occasionally dared to challenge Dado, especially shielding Dan from paternal tongue-lashings and worse. Approaching manhood, brother John ordered Dado to back off when his words to other family members became too cruel. On at least one occasion, father and son battled each other with their fists.

With the Depression's arrival at the end of 1929, Thomas Berrigan's struggle to support the family became more challenging and required more time away. The car had to go. When one job collapsed, another had to be found—and quickly. For a while he was digging holes for telephone poles, and when that gave out, he got work polishing car bodies at the Franklin Auto Plant. In 1933 he was one of the millions of unemployed men hired by the federal government's Works Progress Administration, the largest New Deal agency, to carry out public works projects. Berrigan helped drain swampland, construct highways, cut stone, and build or maintain bridges.

At home Frida cleaned and mended clothes. Not a scrap of anything potentially useful was wasted. Dietary mainstays included potatoes, sauerkraut, home-baked bread, salt pork, and canned fruit from the garden. Not only did no one go hungry, but Frida provided what she could to hat-in-hand hobos who appeared at the door and at times even sent the boys out to deliver food to hard-hit local families.

Both parents were people of prayer, but Frida especially so. "During the day," Dan remembered, "we would [often] find her praying by herself." The usual locus was before a household statue of the Virgin Mary. When in Syracuse she invariably stopped to pray in the cathedral.

Along with prayer was the importance Frida placed on seeing to it that her boys were literate. She was a familiar face at the Syracuse Public Library, returning classics (Dickens was a favorite) and borrowing ever more volumes for her book-hungry sons. She nourished body, soul, and mind. Again and again it is to Frida that Dan pays his greatest homage: "Whatever substance has accrued in our lives, whatever goodness, must be laid at our mother's feet."[20] She "accepted her life," Dan observed, "not as fate, but as vocation."[21]

That the brothers would attend Catholic schools was a given. Discipline was rigorous. One of the nuns punished students who displeased her by making them hold a stack of books at arm's length until the books crashed to the floor. On Saturdays the kids lined up to confess their sins—"mortal sins first," they were reminded—and roll was taken again Sunday morning to make sure no one was failing to attend Mass. Remarkably Dan went to Mass more often than was required; the scent of a priestly vocation was in his teenage nostrils.

In 1938 Dan's best friend in high school, Jack St. George, told Dan that he was thinking of going to the seminary to become a priest. Dan decided to do the same. Using the local diocesan vocation guide, they agreed to write to various religious orders for information, then make their own decisions, and when they were ready to tell each other what they had decided. Both chose the Society of Jesus. Interviews followed. Both were accepted. At age eighteen, Dan was about to begin a participation in the Society of Jesus that would last—at times just barely—the rest of his long life.

*"There could have been, God knows, a better marriage; there could also have been less contentious, clamorous offspring. . . . All this is true. And yet I remember also, for this is the chief point of her story, its commendation— her life struck others as a gentle, a rhythm of peace, and spiritual plenty."* —Portraits

Dan at summer camp. Courtesy Berrigan family

# The Long Black Line

I once asked Dan what had drawn him to the Jesuits. "It had nothing to do with knowing Jesuits—I knew not one," Dan replied. "It was their bare-bones undersell. A friend and I had written off to several religious orders—Franciscans, Dominicans, and various others—for basic information and received glossy brochures with photos of pretty buildings, swimming pools, rec rooms, and basketball courts. Summer camps! But the Jesuits sent the opposite—a very plain folder, no photos, and an austere text that featured some tough quotations from St. Ignatius Loyola! The real thing. No icing."

The order had its start in 1534 when St. Ignatius Loyola, a Basque nobleman who had reenvisioned his life after nearly dying in battle, and six friends vowed themselves to poverty and chastity, calling themselves *la Compañía de Jesús*—the Society of Jesus. Six years later, their initiative obtained the approval of Pope Paul III. The Compañía grew rapidly. Members were ready to accept orders to go anywhere in the world where they might be needed and were prepared to live in harsh conditions. The founding document declared that the society was instituted for "whoever desires to serve as a soldier of God to strive especially for the defense and propagation of the faith and for the progress of souls in Christian life and doctrine." Launched just before the Counter-Reformation, the Jesuits sought to "help souls," a broad term that led to a wide variety of ministries. At the time Dan joined, there were six thousand Jesuits in the United States, more than a fifth of the Society of Jesus worldwide.

Dan entered Saint Andrew-on-Hudson Novitiate in Poughkeepsie, New York, in the fall of 1939, one of seventy novices. His new home was an isolated manor house with smaller adjacent buildings at the end of a tree-lined road on a seven-hundred-acre property. Beyond a bluff lay the Hudson River. In the years that followed, Dan would lead an all-but-monastic life in which almost every minute of the day was structured, from early rising to turning off the light at 9 or 9:30 p.m. It was, Dan summarizes, "a plunge into silence; penance; disciplined comportment; stereotyped, coarse, lookalike clothing; meditation and manual labor and regulated hours. The days were disposed of as though by a relentless metronome: come when told, come when bade, follow the bell, join 'the long black line.'"[22]

The goal from day one onward was to live a Christ-centered life free, in the words of Ignatius Loyola, "of all disordered affections." Mass was celebrated each day, in Latin of course, and none but the ill were absent. There was also daily rosary and times of private prayer. An ascetic regime was a key element, minor aspects of which were cold-water showers and plain food eaten during meals while listening to a reading. In addition to demanding studies and frequent exams (an obligatory syllabus came from Jesuit headquarters in Rome) there was plenty of farmlike labor for one and all, as St. Andrew's was self-supporting. Meals were cooked by those who ate them. The community barber cut hair. The students did all the gardening and the groundwork, raking, painting, cleaning, washing, ironing, and scores of other chores.

A fifteen-year period of formation stretched before Dan. First there were two years in the novitiate, at the end of which he would make (if he was still there) vows of poverty, chastity, and obedience, to be followed by a two-

Dan at St. Andrew-on-Hudson Novitiate. Courtesy Berrigan family

St. Andrew-on-Hudson
Novitiate. (Today the Culinary
Institute of America.) Rev. John Brosnan, S.J.
(Georgetown University Archives)

year juniorate, during which he would complete a bachelor of arts degree with a concentration on classical studies. Next would come the three-year philosophate, a program that ended with an oral exam given in Latin, in which it was expected he would now be fluent. The Jesuit's next three years were called regency; he would be assigned to a full-time ministry, usually in a high school or foreign mission. The theologate followed—a four-year program in theology, during which he would be ordained a priest.[23] At the end of the journey came tertianship, a year during which the individual steps back to critically assess his experience of living and working in the Society of Jesus. During this time, the Jesuit in formation undertakes an "apostolic placement" of teaching or service. The society does not make its formal commitment to an individual Jesuit until that person has been with them for at least fifteen years.

Far from being unhappy or feeling cramped by this intensely structured life, Dan felt an at-homeness at Saint Andrew's he had never experienced. He rejoiced in all the challenges. Also he was at last free of his father's disapproving gaze. "The memories of my first years are particularly vivid," Dan recalled. "They gave me a deep sense of the presence of God in the world, and most especially in human community. I fell in love immediately and incurably with the Jesuit style. . . . It appealed to me . . . as a ground for my boundless idealism, and I found in the talents and youth and drive around me a constant spur to make my own life count."[24]

Dan had been born into one family and now was being grafted onto a second. "A Jesuit is not in existence for himself," Dan said of his adopted family in a letter to Phil, "he is an instrument of our Lord sealed and set apart as the servant of men—to bear their burdens and forget his own."[25] On the feast day of Saint Ignatius, July 31, Dan wrote his mother, "I always thank him [the Jesuit founder] in profound humility for singling me out from all the more fit ones to be part of his great family."[26]

In a letter sent to Phil in 1940 Dan provided a sketch of life at St. Andrew's:

> There's never time heavy on your hands here. . . . You really feel grateful when a half-hour is given in which to do a little extra letter writing, etc. I figure we have about 30 more or less cut and dried periods each day, excluding meals. But something is always coming up—recreation after dinner and supper by the now tightly frozen Hudson is something to thank God for. You can imagine for yourself what takes place when 68 [two fewer novices than had been there on day one] up-to-then silent tongues are loosened for the first time after dinner. Then there's the deep element, two daily meditations, daily Mass and Communion, these three are your driving force and with your 7 or 8 visits to the Blessed Sacrament have melted even this black heart so that now his greatest fear is that he finds himself so terribly unworthy to be in such a Company as that bearing the Name of Jesus Itself. Father gives us our daily Confession in which we come to really know the Society and its spirit, encouragement, love.[27]

Taking great pride in being a Jesuit, even in letters to Phil he signed "Dan, S.J." Later in life Dan would be embarrassed at how readily he took to clericalism as a young man.

It was a far-from-easy path. By Jesuit academic standards, Dan was not well prepared: "When I entered upon my studies it became clear that I had a great deal of ground to catch up and win. Practically all of my classmates had graduated from Jesuit schools in the New York or Buffalo areas. They were invariably far ahead of

Dan with his mother on vow day at St. Andrew's, August 15, 1941.
Courtesy Berrigan family

Study hall at St. Andrew's.
Rev. John Brosnan, S.J. (Georgetown University
Archives)

me on almost every criterion that counted for achievement in our [brotherhood]."[28]

There were brief but often intense daily meetings with the novice master, who was referred to as "Father Master," the senior priest who supervised all the novices' progress. One evening this august elder raised the terrifying question: Was Dan truly one of "the Company"? Did he really have a Jesuit vocation? "Go to the chapel and pray about it," Dan was instructed, "and come back and tell me what you've learned." When he finally returned from the chapel, holding back tears, Dan said, "I won't go. I'm staying." Father Master nodded his head.

Not only did Dan stay with the Jesuits and remain focused on eventual ordination to the priesthood but advocated a similar path for Phil, who had finished high school and was now saving for college by scrubbing soot off railroad engines and also being paid to play first base on a local semiprofessional baseball team.

"I write to you as one who can be more than a brother," Dan wrote Phil in October 1942. "My great dream and never flagging prayer is that you will embrace the priesthood—the life of true joy and of satisfaction in loving and living Christ. You have all the gifts and talents required—that in itself, plus your good will, constitutes a vocation. St. Ignatius once said that it was much more sensible to look for an extraordinary sign from God telling one to remain out of Religion than to ask one to enter Religion since the first is so much more fraught with danger than the second. This determination to enter at the end of this year will give point and purpose to your study and assure you of God's help in your work."[29]

Dan's frequent letters home were dense with Catholic piety and lacked intimacy. In that era, even within tight-knit Catholic families, an institutional formality often stood like a stone wall between religious (those in religious orders, whether male or female) and the laity. I wonder if Phil didn't miss his teasing, playful, pre-Jesuit brother?

Unsure about his long-range goals, in the fall of 1942 Phil began classes at St. Michael's College in Toronto, but whatever thoughts he may have had of possible ordination to the priesthood were quickly blown away by the war going on in Europe and the Pacific. After only one semester at St. Michael's, Phil received his draft notice early in 1943, about the same time his brothers Tom and Jerry got theirs. (John had already enlisted, Jim was found medically unfit due to a serious back injury, while Dan, as a seminary student, was automatically exempted.)

Phil in uniform, 1943.
Courtesy Berrigan family

If later in life Phil would become an advocate of conscientious objection to war, at age nineteen he was eager "to charge pillboxes, blow up machine gun nests, and fight hand-to-hand with my country's enemies."[30] His last civilian activity before reporting for basic training was to stop at St. Andrew's for a four-day retreat plus the opportunity to see Dan. Then began a year of learning the crafts of war that brought Phil from Fort Gordon in Georgia to Fort Blanding in Florida to Fort Bragg in North Carolina, where he was promoted to sergeant.

For Dan the catastrophe occurring in Europe and the Pacific was a remote event reported in occasional letters from home plus newspaper reports—the front-page

Top: Mass at Woodstock College.
Rev. John Brosnan, S.J. (Georgetown University Archives)

Above: Dan.
Cornell University, Division of Rare and Manuscript Collections

of a two-day-old *New York Times* was tacked to the community bulletin board each morning. The war reached the students at St. Andrew's, Dan wrote, "only as distant rumor." Even so the conflict was the inspiration for Dan's first published poem, "You Vested Us This Morning," which he dedicated to his "four soldier-brothers."[31] The poem, published by the Jesuit magazine *America* in October 1943, raised no disquieting questions about the morality of war, an issue that would later dominate so much of Dan's writing and public activity. The second of the poem's three stanzas envisioned Christ leading his faithful followers into the high noon of battle:

Not ours is fear of failing
In deathly hot high noon,
Nor dread of swift shafts hailing
On armor hatred-hewn—
But may your love sound warningly
By gaping tarn and fen,
When choked ways we cannot see,
King, may we see You then
Riding the uplands perilous in forefront of Your men?

The poem was skillfully crafted even if the sentiments prosaic. In fact, few and far between were Catholics who judged the methods being used in the war, including city destruction, as violating the Church's conditions of a just war. Rarer still were those who regarded war, of its nature, as an unchristian activity. The exceptions included two people who would later play a significant role in both Dan and Phil's lives: Dorothy Day and Thomas Merton.[32]

In one of the few surviving wartime letters Dan sent to Phil, he wrote in glowing terms of the war-making his brothers were engaged in:

To realize that the soldiering of this war is a vocation too—that would solve some of your difficulties and loneliness and the vague worries too shadowy for definition, wouldn't it, Phil? To believe our Lord wants you as surely in a field artillery . . . just as surely as he wants fifteen years of study and sweat from me—that's a grand faith and trust and high outlook that will solve a great deal, clear up a lot of moral issues, turn the whole situation (which is otherwise a pure mess) into part of the great plan to bring souls back to God their maker—the only thing that counts in life. And your part is to play the game (as you are doing superbly) looking on Him Who was a good Soldier—unto death."[33]

By this time Dan had taken his first vows and had begun the second phase of his formation, the juniorate, a transition that brought him and his classmates to Woodstock College in Maryland where, in a single terse paragraph in a compact autobiographical essay, "Open, Sesame," Dan acknowledges spending "three miserable years . . . studying philosophy. It was simply not my dish. So I languished like an unhappy three-year freshman, trying with varying degrees of desperation and moodiness to find myself in a thicket of logic and metaphysics. I finished that period with an almost entire lack of distinction."[34]

In *To Dwell in Peace*, he expands on the frustrations of that period: "If we studied, we would prevail; not because the studies were inherently fascinating or soundly presented. They were, in the main, neither. . . . We were to study because, at this stage of life, philosophy was the divine will. It was as though God were attending uneasily to our attempts to prove, from unaided reason, that He exists. . . . Something of substance, something infinitely precious, was lost in the Woodstock years. . . . Life for most of us was reduced to mere endurance."[35]

In July 1944, less than a month after D-Day, Phil arrived in England and was assigned to a company searching for salvageable equipment in the blitzed cities of

*"The Society is very much like her mother the Church—in her timelessness; and in order to mould a perfect human instrument for souls' salvation, will wait and work—and wait again."*

—Letter from Dan to Phil, December 1941

Chapel at Woodstock.
Rev. John Brosnan, S.J. (Georgetown University Archives)

Top: Dan and Phil at Woodstock, 1946.
Cornell University, Division of Rare and Manuscript
Collections

Above: London under the Blitz.

London, Coventry, Birmingham, and Sheffield. For the first time he was face-to-face with the merciless reality of modern war— "children suffocated in the rubble, old people burned to death in firestorms, survivors crippled for life."[36]

His artillery unit was soon dispatched to the continent—first in France, then Holland, finally Germany. Phil was fortunate to survive the intense combat in which he took part. One day, while guarding German prisoners, he decided to take the next step in fighting "against those [Nazi] bastards" by signing up for Officer's Candidate School. He graduated the ninety-day program as a second lieutenant and was posted as a platoon leader to an infantry division outside Münster. It was a high-risk assignment; platoon leaders tended to die within two months. But then suddenly the war was over: no more playing tag with death on the battlefield, though there was still death to inhale for soldiers like Phil patrolling the devastated city. "A sweet stench [hung] over Münster," Phil remembered, "a vast accidental cemetery where people rotted where the explosives had caught them—in homes, offices, even churches."[37] It was too much to take in. Phil was far from the only soldier drinking heavily.

With combat soldiers no longer needed in Europe, Phil was among the many thousands shipped back to America to train for the invasion of Japan. But then the Pacific war ended in August, and all four Berrigan brothers were demobilized. Remarkably each had survived the most destructive war in human history. On his return Phil hitchhiked to Woodstock to celebrate with Dan and to join in a celebration of peace. "We sang, toasting the war's end, patting ourselves on the back," Phil recalled. "I carried the flag as we marched around the main building, a couple of platoons, two hundred Jesuits, friends, family, kids, all cheering our country's victory."[38]

# A Poor Man's Paradise

In May 1946 Dan passed his final exam in philosophy and, feeling like a prisoner who had been paroled, "departed Woodstock, without a vagrant tear, and forever."[39] And now a great adventure began: during the next three years, his regency as a Jesuit, he would become a teacher. His assignment brought him to the heart of a big city slum, St. Peter's Preparatory School in Jersey City, New Jersey. The boys, Dan found, "were unwilling and intractable and altogether delightful." He taught French, Latin, English, and "what was fondly called, at that time, religion. Everything I had believed or hoped about myself, by way of being a contributory creature in the real world, began to come true. I struck out in every direction, like a belated flower child. And this at the hands of some three hundred rough and tough Jersey kids. It was indeed the first of many miracles."[40]

St. Peter's Preparatory School.

To his surprise Dan discovered he had a talent for presiding in a classroom and connecting with students whom other teachers had found the most impenetrable, the least promising. He experienced in himself "the emergence of various gifts long suppressed: instincts, *simpatico*, love of the young." A dam within himself had been breached. The face he saw in the mirror revealed

Top: Yearbook of St. Peter's Prep.
Cornell University, Division of Rare and Manuscript Collections

Above: "Daniel Berrigan, S.J., Latin, English, Moderator of Freshman Debating." Cornell University, Division of Rare and Manuscript Collections

a self he hadn't known was there. "Was I human; and a gifted teacher after all? . . . Could it be that life was a celebration?"

Dan's long days began at dawn and lasted till midnight. Actual teaching was only the core element. There were student clubs to monitor, debating teams to meet with, and newspaper and yearbook meetings to attend, as well as classes to prepare, papers to correct, students to talk with individually. From time to time he brought groups of students to New York City to visit museums and see plays.

It was a no-frills life. Jesuit scholastics in regency like himself "slept in attic rooms, consumed plain food, [and] said our prayers in a fog of exhaustion." Yet Dan found himself in "a poor man's paradise."[41]

Remarkably Dan managed to find scraps of time for nonobligatory reading. Among the authors he was drawn to was the English Catholic priest, scholar, and biblical translator Ronald Knox, whose recent book *God and the Atom* raised troubling questions that were new to Dan. Like nearly every American, Dan had seen the atom bomb as having shortened the war and saved tens of thousands of American lives; God bless the bomb. Knox argued that dropping the atom bomb—causing the incineration of two Japanese cities with their mainly noncombatant populations—was not only a morally atrocious event but the destruction of a worldview, making faith more difficult, undermining hope, and threatening love. What a pity, Knox wrote, that America had not exploded the bomb on an uninhabited island to demonstrate its power without killing the innocent. For Knox the very existence of such a world-endangering weapon was not only a political challenge but an urgent call to holiness, "for the saint is, like the atom, incalculable in his moment; [and] holds, like the atom, strange forces hidden under a mask of littleness."[42]

In what would prove to be a modest first step in pursuit of nuclear disarmament, Dan read a few passages of

Cornell University, Division of Rare and Manuscript Collections

*"Everything I had believed or hoped about myself, by way of being a contributory creature in the real world, began to come true. I struck out in every direction, like a belated flower child. And this at the hands of some hundred rough and tough Jersey kids."*

—No Bars to Manhood

Knox's book to a class of fifteen-year-olds only to discover he had stirred up a hornet's nest: "With considerable heat I was informed that I scarcely knew my arse from my elbow. . . . We did good [said the kids]! We saved lives, didn't we? It was them or us, wasn't it?"[43] It was a response Dan would hear over and over again in the decades to come. At the time Dan was no radical, but he had become one of those rare priests asking questions few wanted to hear.

That weapons of mass destruction, it slowly dawned on Dan, could be embraced so uncritically by so many Catholics revealed a disturbing fact: that one might have the best of Catholic educations, go to Mass every Sunday, learn the Beatitudes by heart, and "still go off to war

. . . [in the course of which] vast numbers of the enemy, whether combatants or bystanders or the ill or aged or newly born would be disposed of by slaughterhouse technique." Through culpable silence if not actual blessing, the Church had become war's chaplain and ally.

Dan concludes this section of his autobiography, "Thus my students became my instructors."[44]

His three years in a paradise of inner-city classrooms came to an end in the summer of 1949. The regency completed, the four-year theologate came next. Along with others in his year, Dan was off to the Jesuit household at Weston, twenty miles west of Boston.

Meanwhile Phil was in motion. When Dan had been finishing his studies at Woodstock before being sent to Jersey City, Phil was back home in Syracuse recovering from war, doing construction work and trying to get his bearings. Frida noted with alarm that Phil was drinking way too much. Was it his way of dealing with what today would be called posttraumatic stress disorder? She pushed him to do what Jerry had already started. In the fall of 1946 Phil followed Jerry to Holy Cross College, a Jesuit school in Massachusetts.

For several years Phil was an older-than-average student at Holy Cross, a tweed-jacketed campus golden boy who balanced studies with dating, golf, and a busy social life. As his studies progressed, questions about faith, conscience, and the social order that were being raised in some of his classes pushed him to ponder his values and long-range goals. A Jesuit theologian taught a class in which the conditions of a just war were a topic; Phil must have been forced to compare tidy theories of war with the actual messy war in which he had participated. There was the question of his own vocation, to discern not just what he *could* do with his life but what he was *called* to do.

Dan's early hope that he might not be the only Berrigan to become a priest was gaining traction. His older brother Jerry entered the seminary of the Society of

Jerry and Phil at seminary in Newburgh. Courtesy Berrigan family

Dan, Phil, and Jerry with parents at Newburgh. Courtesy Berrigan family

St. Joseph in Newburgh, New York, the one American order committed to serving Catholics of African descent. Its priests were known as Josephites. It was a path that rang bells for Phil. In the year he had spent in the Deep South training for war, Phil had repeatedly witnessed a twentieth-century racism that was little different from pre–Civil War slavery. While stationed in Georgia he recalled "marching past little tarpaper shacks flapping in the wind, smoke coughing out of metal chimneys sprouting from their roofs . . . [yet] the blacks didn't own their shacks, and they didn't own the land they worked from sunup to sundown. They rented these from white men, bought seed and other necessities from white men, borrowed money at usurious rates from white men."[45] He recalled too how white troops being ferried to Europe were lodged in cabins while black soldiers had to endure the harsh weather of the North Atlantic sleeping on outside decks. He had witnessed the abuse of black soldiers by white soldiers,

Weston Seminary.

*"The question arises: for what were we being prepared? It could be adduced that we were being fitted and joined to stand immemorially in the Stonehenge circle. To stand there, while the Vandals wreaked their worst . . . or in secular, and necessarily partial, terms: we were being prepared to work as loyal, unquestioning civil servants; in whatever capacity might be determined, by others, in light of talent and temperament."*

—To Dwell in Peace

though all were clad in the same uniform. Racism was a social disease that neither Jerry nor Phil could dismiss as someone else's problem. Graduating from Holy Cross in June 1950, that September Phil followed Jerry into the Josephites. He was off to the seminary in Newburgh, New York.

As Phil was entering seminary, Dan was starting his tenth year as a Jesuit and his second year at Weston in Massachusetts. The curriculum was, he later wrote, "a hatful of watch parts . . . the schemata, sequence and subjects [of which] were inviolate": canon law, ministry, sacraments, discipline, morals, scripture old and new, liturgical regulations, and more. Once again he was part of the long black line, a procession of Jesuits that later in life Dan judged was better connected to Stonehenge than to the postwar, Cold War world.[46] European theologians such as Henri de Lubac, Jean Daniélou, Yves Congar, Karl and Hugo Rahner—whose voices would be significant at the Second Vatican Council—were all under a dark cloud of suspicion in a Church led by Pope Pius XII, and their books were conspicuously absent from the required reading lists at Weston. "Through one decree or another," Dan mourned, "they were pushed beyond the pale." Jesuits in the theologate like himself, Dan wrote, "were being prepared to work as loyal, unquestioning civil servants" who obediently did and said whatever "might be determined by others."[47]

How critical was Dan of the content of his theological studies at the time? His autobiography was written four decades later, by which time his reproaches of both the Church and the Society of Jesus rolled freely. All one can say is that what became open disparagement was a later development, yet there is a sense that, as he began his second decade as a Jesuit, he had an itchy awareness that the old theological answers then being presented in Weston's classroom were too pat.

Dan was by now close to fluent in French, one of the subjects he had taught in Jersey City. Reading French

Catholic journals, he was conscious that theological debate was much more vigorous in the French Church than in the United States. In *To Dwell in Peace* Dan mentions hearing that his counterparts in France were reading the unpublished notes of Pierre Teilhard de Chardin, a Jesuit paleontologist, geologist, philosopher, and theologian whose writings on evolution and the human phenomenon had been condemned by the Vatican, and whose books would appear in print only years after Teilhard's death in 1955.[48]

Pierre Teilhard de Chardin, S.J.

At the end of their third year Dan and his classmates had at last reached the day—June 19, 1952—of priestly ordination. "The event was accounted at the time as grace," wrote Dan, "and it still is. . . . For all that was to follow . . . the anointing of ordination was a momentous healing and enlightenment. It justified the long haul and its sweat and tears, it struck a light that has never been extinguished." The archbishop of Boston, Cardinal Richard Cushing, presided at the event, doing so "at a tornado pace and pitch . . . When his great bassoon [of a voice] sounded, announcing this or that stage of the proceeding, one could entertain no doubt that the gift offered was in fact conferred. The chariot swung low and swept one up. . . . I had at last become what I was called to be. . . . It was Year One of my life . . . the first day of a new creation."[49]

Testifying at the Catonsville Nine trial sixteen years later, once again his thoughts turned to that special day: "I remember a kind of desolation, the cold of the floor on which I stretched like a corpse, while the invocation of the saints went over me like a tide, a death. Would these bones live? I arose to my feet and went out into the sunshine and gave my blessing to those who had borne with me, who had waited for me. A most unfinished man. What would it mean to be a Catholic? Who would be my teacher?"[50]

One year in the theologate remained. While not yet a rocker of boats, the recently priested Father Dan was one of the young Jesuits prepared to slip quietly past the

*"In a minor way, I was launched. No full-masted vessel, no tall ship; rather in the nature of a rower's skiff, fit for inland waters. But still, something."*
—To Dwell in Peace

**Saying Mass.** Cornell University, Division of Rare and Manuscript Collections

"no trespassing" signs: "More or less on our own, [some of us] read the forbidden Europeans, met for discussion, pondered, opened our casements and breathed the fresh air."[51]

During his fourth year, a paper he wrote on the nature of the Church, in part inspired by the writings of Henri de Lubac but prudently leaving de Lubac unmentioned in the text, won the enthusiastic praise of one of the professors at Weston, very likely a man who recognized de Lubac's themes even when uncited.[52]

"My mentor insisted that, on the strength of this essay, I must apply for European studies. The praise and attention were a balm." For the first time Dan could look in the mirror and see someone who "might offer something substantial in matters theological."[53] Taking up his professor's suggestion, for his Tertianship—the yearlong final stage of Jesuit formation—he applied and was accepted for European studies.

Dan's next stop was France. Even before putting a foot on French soil, he felt he was heading for his spiritual home.

# Paray-le-Monial

In July 1953, to Dan's "dumbfounded delight," he departed from Weston for the Jesuit house in Paray-le-Monial, a Burgundian town northwest of Lyons whose roots lay in the foundation of a Benedictine monastery in the year 973. A magnificent church dominates the town center, a Romanesque basilica whose construction began in the twelfth century. For Catholics, the town has one more major attraction. To this day a river of pilgrims is drawn to Paray-le-Monial as the place from which, due to the visions of St. Margaret Mary Alocoque in the late seventeenth century, devotion to the Sacred Heart of Jesus took root. There is a Jesuit connection to this devotion

*"What I discovered in France for the first time in my long experience of Catholic community was so simple a thing as personal freedom. It was an invitation to become a human being by way of others. . . ."*
— No Bars to Manhood

Basilica in Paray-le-Monial.

as well. St. Margaret Mary's spiritual director was a Jesuit, Claude la Colombiere, himself doing his tertianship. It was he who ended up spreading the devotion, so closely associated with the Jesuits, that emphasized Christ's passionate love for humankind.

Dan was one of thirty-five Jesuits in their final year of formation. The others came from Germany, Italy, England, India, Malta, Argentina, Brazil, Venezuela, and parts of Africa. For the first time Dan was grafted into a community that was not defined by borders.

Their house of studies—a chilly, gray-stone building behind a high wall topped with broken glass on the town's main street—was, Dan recalled, "as poor as any church mouse dwelling. But we had a sense of sharing in something extraordinarily painful in France at large. Many of my compatriots were survivors of German exploitation, and had worked in labor camps and factories under the occupier. Almost everything I experienced was being experienced for the first time. I felt in many cases as though I had landed upon a new planet, and was being asked to operate in an entirely new way, to rebuild my senses, my very soul. It was not merely a matter of fumbling about with a new language and slowly gaining confidence in it. The truth was that the language offered new ways into the world of other human beings—and that these others, penetrated and formed by a thousand-year history expressed in their lucid and vivid language, were also new beings, into whose community I was invited to enter. The invitation was austere but irresistible."[54]

*"The walls of the old house on the main street of Paray were of gray stone, sweating with perennial damp. The weather, as winter deepened, was a soul-chilling bloom; one's room in consequence, was outfitted for a tomb. Toward dawn or dusk, a wisp of what might pass for heat huffed out of ancient iron pipes. But for the remainder of day and night, a deadly chill rode the air."*

*—To Dwell in Peace*

Though Dan was assigned certain duties in local parishes and convents, his responsibilities were not heavy. "At a stroke," he wrote, "fourteen years of academic burdens lifted [and] new horizons beckoned."[55] Although he did not realize it during the first few months, Dan's "real mind was being implanted, the future was being furiously sown."[56]

The newly arrived Jesuits had a hard landing. While Paray-le-Monial was a mecca for pilgrims, much of the local population, indeed the French in general, was deeply alienated from the Catholic Church. Relatively few attended Mass. When groups of black-clad clerics walked together down the town's cobblestone streets, some of the more hostile locals would caw like crows. The welcome mat was not out.

Dan soon began to understand the roots of anticlerical enmity. For too much of its history, the Church in France had been closer to the rulers than to the ruled. Also the bishops and priests who had been active with the resistance during the German occupation had been few. Rather than considering what Christian witness might require in postwar France, many Catholics looked back with nostalgia to a romanticized, long-gone Age of Faith. "There was too much prudence, too little courage. . . . For years now we've been waiting for the greatest spiritual authority of our times [the pope] to condemn in clear terms the ventures of dictatorship," Albert Camus had written in 1944 for the resistance newspaper *Combat*. "For this condemnation may be found in certain encyclical letters if they are read and are correctly interpreted. . . . [But the language in which they are written has] never been very accessible to the vast majority of people. . . . The great majority has waited all these years for a voice to raise itself and clearly state . . . where evil lies."[57]

Yet the bread was rising. Nothing he encountered impressed Dan so much as a remarkable experimental effort the French Church was making, the mission of the worker-priests, which sought to repair relations between the Church and the French working class. It had been launched in 1941 when a Dominican priest, Jacques Loew, was given permission by his superiors to find work on the docks of Marseilles. Another key figure was a Jesuit, Henri Perrin, who, hiding his priestly identity, went to Germany in 1943 to work as an invisible chaplain among Frenchmen doing forced labor. After the war, with the fervent support of the archbishop of Paris, Cardinal Emmanuel Suhard,[58] the initiative became an

Top: Albert Camus.
Above: Cardinal Emmanuel Suhard.

The fall of Dien Bien Phu in May 1954.

officially sanctioned movement. A worker-priest was any priest who had been freed from parochial work by his bishop or superior, lived by full-time labor, and was in clothing indistinguishable from an ordinary working-man. Yet controversy about clerics in mufti was reaching the boiling point. To the outrage of factory owners, many worker-priests played an active part in union campaigns for better pay and work conditions. Disturbed at how "leftist"—meaning, in fact, how allied with the workers—many worker-priests had become, the Vatican decided that the experiment had to be curtailed. Pope Pius XII suppressed the movement entirely in February 1954. (Later in life, whenever Pius XII was mentioned, Dan tended to refer to him as "the icebox pope.") In 1963 Pope John XXIII, sailing by a different wind, once again allowed priests to return to industrial workplaces.

All this was front-page news in France at the time, but the French were thinking less about the trials and controversies of the Church than about the beating France was taking in Vietnam, the last battle of which occurred at Dien Bien Phu in May 1954. With this calamitous David-versus-Goliath defeat of France in its Indochina War, "the end of the Indo-Chinese colonial adventure was at hand," Dan wrote, "and the republic was stricken at the heart, to a degree it had not known since the [German] occupation. . . . It was a year of national humiliation and turmoil." Following the news closely, Dan became one of the relatively few Americans for whom "Vietnam" was a familiar word in the mid-1950s.

Not all his tertianship, as it turned out, was spent in France. During Lent 1954 Dan was sent on mission to West Germany to assist a Jesuit military chaplain. Dan was later amazed at how few questions he had at the time regarding the US military presence in so many countries. Dan recalled in an autobiographical essay, "I preached and heard confessions and counseled innumerable soldiers and never once brought up, or had brought up to me, the question of modern war, the question of why we were in Germany at all. I do remember writing home from Germany that the endless expenditures and installations, including the first nuclear installation in Western Europe, reminded me ominously of the advance of the Roman Empire. In order to come up with such a thought, I must have entertained at the time rather serious misgivings about the whole adventure. But I cannot claim an acuity of conscience that was only to come to me much later. The fact is that at the time I enjoyed those months. I thought the soldiers who crossed my path and with whom I dealt were unusual and delightful fellows. As undoubtedly they were."[59]

Nor was Dan as yet scandalized by the auxiliary role played by the Church in these far-flung outposts. Chaplains, all of them commissioned officers whose first obedience was to their military superiors, were the face and voice of Christianity for those in uniform, but it was a voice that, in Dan's experience, raised no hard questions about war or conscience and the dangers of blind obedience. "I remember that [every chaplain I met], without exception, was totally militarized," Dan wrote. "They wore their uniform not solely upon their frame, but upon their soul. It was a symbol of the state of their spirit. They were as military as their colleagues in the Officers'

*"It was a measure of my unawakening that I traveled for forty days through American camps and installations, exhorting soldiers and officers to shore up their observance of the faith. And not once did I refer to the fact that nuclear weapons studded the landscape. I met constantly with chaplains and military personnel and their families. And the question of war never once, according to my memory, surfaced as a moral question. One and all, we slept on, the military and I, in an enchanted cave: the workshop of Mars."* —To Dwell in Peace

St. Ignatius Loyola, founder of the Society of Jesus.

Clubs. . . . Indeed, it seemed to me even at the time that several of them made an especially severe push to project themselves as military men to the core."[60]

This was not to say the chaplains were lacking in pastoral concern for those in their care.[61] The head chaplain, a New York Jesuit, especially impressed Dan:

> He was a lieutenant colonel, a tireless worker, and had an astonishing influence over the young soldiers. He used to drive all night . . . with groups of them to preach a retreat that many of them declared had brought their lives to rebirth. He would drive back with them through the night following the close of their spiritual exercise. Alas, he died later of overwork, and I have no doubt that judgment upon him is merciful. But it seems to me [as I look back] . . . that he was a captive of the military system, that his life never once raised the questions that lie at the heart of the gospel.

One aspect of his year in Europe had been participation soon after arrival in a retreat led by their tertianship director, Père François Charmot, whom Dan venerated as "the best and tenderest of masters." Using the Spiritual Exercises of St. Ignatius Loyola, "we meditated on the old-fashioned truths, truths the new theology had by no means held in contempt: sin, death, heaven and hell, the judgment of God, the mercy of God." The thirty-day silent retreat, only the second time Dan had done the Long Retreat after the novitiate experience, ended with meditation on God's kingdom. "We dwelt on [Christ's] meek manifesto, the Sermon on the Mount, and were refreshed at last." Such a regrounding drew the almost-finished Jesuits back to the person whom they were attempting to follow. The black cassock and the initials S.J. after one's name were of no account apart from Jesus.

Thanks to Père Charmot, it had also been a year of important encounters, including meetings with some of the controversial theologians Dan had been reading since he was at Weston. One of Père Charmot's visitors was the Dominican theologian Yves Congar, an early advocate of dialogue with both the Orthodox Church and Protestant Christianity. "To be part of a conversation with Yves Congar," Dan once told me, "was like having cognac for breakfast." Congar promoted the concept of a "collegial" rather than a monarchal papacy and, while advocating the role of laypeople in the Church, criticized the clerical pomp at the Vatican. Following publication in 1952 of Congar's *True and False Reform in the Church*, Rome banned further printings of the book. After publication of an article in support of the worker-priest movement, Congar was prevented from teaching or publishing.

Dominican theologian Yves Congar.

"To say Congar was under a cloud," Dan told me, "would be like saying Joan of Arc felt warm when the bonfire was lit." It was only after Pius XII's death that Congar's reputation recovered and his freedom was regained. In 1960 Pope John XXIII asked Congar to serve on the preparatory theological commission of the Second Vatican Council. Congar has since been described as the single most formative influence on Vatican II. Pope John read and heavily annotated his personal copy of *True and False Reform in the Church*. According to Dominican Paul Philibert, a Vatican II scholar, Congar's book "may claim to being Pope John's inspiration for convoking the council."[62]

In 1994 Congar was named a cardinal by John Paul II.

Another significant event was participation in a three-day retreat led by a Jesuit worker-priest from nearby Lyon, Père Paul Magand. In a letter to Phil, Dan reported,

> [Magand] has been in the factories there for some eight years, so can speak with authority. My admiration is unbounded for these men, who are carrying the world on their shoulders, often with such withering fire from the sidelines. He spoke with real passion, not so much on his own job, as on the need of charity, of justice, of poverty. It was unforgettable. He had come in on the evening train, in his old worker's clothes, spoke to us in the same, even said Mass in them, without a cassock. He also brought to mind many things which have been simmering with me for some time; spoke for example of the "unreality" of French Catholics, in the sense that so much theorizing, analyzing, orating, is done about conditions— and so little action. This is true of their churchmen as well; for whom *elan*, *milieu*, *incarnation*, *esprit*, and all the rest become, after a period of genuine freshness, a series of wearying catchwords as old as the clichés they began by replacing. And that is why the priest workers represent such a marvelous and sacrificial and admirable departure; they are one of the few steps taken to put a tether on all the billowing theory and drag it to earth.[63]

Dan returned to America from France in the late summer of 1954 with a sense both of homecoming and home-leaving. "What I discovered in France for the first time in my long experience of Catholic community was so simple a thing as personal freedom. It was an invitation to become a human being by way of others, immersed as we all were during that year in the tradition of our scripture, as well as the experience and history of our order."[64]

*"What an unfinished human I was, for all the years of Jesuit life, the study, asceticism, sacraments, choices and byways, teaching, exhortations, and retreats, scrutinies and testing. I remember the words of Joan of Arc, in the poem of Péguy, her mourning how long it takes to create a human, how quickly a human is destroyed. And how long, too, the clumsiness and groping, false starts and cowardice, the good, bad, and indifferent in the human meld."*

—To Dwell in Peace

# Brooklyn Prep

Dan was a fully professed Jesuit when he returned to America in the autumn of 1954. His first assignment was to teach at Brooklyn Preparatory School, better known as Brooklyn Prep, a Jesuit institution whose students—many of them second-generation immigrants—were stretched "till our bones cracked," as one of Dan's students put it.

Academic standards were high. In the honors program, where Dan was placed, students in their senior year were expected to read Homer in ancient Greek, Cicero in classical Latin, Dante's *Divine Comedy* in early Italian, plus know fifteen to twenty of Shakespeare's plays. In translations of classics, Dan wasn't as interested in linguistic exactitude as in attempting to communicate the text's art and drama. Not surprisingly, given so solid a grounding, some of the school's students went on to distinguished careers as scholars, but what Dan was mainly seeking of the kids he taught was, as he once told me, "to catch fire and burn. I wanted them to get more out of life than an upward ride on the golden escalator to nowhere." Part of his focus in that period was to create groups of students to make contact with hard-pressed Puerto Ricans living not so far away. He made contact with Jesuits at Nativity Mission on the Lower East Side of Manhattan, a parish that served many Puerto Rican families and also happened to be near the Catho-

*"I was aback in the hustings, with a vengeance. With an enterprising team of laymen and Jesuits, we started honors courses in classics and English literature. I sojourned regularly with students to the Lower East Side of Manhattan; there we made ourselves useful at the Nativity Center, whose open doors were welcoming the great influx of Puerto Ricans."*
—To Dwell in Peace

HAT TAKETH
HE SWORD
HALL PERISH
BY THE SWORD
Jesus

Dorothy Day, founder of the *Catholic Worker,* protesting for peace.

lic Worker house of hospitality, St. Joseph's. "This is how I began to know Dorothy Day and people working with her," Dan recalled. "I had grown up with the *Catholic Worker* in the house and here was its founder, a woman glad to talk not just to me but also to my students and welcome them into volunteer work. It was life-changing for all of us."

Meeting Dorothy Day was a major event: "She taught me more than all the theologians," Dan said half a century later. "She awakened me to connections I had not thought of or been instructed in—the equation of human misery and poverty with war making. She had a basic hope that God created the world with enough for everyone, but there was not enough for everyone and war making."[65] But the process of understanding and embracing Day's radical rejection of war took Dan several years.

Dan, though working hard to shed the dark weight of clericalism, was still every inch a Jesuit priest of the 1950s, one of "the Jesuit gods," as one Brooklyn Prep student put it. "The word 'Jesuit' in those days," said a former student, "was a synonym for brains and excellence and also, it has to be said, ego." Jesuits were widely seen as the aristocracy of the Catholic priesthood. Some students were critical. A graduate recalls, "Father Berrigan always came across [to me] as a pompous person, a little intolerant of persons not up to par."[66] Dan Berrigan pompous? Perhaps he was. I have to take the witness's memory seriously, though I never encountered that trait in him. But sharp-tongued, yes—capable of searing and wounding sarcasm when his inner winds blew from the east. At his best, however, he had a rare ability to connect with those his colleagues found hopeless.

Novelist and former Jesuit Joseph Roccasalvo, once a student at Brooklyn Prep, was witness to one such instance:

As a member of the [Brooklyn Prep] sophomore Sodality of the Blessed Virgin, I found myself in Father Berrigan's company taking a Brooklyn bus to the Gold Street Mission. Dan had been asked to substitute for the moderator, who was tutoring students in the lower mysteries of plane geometry. I knew Dan by sight as the priest with the abstracted air who did not so much traverse school corridors as waft through them. . . . His preaching at the first Friday Mass was my exposure to his beguiling way with words. I recall one sermon in which he warned the students against "the illusion of the obvious." Opaque to me then, this phrase has since become demonstrably clear. On that March day . . . I recall how he put me at ease, and how swiftly we seemed to arrive at our destination.

Dan and I walked to the mission and entered a ramshackle building where the security guard directed us to the auditorium. Chairs in clusters encircled the room in which Catholic students were catechizing their charges. Dan left to explore the premises while I joined my Communion class. Five students from the previous week were dutifully waiting, but I noted a sixth had been added—Winston. Five feet tall and wiry, he was dressed in the oversized clothes of an older brother. Dark complexioned with huge eyes and coal black irises, he did not so much sit in his chair as squirm in it. He muttered aloud as his eyes looked distractedly ahead. Here was a needy child. I hoped to explain how Catholic Mass incorporated the Jewish Passover. I never got that far. Winston twisted and turned, waving both hands, or interrupted with pointless remarks. When to the cheers of the class he landed on the floor with his collapsible chair alongside, I lost my patience.

*"How could it be that the work of teaching, and the communitarian life of the schools, so often narrowed the vision of teachers, dug a furrow that in time, became a very grave? . . . And at the far end of our efforts, how did it fare with our graduates, those darlings of our long belaboring? Were they notably superior in moral understanding for having been exposed to our ethos over the years? Had their imaginations taken fire from our own? Or were we, and they, merely sedulous instances of a cruel and wounding culture?"*
—To Dwell in Peace

"Rev. Daniel J. Berrigan, S.J., Religion, Latin, English, Senior Sodality."
Cornell University, Division of Rare and Manuscript Collections

At Brooklyn Prep, "Father Berrigan explains the use of the sacred vessels of Mass to the assembled Senior Sodalists." Cornell University, Division of Rare and Manuscript Collections

I did not notice Dan watching from a distance. He walked over and without explaining asked Winston: "Would you like a soda?" He nodded yes, eager to exchange my presence for a newcomer's. Order returned, and my class moved peaceably to its close. I glanced across the room to see Winston sipping his soda. Dan sat alongside with a smile compounded of kindness and genial irony. I gave my students their assignment and dismissed them, then walked over to Winston, who was slurping the remainder of his Coke.

Without soda to distract, I thought, who will calm his antics, for he had now inserted a finger in the neck of the soda bottle, and was banging it against the chair. Dan turned to him. "Winston, would you like to hear a story?" "What story?" he asked. "About the genie in the Coca-Cola bottle." "What's a genie?"

I excused myself and walked away, having decided that the improvised tale was between Dan and Winston. I regret not staying for the story of a genie locked in a bottle, but eager for freedom to benefit the conjurer. At five o'clock the security guard sounded the bell that signaled the building's close. I saw Dan holding Winston's hand as they approached his mother waiting at the door. "Were you good today, Winston?" she asked. He nodded affirmatively while Dan smiled in confirmation. Winston waved good-bye as we left the building, and then Dan and I returned to Brooklyn Prep.[67]

If Dan's life during his three years at Brooklyn Prep centered on students, the borders of his engagements reached a widening circle. He celebrated Mass and preached at several parishes. He served as chaplain of a Brooklyn chapter of Young Christian Workers, a movement with European roots whose goal was "reconciling [Christ's] Church with the industrial workers of the world." The group met over a Flatbush grocery store to do scripture study before engaging in community service in poor neighborhoods. Dan also became active with the Walter Farrell Guild, named after a Dominican priest who had died in 1951, in which both clergy and laypeople met to discuss literature and theology. Moreover, he was doing a monthly broadcast on a Jesuit radio program, *The Sacred Heart Hour*. He was beginning to be sought out as a retreat leader. His was an intensely social life, at the core of which was solitude.

"I was dwelling at the eye of an urban hurricane," Dan wrote in *To Dwell in Peace*. "I would walk long distances in the city, invariably alone, usually late at night; then return for a quiet hour in the chapel before sleep. I was communitarian by discipline, a loner by instinct. I cultivated my soul with a fierceness that could be understood only as a passion for survival. I read widely and wrote as I might. . . . I took it for granted that someday I would be known as a poet and a chronicler of the times."[68]

Poems by "Daniel Berrigan, S.J." were appearing in more and more journals. Some caught the eye of an editor at Macmillan, Betty Bartelme, who in turn contacted Dan, inviting him to submit what he regarded as his best work to date. Dan christened the submission *Time without Number*. One of the text's readers was the celebrated poet Marianne Moore. She had, Bartelme reported, "taken the manuscript to heart." Macmillan sent a contract.

Dan and Phil with their parents.
Cornell University, Division of Rare and Manuscript Collections

# Father Phil

Phil on the day of his ordination, with Dan and parents. Courtesy Berrigan family

As 1954 began, Jerry Berrigan made the difficult decision that the priesthood, with its obligatory celibacy, was not for him. He opted for marriage. Phil, meanwhile, pressed on in seminary. His ordination came in June 1955, a ceremony held at the Shrine of the Immaculate Conception in Washington, D.C. For the occasion Dan wrote a celebratory poem, "The Innocent Throne." It began,

Philip, since all is summed in you,
I am a wastrel of fair words
to send them loud and purposeless
all frantic as a cage of birds.
Possessing not my heart, my voice,
they fret the lovely, listening day:
then do not heed them. My word for you
no word of mine will ever say.[69]

Phil's first assignment was in the city of his ordination. He became assistant pastor of Our Lady of Perpetual Help, a solidly black parish in the Anacostia district. During the year he was stationed there, while Phil taught Catechism and Scripture, his parishioners taught him "the real meaning of hate, fear and discrimination

. . . Blacks lived in battered neighborhoods, went to rundown schools and worked at rotten jobs. . . . Whites owned the banks and businesses; blacks mopped the floors."[70]

Phil increasingly questioned the gradualist approach to racial justice advocated by the Josephites and many others. Gains in integration, education, housing, and other race-stamped issues came at a snail's pace if at all. Below the Mason-Dixon Line, even Catholic parishes tended to be of one color or, if otherwise, with blacks in the back of the church just as they were at the back of the bus.

While his antisegregation message was judged as outrageous by most whites, black audiences listened with surprise and gratitude. Phil began to develop a reputation as an eloquent public speaker, and with the civil rights movement gaining momentum, his was a voice more and more people wanted to hear. The fact that he was a Catholic priest added to his appeal even among non-Catholics. Phil earned a reputation for never saying no to an invitation.

In 1956, after a year in Washington, his superiors decided to transfer Phil to New Orleans, this time to teach religion and English at St. Augustine's, a highly regarded all-black, all-male Josephite high school in the city's French Quarter. Here he found he was not a voice crying in the wilderness; the local church was exemplary on racial issues. In 1953 Archbishop of New Orleans Joseph Rummel had issued a pastoral letter condemning any form of segregation in the diocese:

> Ever mindful . . . of the basic truth that our Colored Catholic brethren share with us the same spiritual life and destiny, the same membership in the Mystical Body of Christ, the same dependence upon the Word of God, the same participation in the Sacraments, especially the Most Holy Eucharist, the same need of moral and social encouragement, let there be

Phil gives a blessing on his ordination day. Cornell University, Division of Rare and Manuscript Collections

*"I entered the Society of Saint Joseph for training toward the priesthood. I lived with Black seminarians. I learned from them in a graphic way what it means to be Black in this country."*
—Phil Berrigan in The Trial of the Catonsville Nine

no further discrimination or segregation in the pews, at the Communion rail, at the confessional and in parish meetings, just as there will be no segregation in the kingdom of heaven.[71]

In his early months at St. Augustine's, Phil avoided controversy by focusing on teaching and his responsibilities with adult and student groups active in charity work. He rose early and was still up after midnight, often putting in eighteen-hour days.

In 1957, when a group of students in his theology class asked Phil what they might do to bring about integration in parishes that remained solidly white, he suggested that the following Sunday they attend Mass in a parish where black faces were missing. Several students took up the proposal and, after Mass, were badly beaten; one of them needed forty stitches. Archbishop Rummel responded with vigor by declaring that no services would be permitted for the parish without repentance for what had been done: "You'll get Mass and the other sacraments when you stop this barbarism. Only when you accept that you have done something gravely wrong can there be healing." When the repentant parish reopened five months later, it was integrated.

Phil with children in New Orleans.
Cornell University, Division of Rare and Manuscript Collections

Phil was grateful for the results of his students' brave action but deeply troubled that he had unwittingly proposed a strategy that had put their lives at risk.[72]

# Le Moyne

The year 1957 was a big one for Dan. The Academy of American Poets honored *Time without Number* with the Lamont Poetry Prize. One of the poems that impressed the judges was "Credentials":

> I would it were possible to state in so
> few words my errand in the world: quite simply
> forestalling all in query, the oak offers his leaves
> largehandedly. And in winter his integral magnifi-
>     cent order
> decrees, says solemnly who he is
> in the great thrusting limbs that are all finally one:
> a return, a permanent riverandsea.
>
> So the rose is its own credential, a certain
> unattainable effortless form: wearing its heart
> visibly, it gives us heart too: bud, fullness and fall.[73]

The book was also nominated for a National Book Award. Dan was well and truly launched as a poet. Such recognition, Dan noted, "was an enormous stimulus upon work that up to then had been wrought mainly in darkness."[74]

That fall, after three years teaching at Brooklyn Prep, Dan was appointed to the post of associate professor of New Testament studies at Le Moyne College,

*"With the publication of my first book my mind exploded. . . . Publishers would now take almost anything I chose to compile; the question of quality was largely in my own hands and my own sense of things."*
—No Bars to Manhood

Le Moyne College.

*"In 1957 I was assigned to the theology department of a young Jesuit college in Syracuse, New York. My poetry was in the public eye, a second book of essays on the way. I would have been regarded by colleagues as a promising gent, a bit to the left of perfect balance, perhaps, but one who could be counted on not to rock things seriously."*

—To Dwell in Peace

a Jesuit school in the Berrigan stronghold of Syracuse.

As Dan recalled in an autobiographical essay, "In a sense I felt that now my life was beginning on an entirely fresh and exciting basis. I was teaching college classes for the first time. The college was only eleven years old and we were, in a rather innovating way, making go as we went. . . . I cannot remember when I was more hardily tested or more blessedly renewed in spirit. For six long years I was riding the crest of a wave toward a shore that continually receded and expanded, showing now its reefs, now its populated and noisy centers, now the human faces upon its shore, inviting or threatening."[75]

His classes were popular despite the fact that his required reading list was "as long as Route 66," as one student complained, and his standards high: "I was accounted stern in the classroom and not solely regarding points of scripture. When assignments were due I poked about in the corners of grammar and punctuation. . . . I sought literacy as well as imagination."[76] Later in life Dan looked back critically on his early years as a college teacher: "My mind was still in a kind of mind-set. I know I always resented being referred to as a teacher of 'dogmatic' theology. But the fact was that I was still, in many aspects, quite dogmatic."

Burning the midnight oil, during his six years at Le Moyne Dan was a productive author, completing two books of poetry, *Encounters* (1960) and *The World for Wedding Ring* (1962), and two collections of essays, *The Bride: Essays in the Church* (1959) and *The Bow in the Clouds* (1961). His readership was steadily expanding as his name became more familiar.

Increasingly aware that his vocation extended beyond the classroom, Dan suggested to Karl Meyer of the Chicago Catholic Worker that he move to Syracuse to take the lead in founding a house in a poor neighborhood to serve the needs of local people, with Dan's students helping as volunteers. Meyer had recently served a thirty-day jail term for refusing to take shelter, along with Dorothy

Day, during an obligatory civil defense drill in Manhattan. Trying to avoid controversy, Dan approached the idea of opening a community house cautiously. At the time, Meyer recalls, "Dan did not want his name or the project explicitly associated with the Catholic Worker. In that period of his life, he spoke out publicly very little, if at all, on the moral or political problems of war and peace, with which the Catholic Worker was so associated."[77]

Though Meyer was willing, the local bishop proved hostile, phoning Dan to threaten his removal from the Le Moyne faculty unless the project was abandoned. "I seemed to have pressed my ear against the crater of an active volcano," Dan told me years later. "How dare I bring to town this 'so-called' Catholic, Karl Meyer, a known pacifist who is part of the Catholic Worker movement? And me a wet-behind-the-ears Jesuit inviting him? Didn't I, a teacher of theology, know that the just war doctrine was a cornerstone of Catholic theology? And what need was being met by a so-called house of hospitality that the parishes in Syracuse weren't already meeting?"

Presumably the bishop's next phone call was to the Jesuit president of Le Moyne with the suggestion that Dan might do better somewhere else. Remarkably Dan's administration and fellow teachers rallied around him— "one of the few times," Dan remarked, "when professors stood by a colleague in trouble"—and the bishop withdrew his threat.[78] Even so, it took several years before an approximation of Dan's idea took shape.

Among Dan's students at Le Moyne was David Miller, a young man who a few years later would claim front-page headlines for being one of the first to burn his draft card as a protest against the Vietnam War. By then David had graduated and become part of the Catholic Worker community in New York.

At least one thousand students passed through my classes in those six years, but it is not to be wondered at that I remember David quite vividly. The question

*"Disease of power is the phrase that occurs. Whether the malaise strikes in church or state, I am not at all certain that it takes a different form. In the ecclesiastical instance, there is a dread and double jeopardy implied: the sword is two-edged. The will of the authorities is presented as God's will. And that weapon of sovereign will removes limbs and heads so cleanly it becomes almost a privilege to perish at such hands—under the Excalibur that whispers as it kills: God's will! God's will!"*
—To Dwell in Peace

Thomas Merton.
John Howard Griffin (Courtesy Griffin Estate)

*"What was [Merton] trying to do? He might say . . . he was trying to clear the rubble, he was trying to awaken people to the truth, he was trying to save what could be salvaged of lives and dignity, he was trying to show that atrophied human parts could indeed be turned on, a very space of anger, indignation, joy, ecstasy even. That these were the proper functions of the soul awake."*

—Portraits

of war had not yet occurred—Vietnam was still a remote and obscure event. David, however, was part of whatever social action was occurring off-campus, or being planned on-campus. . . . My name has been associated with him in the years that followed, and I am indeed proud of whatever that may be construed to imply, even of guilt by association. The fact is that we never discussed war and peace. We often discussed civil rights and tried to do something about the horrendous ghetto conditions of downtown Syracuse. I can only reflect upon the mystery that has since become a little more apparent. That is to say, David's life was fertile soil upon which the good seed fell and flourished.[79]

One of the writers Dan most admired was Thomas Merton, the Trappist monk to whom Dan had sent an appreciative letter after reading his autobiography, *The Seven Storey Mountain*, shortly after the book's publication in 1948. Flooded with fan mail at the time, Merton didn't respond, but when Dan next wrote, in October 1961, an intense and intimate correspondence began that lasted until shortly before Merton's death seven years later.

Dan's letter was prompted by publication in the October issue of the *Catholic Worker* of "The Root of War Is Fear," an essay in which Merton declared that "the duty of the Christian [in a world gearing itself for nuclear war] is to strive with all his power and intelligence, with his faith, his hope in Christ, and love for God and man, to do the one task which God has imposed upon us in the world today. That task is to work for the total abolition of war."[80] It was an article that led some of its Cold War critics to accuse Merton of being "used by the Communists."

No reader was more challenged by Merton's essay than Dan. By then he had learned of the effort then under way by several people (I was one of them) to launch an American branch of the British Pax Society, and told Merton about it. Pax was a Catholic association whose

Cover of October 1961 issue of *The Catholic Worker*, featuring Merton's essay, "The Root of War."

members had either rejected war altogether as incompatible with Christianity or had concluded that warfare, given the destructive capacity of modern weaponry, could no longer meet the conditions of a just war.

The great problem, said Merton in his response, "is the blindness and passivity of Christians." American Catholics "are almost in the same position as the Catholics before the last war in Hitler's Germany." Merton's letter included an invitation to visit his monastery, the Abbey of Gethsemani in Kentucky. "Next year," Merton proposed, "you and some other peace people must come down."[81]

Ten months later, in August 1962, the two had their first encounter. In a journal entry Merton found his guest "an altogether winning intelligence, with a perfect zeal, compassion and understanding" in which he recognized "the true spirit of the church."[82] There were to be four more face-to-face meetings in the years ahead.

Dan's most significant extracurricular initiative at Le Moyne was the founding of International House, an off-campus residence where Dan lived with a community of students preparing for future endeavors that connected their faith with work for social justice. "Toward the new

*"Father Dan Berrigan is an altogether winning and warm intelligence and a man who, I think, has more than anyone I have ever met the true wide-ranging and simple heart of the Jesuit: zeal, compassion, understanding, and uninhibited religious freedom. Just seeing him restores one's hope in the church."*
—Thomas Merton in Conjectures of a Guilty Bystander

year of 1962 I was granted a go-ahead with a project of living off-campus with fifteen students who would prepare themselves for Peace Corps–type of work in rural areas of Mexico. We got the house off to a flying start . . . and settled into the chancy business of making ourselves into a community. It went well. By the time I left Le Moyne . . . the first team had already gone south."

International House had its own chapel. "It was," Dan wrote, "a simple necessity . . . no more a luxury than a kitchen. The chapel must express something of our faith and hope, the work we were pledged to. The week we moved in, we came on an abandoned room in the basement, untidy, unfinished, the joints and two-by-fours exposed, baggage and trunks and trash piled ceiling high, raw concrete underfoot. Just the place. We labored like motivated ants. Slowly things took shape. . . . We laid a floor of flagstone, installed lighting, enlisted an artist to paint a mural. Vessels and vestments were designed and donated."[83]

"The jewel of the place," said Dan, "was the altar." Its designer and builder was none other than the family patriarch, Thomas Berrigan, now nearing eighty. Making it must have been the elder Berrigan's gesture of belated pride in a son he had once regarded as physically unfit to bear the family name but who had grown up to become priest, professor, and published poet.

The altar was a work of love and craft—"not a nail [was] driven," Dan recalled appreciatively, "the lengths of wood were . . . pegged together, rough and true." The altar cloth was his mother's gift: "It was her table linen, a gift at her wedding . . . [still] dazzling white after more than fifty years. It unrolled luxuriously and fell to the floor like a snowfall."

It must have puzzled Thomas Berrigan that the Masses at which his son presided were in English rather than Latin. In matters liturgical, Dan was several years ahead of the switch to the vernacular that would be authorized at the forthcoming Vatican Council.[84]

One of the major pluses of Dan's years at Le Moyne was being able to see so much of his family. Jerry and his wife, Carol, had settled in Syracuse, and his parents remained there as well. While the bond with Frida was especially strong, Dan spent many Sunday afternoons sitting on the porch or in the living room with his father, whose attention span was shrinking. Contact was still strained but much better than it had been earlier in life.[85]

Starting in 1960, Dan's bond with Phil began to develop into a vocational partnership, with Le Moyne students going to New Orleans to participate in civil rights projects and Phil identifying promising black students for Le Moyne scholarships. The two of them also tried to take part in a Freedom Ride in 1961 but were blocked by their superiors, as happened again two years later when they sought to join with other clergy in integrating the Jackson, Mississippi, airport. (The Catholic bishop of Jackson threatened to remove all Josephite clergy working in his diocese if Phil was not recalled.)

Phil, Dan, and Jerry Berrigan, Niagara Falls, 1957. Courtesy Berrigan family

Another area of tension had been a decision from Phil's superiors barring him from co-authoring a book with Dan. (Instead, two books emerged, Phil's *No More Strangers* and Dan's *They Call Us Dead Men*.) Dan was so disheartened by the restrictions imposed by his superiors that he seriously considered disobedience, thus risking dismissal from the Jesuits. He wrote Merton for guidance and received the advice that, unjust though the orders were, he would achieve more in the long run by compliance.

"You have to consider the continuity of your work as a living unit," Merton wrote. "You must be careful not to rupture that continuity in a violent and drastic way without having an exceptionally grave reason and a rather

Phil preaching. Courtesy Berrigan family

evident sign that this is required precisely of you. By this I refer to the fact that a violent break with superiors would tend to cast discredit on all the initiatives you have so far taken and render them all suspect as part of a dangerous process leading inevitably to radicalism and defection. If you allow this to happen (of course it might have to happen in some cases) you must consider that you are turning adrift those who have begun to follow you and profit by your leadership. And you are also at the same time wreaking havoc in the minds of superiors, who were perhaps timidly beginning to go along with you."[86] Dan found Merton's guidance persuasive.

But, as Phil's work in New Orleans made clear, there were many other ways of tackling race issues and doing so without going south. Dan felt challenged to consider what could be done about race and poverty issues right where he lived. One result was his proposal that students who belonged to the sodality[87] he had founded investigate local slum housing in Syracuse. "Who," Dan asked, "was accountable, say, for an uninhabitable derelict building, a crowded slum block? Who collected rents and refused to make repairs?"[88]

When they discovered that some of the landlords were Le Moyne College benefactors, the researchers publicized their findings, much to the annoyance of the college administration. Protests followed. "We were on touchy ground," Dan recalled. "The [city's] monetary mandarins were influential not only in the political establishment, but in the church as well. They oiled the gears of the city; they were also conspicuous consumers of parish services." For the implicated donors it was obvious that the college would be better off if Dan Berrigan were assigned elsewhere.

The yearlong sabbatical in Europe that Dan was given at the end of the spring semester in 1963 may have been a gentle way of getting a troublesome priest off the campus. "From some few among the faculty," Dan wrote, "there was an all but audible susurration of relief [but] from myself a deep breath . . . of gratitude for all that had been. What was accomplished at the college was as permanent as anything could claim in such times. It would bear fruit. . . . I had gained a precious grounding—in innovative worship, in community, in the joining of conscience to professional skill."[89]

Whatever the reasons, Dan was not invited to resume teaching at Le Moyne when his sabbatical ended. In fact, "Never again would I be, for any appreciable time, a member of a Jesuit faculty."[90]

*"More than the Le Moyne years were ending. It came almost like the sounding of a knell; but the tolling was so deep and gentle as almost to merge with the murmur of life itself, and be lost there. Who could tell what changes were being rung, what death and birth? And by no means my own solely: beloved friends on the faculty, young women and men entering convents and seminaries.*

*And more: the tonality and travail of academic life, the near ecstasy of friendship and work and worship and life together; the fabric of things, so dear, so closely woven, and (as I was discovering) so easily raveled."*

—To Dwell in Peace

# Paris and Eastward

"Europe is obviously the next step," Merton had concluded in a June 1963 letter to Dan, "because over there you may find what's what. And you need to. When you do, let me know."[91] A few weeks later Dan was searching for a small apartment in Paris that wouldn't overburden his five-dollar-a-day sabbatical budget and found it in a *Maison des Etudiants* (a house for students) at 61 rue Madame on the Left Bank. There was no charge for bed-and-board if he would agree, when not traveling, to serve as chaplain, taking his meals with the students, being available for counseling, and offering Mass on Sundays. Gladly, said Dan.

Dan did do some traveling during the first half of his sabbatical, although mainly he was in Paris. Prague and Budapest were the most important stops. In his autobiographical essay "Open Sesame," he described what drew him east:

By Christmas [1963] I had decided that . . . if I was to get anything out of the year I had better launch . . . eastward. And so I did. At Christmastime I visited Czechoslovakia and Hungary for periods of about one week each. It was my baptism in Marxist society. I was particularly moved by the evidence that the churches in those countries, especially the Protestant communities, were finding ways of survival in most difficult circumstances. I returned to Paris by way of Rome, in order to inform the Vatican on what I had discovered in Eastern Europe. It amounted to support of a strong recommendation on the part of the Protestant communities that the Vatican begin to take a more practical interest in the religious and social situation in Marxist Central Europe. I reported to Cardinal Bea's assistant, . . . [a man who] gave me a sympathetic hearing. I was trying to interest the church officials in the idea that I should be appointed a Vatican observer at the Christian Peace Conference to be held in the summer of 1964. . . . [Though not appointed as a Vatican observer] I did get to Prague in June 1964 [to take part in the Christian Peace Conference] and [afterward] proceeded with a group of American theologians into the Soviet Union, by invitation of the Orthodox and Baptist communities there. The impact of that trip is ineradicable upon my spirit. I was discovering for the first time, and at firsthand, the radically different social forms by which other decent men and women were living. I was discovering peaceable communities of faith, surviving and even thriving in most difficult and trying circumstances. I was seeing at firsthand the damage wrought to the human spirit in the West as a result of the Cold War.[92]

Getting approval to travel in Communist countries had not been easy.

No Jesuit superior in France would grant permission for my venture. The authority at [Jesuit headquarters on] rue de Grenelle was sympathetic but firm. He

Cathedral of Notre Dame in Paris.

Cathedral in Prague.

would relay my request to the general of the order in Rome. Christmas approached. I bit my nails and fretted, and not a word. And finally, on December 23, the day of proposed departure, permission was granted. I ran for the plane at the last moment. . . . I landed in Prague toward midnight. The city was windless, still, dead cold. I was conducted [by a professor at the Comenius Theological Seminary] to a hotel, unheated and dank. There was little fuel in the city and less food. I slept in my clothes.[93]

While being shown the city by his host in the days that followed, Dan was impressed by the serious attempt the state was making to suppress Christianity—Christmas was made an ordinary workday, there were no Christmas decorations, those active in church life were excluded from the professions—but impressed even more by the vitality of Christian life in such harsh circumstances. "I had moved among Christians who lived their faith with steadfastness, under a shadow of disrepute and disenfranchisement. They refused the quick fix—to flee to the West. . . . [They were] marked by a dogged sense of patience and resolve. They chose to live in circumstances, however harsh, which they believed [were] permitted by God."[94]

"The Christians I met in Prague and then in Budapest," Dan later told me, "were miraculous flowers that flourish in winter."

# Meeting Dan

It was in Paris that my friendship with Dan began, though we had met nearly three years earlier, in October 1961, when I was part of the Catholic Worker's Manhattan household. On that occasion Dorothy Day had brought me with her to a small meeting that Dan had come down from Syracuse to attend. We gathered in the living room of an apartment on the west edge of Harlem. Our host was William Robert Miller, jazz critic and then editor of the Fellowship of Reconciliation's magazine, *Fellowship*. John Heidbrink, another key FOR staff member, was also present.[95]

Dan was a lean, wiry man with closely cropped black hair and pink skin dressed in tailored black clericals and a Roman collar. He was introduced to us as a poet who had won the Lamont Poetry Prize and was currently teaching theology at Le Moyne. He also had founded an "international house" at which students lived in community in preparation for justice-oriented work in Latin America.

Heidbrink, a Protestant minister, remarked on the ecclesiastical thaw that was astonishing the world as Pope John XXIII began proving to be something more than a pope between popes. "This pope is a parade of surprises," said Heidbrink, "not just a breath of fresh air but a hurricane, and Father Berrigan is part of that hurricane."

Introductions over, my memory is doubtless com-

Dorothy Day with Catholic Worker staff. Marquette University Archives

*"Many years before Vietnam housebroke our souls, [Dorothy Day] said no to war—once for all, unequivocally. Once was enough perhaps. But she repeated it month after month in her paper, The Catholic Worker. . . . She said no without contention or malice or dour judgment against tardy, commonplace minds like our own, as we ventured toward the truth—our own devious dance, two steps forward, two back—our second thoughts, our backward glances."*

—To Dwell in Peace

pressing what actually happened half a century ago in having Dan immediately pull a sheaf of paper from an inner jacket pocket and proceed to read aloud an analysis of Catholic social teaching and the impact of Pope John. Undoubtedly it was an excellent essay, suggestive in style and content of all that would, in the coming years, become so widely appreciated in Dan's writings. His prose bore the stamp of his poetry. For better or worse, however, honesty requires the admission of my having to fight off a nap; I must have had too little sleep the night before. I fear my eyes and ears were more closed than open until the discussion began, but by then it was late and the exchange too brief. All I can remember is that we talked about the urgent need to challenge Catholic at-homeness with war.

Dorothy was normally a good and appreciative listener, but I recall she was annoyed as we closed the apartment door behind us and began making our way back by subway to the Lower East Side. "Just like a priest!" she snapped. "He didn't leave room for anyone else to talk!" On the subway she became more positive, recalling Dan bringing Brooklyn Prep students to the Catholic Worker in the mid-fifties. The next day she asked me to write "Father Berrigan"—she never referred to priests informally—and request a copy of his paper. "I need to read it again. It might be something for us to publish." This was a pattern I gradually came to anticipate in Dorothy, irritable one day, with more positive second thoughts the next.

After that first encounter, I didn't see Dan again until mid-June 1964 when he was on sabbatical and I was among the several Catholic participants in a Fellowship of Reconciliation–sponsored European seminar. Hermene Evans, one of the few Catholic members of the FOR at the time, had underwritten the costs of the small Catholic contingent that was part of an otherwise Protestant group.

Dan was already in Paris, our first stop, when we

arrived. We found him standing in the lobby of a posh hotel at which John Heidbrink, the FOR staff member who had organized the seminar, had booked rooms at a bargain price.

At first sight I didn't recognize him. The tailored clericals and Roman collar had been replaced with a black cotton turtleneck, trim black chino slacks, a faded green windbreaker jacket, and a suede leather tote bag slung over his shoulder, his mobile library and wine cellar combined.

The transformation of clothing was less striking than Dan's face. Three years of breakthroughs and setbacks had marked Dan. In 1961 he had struck me as a well-scrubbed, pink-faced American cleric taking root in academia like so many bright upcoming Jesuits. Now his face seemed blizzard-worn, the pink blown away. In its place was bleached Maine rock etched with experiences of winter. The Roman collar had evaporated.

What had brought him, I asked, from Syracuse to Paris? It was due, he replied, to his liturgical innovations—saying the Mass in English well before such usage was officially authorized—and his engagement in the local civil rights movement, jeopardizing contributions to the university. These impolitic activities had caused tension between him and his superiors, a tension further aggravated when permission could not be obtained for Dan to coauthor a book with Phil. After six years teaching theology at Le Moyne, Dan had been given a yearlong sabbatical in France. I asked, "Was this meant as a sugar-coated exile?" "Very likely," Dan responded, "but what a place to be!"

Our three-day Parisian stay included street searching, river walking, bread buying, and wine sipping, plus meetings with several remarkable people, one of whom was Jean Daniélou, fellow Jesuit and eminent scholar of the early church. Daniélou spoke to us about theologians of the first centuries of the Christian era, such saints as Gregory of Nyssa and his brother Basil the Great, who,

Jesuit scholar Jean Daniélou after he was made a cardinal by Pope Paul VI.

using a modern term, could be described as pacifists—people for whom killing other human beings for any reason was a rejection of Christ and his gospel.

Dan also introduced us to two worker-priests, both Dominicans. Impressive men. That they were priests caught me by complete surprise. We met them at the Grail house, a community of Catholic laywomen. The smell of paint in the building had led me to assume these two men were painters who happened to be taking a break in the room into which we had been ushered. One of them was brawny, with a butcher's arms and back, the other lean and quick, with a knife-fighter's tense alertness. Both were formidable. It required Dan's introduction for me to absorb the notion that they were priests, but I was again in for a surprise as I assumed, gruff men that they appeared to be, that they would talk in a gruff way. Instead they were very much like Dan—and, again, like Dan, shattered stereotypes. I had never imagined such a priesthood, never thought such a worker-scholar synthesis (to use a Catholic Worker's phrase) could bridge the lay-clerical divide. These plain-clothed clerics, working full-time in factories, were attempting to reconnect the Catholic Church in France with the post-Christian working class who viewed the Church as an ally of the comfortable class.

On our last morning Dan took us to have breakfast with a crowd of university students who were running a Catholic Worker–style hospitality program in the thirteenth-century crypt of St. Severin Church near Notre Dame in the Latin Quarter. The church's ancient cloister was being used as a soup-serving area once each day, and the students had created a number of paid jobs for their guests; scrubbing grave markers and stonework was one of them.

Before breakfast, we trooped into the church and, with Dan presiding, proceeded to celebrate a Mass in English, my first such experience. Presbyterian John Heidbrink read the Gospel, and everyone—Protestant, Quaker, Catholic—joined in sharing the consecrated

Church of St. Severin in Paris.

bread and wine, "the living bread which has come down from heaven," as Dan announced with a joyous face. "Taste and see how good the Lord is."

There are circumstances even in liturgy, Dan found, that warranted "holy disobedience." Amid worshipers who knew little Latin, Dan's celebration of Mass climbed over several of the fences in canon law, not disrespectfully but in recognition of the pastoral needs of those attending Mass. We walked out of St. Severin's cool stone interior into the summer light to see Notre Dame lifting her spires above the green treetops, very much as our own spirits had been put to flight by our breaking of the bread of Christ.

That night our pilgrimage group, having flown to Rome, made ourselves at home in a pilgrim hostel on the Piazza Navona run by Dutch nuns. Here Jim Douglass, a theological adviser at the Second Vatican Council who occasionally wrote for the *Catholic Worker*, joined our traveling seminar.

Over the coming days we had walks and meetings, one in a regal palace library that had once been the study of a Renaissance cardinal. One afternoon we wandered about in the archaeological excavations beneath San Clemente, a church near the Colosseum where water was still rushing through stone channels fitted together before the angel declared unto Mary.

One of the meetings Jim Douglass had arranged was with Cardinal Augustin Bea, head of the recently created Vatican Secretariat for the Promotion of Christian Unity. Bea, a German Jesuit and biblical scholar, was one of the bishops most closely linked with Pope John XXIII's aspirations for the council. Welcoming our small group, he said how pleased he was to see Catholics and Protestants collaborating in peace work, including—nodding to Dan—a fellow Jesuit. Responding to questions about the council, he remarked on the divisions that existed among some of the bishops regarding the proposed condemnation of nuclear weapons and recognition of the right of refusal

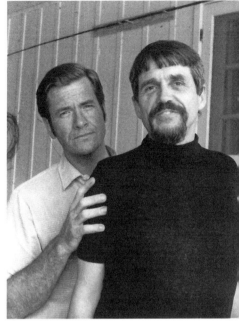

Dan with John Heidbrink of the FOR.
Courtesy Berrigan family

Cardinal Augustin Bea of the
Vatican Secretariat for the Promotion
of Christian Unity.

*"We also attended sessions of
the Christian Peace Conference
in Prague. There, in an immense,
bare hall, several hundred
delegates from mainline
churches, East and West, talked
interminably and debated
resolutions, in the manner of
their kind. Earnestness and
political savvy and a measure
of religious passion were in the
air. . . . Little or nothing
accomplished (we thought at the
time), for all the grandiose air
and solemn ceremony, the grave
debates and resolutions, recorded
word for word, as though the
fate of the world hung on the
outcome."* —To Dwell in Peace

to condone or participate in war in any form. "There is resistance among some members of the American hierarchy to the council taking a new direction in these matters," said Bea. The several Catholics at the meeting laughed at his polite understatement. "Your efforts are needed," Bea added, raising his hands and eyes toward heaven.

The experience most deeply engraved in memory is a trolley ride to the Vatican during which Dan astounded the Roman citizenry on board by announcing that the least we Americans could do for international goodwill was provide some music. Dan immediately led us in singing one of the newly minted anthems of the sixties, Bob Dylan's "Blowin' in the Wind."

Events in Vietnam had been much more on view in the French and Italian press than in our own. Dan was one of the first Americans I knew who was talking about "the Americanization" of France's failed war in Indochina. The Catholics in our group became increasingly aware of the need to organize American Catholics to challenge the war in Vietnam, which so far enjoyed the automatic backing of the US hierarchy, and for most laypeople was a ho-hum issue. For those Catholics paying attention to events beyond America's borders, support of the Saigon regime—then led by a Catholic—was part of a life-and-death struggle with demonic Communism.

Heading northeast from Rome, our seminar took us across the Iron Curtain to Prague, where we participated in the Christian Peace Conference, one of the rare East-West encounters for religious dialogue in that decade. At the time Czechoslovakia (today two states: the Czech Republic and Slovakia) was experiencing the Prague Spring—"socialism with a human face" was the widely used phrase. Our hosts proudly showed us a vacant pedestal on which a giant statue of Stalin had long stood but had lately been removed by a blast of dynamite. (Four years later, Soviet tanks would crush the Czech experiment with nonrepressive socialism.)

One of the memories that still haunts me is walking

with Dan and others in our group early one evening to Prague's one surviving synagogue. It was surrounded by ancient gravestones crowded together and tilted in every direction. Inside the building we met with the rabbi, a bearded man old enough to have known Abraham. He spoke with us about the Holocaust, which few Czech Jews had survived. Before we left he begged our prayers that a younger rabbi might emerge to take his place.

The formal speeches given at the Christian Peace Conference itself were profoundly boring set pieces that rocked no boats. "I feel," Dan commented, "like we're trapped in a mimeograph machine." As is often the case at such meetings, what happened between the speeches was what really mattered. The FOR contingent plus some Czech friends were rescued for a day by Dan, who led a mini-retreat in an ancient church that our hosts had made available to us. His theme was a line from Genesis about Abraham "going to a place which I [God] will show you." The core idea was that, like Abraham, we who seek peace are traveling in faith and know as little as Abraham did about where the path we're on will lead us. "We pack up," Dan said, "and start off, and trust to God to keep us more or less on the right track."

While having a meal under medieval Gothic arches in a restaurant cellar in Prague's old city one evening, Dan, Jim Douglass, and I resolved to found the Catholic Peace Fellowship on our return to the United States. While we had spoken about this in an exploratory way both in Paris and Rome, that night it became a promise. We talked about what its focus should be and what we had to do to make that work possible. Our main goals, we decided, were to organize Catholic opposition to the Vietnam War and launch a program to make known the fact that conscientious objection to war was an option not only for members of specific peace churches but for Catholics as well. We envisioned setting up a speakers' bureau and developing study kits for use in schools, universities, and seminaries. As Jim Douglass talked about

Synagogue in Prague.

what a Catholic Peace Fellowship might try to achieve, Dan whispered to me, "When I listen to Jim speaking, the four winds of the universe blow through my head. He is a born contemplative."

Having agreed to launch the Catholic Peace Fellowship, the only problem was that we had no staff, no office, and no money. "But money will be forthcoming," Hermene Evans promised. She pledged a thousand dollars toward start-up expenses, quite a large gift in 1964. John Heidbrink also pledged to find support from the Fellowship of Reconciliation. I agreed to act as part-time secretary, at least to get things rolling.

From Prague, Dan and the rest of the seminar participants left for a visit to Moscow hosted by the Russian Orthodox Church as well as Russian Baptists. My vacation used up, I flew back to New York where I was then working as a journalist.

Dan's sabbatical in Europe came to an end in the early autumn of 1964, just after one final journey, this time to take a close look at apartheid in South Africa. No longer assigned a university teaching position, he was posted to the editorial staff of *Jesuit Missions* magazine and given a room at a Jesuit residence on East 78th Street in Manhattan, a townhouse that had once been home to Emily Post, guide and guardian of American etiquette. From that unlikely address, Dan was on the brink of a very different life than he had envisioned before his departure for Paris a year earlier.

> I returned to the United States convinced of one simple thing—the war in Vietnam could only grow worse. The course we had set at the initiative of [President] John Kennedy, and more remotely by [Secretary of State John Foster] Dulles's brinkmanship and by the nuclear fervor of [former president Harry] Truman—all of this was about to turn in the direction of a war which [American leaders] were in no mood to limit. . . . [W]e were about to repeat the al-

*"For me, the conference was a delayed fuse, or a damp fuse, or perhaps something of each. But in any case, it would detonate at some time in the future, and my former life would be blown to pieces. The trouble with the would-be peacemakers, I reflected as these flocked together for such gatherings, was a grievous one. They had no true center. Many souls, a multitude of good souls; but no soul."*
—To Dwell in Peace

Prague.

ready bankrupt experience of the French, with a new provocation and a new rhetoric. . . . We had nothing like the colonial interests that France had had in Southeast Asia, but we were determined . . . to prove our manhood and to put to the test our formidable military machine. It is extraordinarily difficult, even years later, to attempt to unravel the tortuous symptoms and motivations that edged us even deeper into that remote morass. . . .

I remember being afflicted with a sense that my life was being truly launched—for the first time—upon mortal and moral events that might indeed overwhelm me, as the tidal violence of world events churned them into an even greater fury. And even in those years, when we were speaking hypocritically of [only providing] "military advisers to the Vietnamese," I had a sense that the war could not but get worse. I felt that we were even then launched upon a suicide course. . . . I felt (and shared this conviction with my brother Philip) that this war would be the making or breaking of both of us.[96]

# The Spiritual Roots of Protest

Cross in front of Merton's hermitage.
Jim Forest

I n late November 1964, six weeks before the Catholic Peace Fellowship (CPF) was to have its own office and, in myself, a full-time staff person, a small group of individuals connected to the CPF and the Fellowship of Reconciliation—Dan and Phil, Tom Cornell, and I among them—arrived at Merton's monastery in Kentucky for a three-day retreat to consider "the spiritual roots of protest."[97]

Merton had envisioned the retreat as unstructured. "Let's make it purposeless and freewheeling and a vacation for all," he suggested to Dan, "and let the Holy Spirit suggest anything that needs to be suggested."

My memories of the retreat begin with place and weather. The monastery was mainly made up of ramshackle buildings, the oldest dating back more than a hundred years, with a spikelike spire rising out of the church. The rolling hills of rural Kentucky were wrapped around the abbey on several sides. The wind brought an occasional whiff of bourbon from distilleries in nearby Bardstown. The air was damp and chilly, the sky mainly overcast, with occasional rain.

Despite the weather, two of our retreat sessions took place at Merton's hermitage, a small one-story structure made of gray cinder blocks on the edge of woods about a mile from the monastery. Perhaps to make the roots-of-protest theme of the retreat visual, Merton had placed weathered, upturned roots from several trees on the hermitage porch. Merton served as the retreat's central but never dominant figure. At each session one of the participants made a presentation, at the end of which wide-ranging discussion took place.

*Domine ut videam*—Lord, that I might see: these three words, from St. Jerome's Latin translation of Mark's Gospel, were the appeal that Bartimaeus made to Jesus to open his blind eyes.[98] This urgent prayer, used by Merton the first day, was at the heart of our retreat. Peacemaking begins with seeing, seeing what is really going on around us, seeing ourselves in relation to the world we are part of, seeing our lives in the light of the kingdom of God, seeing those who suffer, and seeing the image of God not only in friends but in enemies. What we see and what we fail to see define who we are and how we live our lives.

Then there was another Latin phrase that Merton used: *Quo warranto?* (By what right?) In the context of the retreat, this question became, "By what right do we protest?" It wasn't a question I had ever before considered. In raising the "by what right" question, Merton forced us to consider that protest, if it is to have any hope of constructive impact on others, has to be undertaken not only with great care but with a genuine sympathy and compassion for those who don't understand or who object to one's protest, who feel threatened and angered by it, who even regard the protester as a traitor. After all, what protest, at its best, aims at is not just to make a dissenting noise but to help others think freshly about our social order and the direction in which we are going. The protester needs to remember that no one is converted by rage, self-righteousness, contempt, or hatred. One has to use the hammer of protest carefully. Protest can back-

Top: Merton's hermitage. Jim Forest

Above: Thomas Merton. Jim Forest

*"As for Franz, he will not go away. He will not go away from the church that sent him on his way, alone. His way, which should have been the way of the church. So he lingers, half unwelcome. Like a speechless mouth, like a mysterious cry hovering on the air, seeking a hearing. Listen: 'Love your enemies . . . Refuse the easy ride, damnation as destination.'"*
—The Bride

Conscientious objector and martyr, Blessed Fränz Jagerstätter.

fire, harden people in their opposition, and bring out the worst in the other. Sometimes this may be necessary—for example, as Merton pointed out, the confrontations that had occurred in Birmingham, Alabama, in which police had responded to nonviolent black protesters opposing racial segregation with tear gas, attack dogs, fire hoses, clubs, beatings, and mass arrests. If it is to be transformative, as in the end it was in Birmingham, protest needs to be animated by love, not love in the sentimental sense but in the sober biblical sense of the word. Hence Christ's insistence on love of enemies. "Until we love our enemies," Merton said, "we're not yet Christians."[99]

"The grace to protest," Merton wrote in his notes for the retreat, "is a special gift of God requiring fidelity and purity of heart." Far from seeing an opponent merely as an obstacle, one wishes for him or her "a better situation in which oppression no longer exists." Ideally, protest aims at changes that benefit everyone.

One of the issues Merton raised was how untroubled most US Christians were by the militarization of American life and the blurring together of national and religious identity. Summoned to war, few say no or even imagine saying no. Merton saw this as a problem not only in the United States but wherever nationalism is the primary shaper of one's identity. Merton spoke of the "pseudo Christianity" Kierkegaard had described in which the individual abdicates "conscience, personal decision, choice and responsibility," yielding himself to "pure myth," a myth that often is a Cinderella story about national identity.

By way of exemplary contrast, Merton reminded us of the life of Franz Jägerstätter, a name familiar to the Catholic retreatants but generally unknown at the time. Jägerstätter was an Austrian Catholic farmer, husband, father, and church sexton who, for his refusal to serve in the army of the Third Reich, was beheaded in Berlin on August 9, 1943. Despite his modest education, Jägerstätter had seen with amazing clarity what was going on around him, spoken out plainly and without fear to neighbors and strangers about the hell Hitler's movement was creating, and finally—ignoring the advice of his bishop to take the military oath—paid for his obedience to conscience with his life.[100]

Why, Merton asked, does contemporary Christianity produce so many who fight in manifestly unjust wars and so few, like Jägerstätter, who say no? "If the Church," said Merton, "could make its teachings alive to the laity, future Franz Jägerstätters would no longer give their witness in solitude but would be the Church as a whole reasserting the primacy of the spiritual." (Little by little Franz Jägerstätter has come to be widely known, the subject of books, plays, and films. His story already had played a part in shaping what the Second Vatican Council declared about conscientious objection, the limits of obedience, and under some circumstances, the duty of disobedience. In 2007 Jägerstätter was beatified at the cathedral in Linz, Austria. Blessed Franz is today recognized as a patron saint of conscientious objectors.)

In a talk given on the second day, Dan returned to the witness of Franz Jägerstätter and the questions raised by his life, emphasizing Jägerstätter's pained awareness that the overwhelming majority of German and Austrian Christians had been willing to yield virtually anything demanded of them by the Nazi regime. Such a pattern of Church surrender to political demands, Dan noted, wasn't unique to the Hitler period nor unfamiliar in the postwar period. Churches tend to preach and act within borders drawn by the state. "What American bishop," Dan asked, "has expressed objections to making, testing, and even using nuclear weapons?" At the time, the answer was none—but in the years to come, that would change. One of the main causes of episcopal silence, Dan ventured, was fear. "The church's fearfulness," Dan added, "is our confession of unconvertedness."

There is no forgetting Phil's attentive stillness during the retreat. Perhaps he was remembering the scenes

Inside Merton's hermitage. Jim Forest

Top: Phil and Dan with Merton and Tony Walsh. Used with permission of the Merton Legacy Trust and the Thomas Merton Center at Bellarmine University

Above: Dan with Merton. Jim Forest

of destruction he had been part of while fighting in Europe. I recall him sitting in the hermitage in T-shirt and black trousers, head tipped toward the floor, as quiet as one of the roots Merton had placed on the porch. He too looked at the Church in Hitler's Germany for parallels with our own situation—our war-complicit hierarchy in present-day America—and saw in Franz Jägerstätter a model for our times.

When I sought Dan out one night for confession, he stressed the relationship between penitence and hope, a hope not easily achieved in the midst of war.

In an interview about the retreat that Dan gave years later to Gordon Oyer, who was writing a book on the subject, he remarked that "the most significant aspect of the retreat was the sense of friendship it created." Dan told Oyer that he had not "previously experienced relationships at that depth as they pertained to ideas on peacemaking, other than perhaps with his brother Philip. The retreat helped create bonds of friendship with Protestants that would be an ongoing source of inspiration. It also fostered trust in where others were coming from and what they were doing."[101]

Our three days together ended too quickly. Many questions had been raised, few if any resolved, but I'm certain all of us were haunted by the conversations in which we had taken part. The name that kept recurring was that of Franz Jägerstätter—a modern martyr whose protest reached the deepest roots of faith. It was in part thanks to the retreat that, in the years that followed, the Catholic Peace Fellowship did so much to promote awareness of the Jägerstätter story as a modern Gospel parable.

# "Let the Lord make of this what he will"

On the first of January 1965, using a twenty-five-dollar-a-month room rented from the War Resisters League at 5 Beekman Street in lower Manhattan, just around the corner from City Hall, I began full-time work with the Catholic Peace Fellowship. Tom Cornell, teacher and former managing editor of the *Catholic Worker*, joined me as cosecretary a few months later, thanks to financial help from Dan and Phil plus Hermene Evans.

The quicksand of Vietnam—"the Land of Burning Children," as Dan would rename that country—was taking ever more lives and bringing to a boil many of America's long-simmering internal difficulties.

At the end of his sabbatical, Dan had wanted to be more of a worker-priest himself. He hoped he might give a day a week to the Catholic Worker, helping with the soup line and the free-clothing room. Instead he spent several hours each week helping the Catholic Peace Fellowship get launched.

A ritual emerged. Tom Cornell and I subwayed uptown for a midday meeting in Dan's room. Putting first things first, Dan celebrated a bare-bones liturgy. Afterward we sorted through letters—reading the more important ones aloud—considered how best to respond, discussed problems and ideas, and had lunch. Many of the letters we discussed came from young men urgently

Jim Forest and Tom Cornell in the office of the Catholic Peace Fellowship.

Maryknoll Archives

wanting to know if, as Catholics, they could be recognized as conscientious objectors, and if so, how to go about it.[102]

The style of our eucharistic bread-breaking was as simple and graceful in line as a Shaker chair and quiet enough to please a Quaker. A prayer for forgiveness was followed by intercession for friends who were ill or in difficulty. We took turns reading the appointed Old and New Testament texts for the day from a paperback edition of "that old book," the Bible, plus perhaps a supplementary reading from Neruda or Auden or Péguy or Teilhard, or Brecht, or Merton. After the readings, silence. Then some reflection, usually initiated by Dan, on the readings. More silence. Then a simple canon prayer from the *Bible Missal*, a Mass book widely used at the time. More silence. Finally, after the unspectacular miracle of consecration came the sharing in that quiet miracle, and more silence, perhaps some more prayer, and an embrace at the end.

Apparently some attentive soul kept a stethoscope to the wall during these liturgical celebrations, for the day came when we arrived to find Dan in considerable distress. Hours before he had been told our informal Eucharists were absolutely not allowed. There had, in fact, been a number of less imperative proddings to the same effect in previous weeks. So we sat forlorn, trying to talk about those things that would have come later. No sandwiches were assembled—we had no appetite.

In the midst of a halfhearted sentence, Dan stood up abruptly, went downstairs, and returned with two slices of rye bread. From its usual place in the file cabinet, a bottle of wine and a water glass were removed, books and papers on the desk pushed aside, the bread and wine put in place, the Bible taken up. I was handed the book and found the readings of the day. We each read a portion.

Perhaps there was some dialogue about the readings. My memories are of silence. At last the bread on its plate was taken in one hand, and the glass with its red wine in the other, silence where a canon prayer would ordinarily have been spoken, until a few intense but quiet words were spoken by Dan, "Let the Lord make of this what he will." And so we ate and drank, and with reverence. It was a communion I will never forget.

In the same period, another memorable Mass took place at the Catholic Worker, with Dan as the celebrant. While he might on occasion choose readings according to what he judged appropriate to the day and the historic moment rather than the church calendar and do some of the prayers with a degree of improvisation, though always preserving the core elements, at the Catholic Worker there was less improvisation. Dan knew Dorothy was made uncomfortable by liturgical innovation.

On this occasion, having forgotten to bring along a chalice from the Jesuit chapel, Dan instead used a ceramic coffee cup and a matching small plate as chalice and paten. I recall glancing at Dorothy and noting a grimace, but she made no complaint and indeed took part in communion and afterward expressed her gratitude. But then, when nearly everyone had gone, she took the cup and plate and said they should be buried as, having held the body and blood of Christ, they should no longer be used for coffee and sandwiches. Where the burial occurred, I do not know.

Soon afterward I was at Mount Savior Benedictine Monastery near Elmira in upstate New York. After telling their distinguished potter, Brother Thomas, what I had witnessed, he gave me one of the chalice sets he had made for sale in the monastery shop, entrusting me to deliver the set to Dan, which I did on return to the city. At the same time I told him about Dorothy's response to the coffee cup Mass. Dan was very touched with the gift chalice and paten and used them—not only at the Catholic Worker—on countless occasions afterward.[103]

*"[Dorothy Day] united in her person, in what I can only call her art, all that the culture serves to tear apart. Holiness and great practicality, life in the spirit, life in the world, responsibility and prayer, God and the neighbor. She healed, and stiffened spines, and taught us lessons as no seminary or retreat had done."*
—To Dwell in Peace

75

# Meeting Phil

My memories of Phil begin in November 1961, about the time I first met Dan, with the delivery to the Catholic Worker of a fat manila envelope postmarked New Orleans. Inside was an essay on Christianity and racism written by Philip Berrigan. Affixed to his name were the initials S.S.J.—the Society of Saint Joseph. At the time, Phil was teaching at a black New Orleans Catholic high school. It included this story:

Recently . . . a young priest was sent to a "white" parish to offer two Masses on a Sunday. . . . In the Gospel, Our Lord was tested by a Doctor of the Law, and from the encounter came the two great Commandments of Love. The priest [a Jesuit whom Phil knew] came armed to preach on this text with an application to the injustice of segregation. He quoted his text and the words of Christ, saying that on these two commandments depend the whole Law and the Prophets, and he was getting nicely launched into his sermon, when there came an abrupt disturbance from the congregation. A man was on his feet in the middle of the church, waving his arms excitedly and shouting toward the pulpit, "Hey! I didn't come here to listen to this junk. I came to hear Mass." The man, with others, finally walked out, shouting back, "If I miss Mass today you're responsible!"

Phil concluded his reflection,

> We show no reluctance in noising about the claims of the Church, we suffer no arbitration of her deposit of truth, we glibly repeat the lofty message of Our Lord, but in the desperately important encounter with those who need us, in the hard and hot work of the vineyard where hope is extended, truth exchanged, solidarity and brotherhood won—it is here that we fall, or fail to be present. . . . If the challenges of our age seem too much for us, if we insist on reliving the nineteenth century, then we ought to question our religion, we ought to renounce our Western culture and the democracy that is so much a part of it, we ought to maintain that God has no part in this world of His, because we have refused Him entrance. And I know that we will refuse to do this.

Phil Berrigan. Cornell University, Division of Rare and Manuscript Collections

Dorothy Day read the essay, then asked me to prepare it for publication in the December issue.

Three years later, in the summer of 1964, soon after returning from the seminar in Europe, at last I met Phil Berrigan face-to-face. I was surprised by his appearance—no resemblance to Dan. Apart from worker-priests in France, I generally expected a certain softness in clerics, even those few of a dissident bent. But here was a tall, striding, blue-eyed man with a powerful, calm handshake, a Gary Cooper grin, a soldier's posture, close-cropped silver hair, looking years older than Dan rather than his kid brother. He made me think of athletes one saw on Wheaties cereal boxes—human antelopes gliding over mountainous linebackers like a paper airplane in an updraft. In popular stereotypes, Phil could have played the stoic and brave town marshal in the television series *Gunsmoke*, or the tough, secretly pious football coach at Notre Dame, or a downed pilot working with the French Resistance. Phil fit such roles—handsome, modest, fearless.

Phil, too hot a potato for New Orleans, had been as-

*"Thanks again, chumly, for everything. I was delighted to know Dorothy and youse were making a team. The great lady wrote me a nice note, and said she is going to publish a letter of mine in the Mar. issue. That shd make some of the boys unhappy. . . . Merton says you shoot a stone in the air and if someone calls out you know it was seen. Love, dear boy and keep em off guard."*
—Letter from Dan to Phil, March 3, 1964

Cornell University, Division of Rare and Manuscript Collections

signed to a Josephite residence in the Bronx, a high-ceilinged, immaculate rectory with portraits of Roman pontiffs on the parlor walls and a large beer- and steak-laden kitchen with a warrior of a housekeeper presiding.

Phil's room, in contrast to the spic-and-span order elsewhere in the house, was cluttered and rumpled. Most impressive were the mountain ranges of books, newspapers, and magazines—stacks of the *I. F. Stone Weekly*, the *New Republic*, the *Nation*, *Commonweal*, ripped-up issues of the *New York Times*, the *Wall Street Journal*, the *Washington Post*. Exclamation marks were noticeable in margins, whole paragraphs underlined. It was my first glimpse of Phil's hunger for data and analysis. Tom Cornell, who had come with me, commented on leaving, "Now there is someone who does his homework!"

I was struck as much by the dissimilarity between the two brothers—not merely a physical contrast (Phil resembling his father, Dan taking after his mother)—as by a difference invading every zone of their lives apart from their shared recognition of religious and historical priorities. Dan's room was a carefully assembled collage of signs, artwork, posters, books, photos, and furnishings that made the room kaleidoscopic; Phil's room resembled a library basement. Contrasting Phil with Dan, it was the difference between a Brooklyn dame and a Parisian *dame* or a gallon bottle of economy Gallo wine and a noneconomy bottle of Chateauneuf du Pape. Dan was imprinted, inside and out, with France while Phil was stamped "made in America." (In a letter to Dan sent in September 1971, Phil describes himself as "a meat-and-potatoes man" while seeing Dan as "a mystic-activist."[104])

Phil was a disarming man. While his convictions were achieved by a patient route and were solidly clung to once established, his style of personal expression reminded me of Spencer Tracy's portrayal of Father Flanagan in the film *Men of Boys Town*. "Love ya, man," was a phrase that often preceded the closing in his frequent letters. The closing itself invariably made reference to the focal point of Phil's commitment: "The Lord's Peace," "In Christ," "In Xto," "Fraternally in Him," "The Savior's inspiration and strength . . ." As we became closer, he more frequently dropped the "Father" from his signature, but the "S.S.J." never was pruned away until, abandoning his own oft-repeated view that celibacy was best not only for priests but for those preparing to do jail time, he fell in love. But that event was impossible to imagine in the mid-sixties. He was outspoken on the benefits of celibacy. "The point of celibacy," he said, "is to be available to others day and night."

Finding Phil so radical in some ways, I was unprepared for how conservative Phil was in certain other respects. In matters liturgical, few priests at the time were less preoccupied with change, apart from exchanging Latin for English. In the 1950s, *Worship* magazine had published an essay of Phil's relating liturgy to the needs of the black community. But in the 1960s Dan's gift and passion in liturgical innovation began to stand in contrast with Phil's. It was Phil who first mentioned to me, with no small disgust, that the Church in Germany had prided itself on its liturgical and theological renewal during the Hitler years with few resisting the Hitler regime or fewer still resisting Hitler's wars.

I found Phil was often angry with high churchmen. When Bishop (later Cardinal) John Wright politely backed off signing a statement of opposition to the Vietnam War, Phil's comment was, "Wright hasn't been out in the rain alone since he was four." Yet his disappointments with hierarchs never reduced his conviction that there were grounds for high expectations from the Church—"that is, you and me," as he added, "not just bishops." For him, "the Church" meant the Catholic Church, in which regard Phil made no bones about being Roman, but his definition was encompassing. A quotation from Bishop

*"I often think that fidelity to Christ means more and more the outside stance, for the sake of whatever remnant is kicking around. . . . The crucial point—it seems to me is this—how to eliminate the last stubborn furniture of the old church, and in the process, get the new one to witness. . . . I believe we have history on our side, and more sentiment than we realize. I feel increasingly that if this is to be done—it will be done by a small community absolutely unanimous in dedication and purpose, and from a position so exposed that we cannot yet tell what it will be."*
—Letter from Phil to Dan, Fall 1964

Gerard Huyghe of Arras was taped over his desk:

> That man is a Catholic [here Phil added the word "Christian"] who opens himself to all and allows the universal love of the Lord to resound in his heart. He is a Catholic who, when he remembers the mercy of Christ toward him, becomes merciful—that is to say overwhelmed with distress, whatever form that distress may take. He is a Catholic who instinctively rejects everything that is a source of division, who cannot meet anyone without tirelessly seeking out an area of agreement. He is a Catholic who sees in each man not the social category to which he belongs, not the label which is applied to him, of unbeliever or Protestant or Jew or Communist, but the brother for whom Christ died and who has been placed in his path in order to receive his love. He is a Catholic who through humility has made himself poor in spirit and is always ready to welcome those who are deprived, whether it be of material goods or the light of faith.

Soon after that first encounter I wrote to Phil with the proposal that he serve as the Catholic Peace Fellowship's chairman. His response was immediate and positive, but a modification was proposed: "It would be good to have a layman in charge—it may be something of an education to clerics in general." We ended up with a cochairmanship: Phil plus Marty Corbin, then managing editor of the *Catholic Worker*. Dan was put on the sponsors list rather than made another cochairman, not because he was less active in CPF than Phil, quite the opposite, but because it seemed peculiar to have two Berrigans—neither of them yet widely known—jostling each other at the top of the letterhead. (Merton, while mentioning his discomfort at being "a name," agreed to be on the CPF's board of sponsors, as did Dorothy Day, Gordon Zahn, Archbishop Thomas Roberts, and a dozen other notables.)

*"The war had commandeered the church; and the war went on. It had not seized church properties or investments, a fact of note. The war had only claimed the consciences of believers, bishops, laymen and laywomen, the lives of the young, one and all pledged to abandon all things and follow the god of war; to kill and die and maim and bomb. This was a small price, purportedly; it had been paid before, and would be paid again. So the war went on, our longest war, for more than a decade."*

—To Dwell in Peace

With the help of friends, Dan and Merton among them, an address list began to take shape. Merton sent a packet of his abstract calligraphies, suggesting we sell them for ten dollars each to raise a little money.

Not long after my first encounter with Phil came a meeting with him that reminded me that Phil had been an infantry officer who made life-risking decisions concerning those under his command. Both he and Dan had been pressing me to give up my professional livelihood, journalism, in order to turn the Catholic Peace Fellowship into a full-time staffed organization. In fact I was ready to be the first staff person but only for a limited time, from January 1965 through August. I had recently been offered a full-tuition scholarship by Berea College in Kentucky that would also have provided food and housing for me and our small family and, four years hence, put a degree in my hands. My days as a high school dropout at last seemed numbered.

Not enthused at all by this plan, Phil called with the proposal that we meet in midtown Manhattan the following afternoon. We walked for a bit, settled in at an Irish bar, ordered some whiskey, and began to argue.

Phil declared with no uncertainty, "Formal education might be the standard track for many, but a better education is available, for those willing to do their homework, in the peace movement—indeed, only in that fray can there be a meaningful linking up of the data and speculation of study with the overwhelming fact of needless human suffering and waste—and only in such a context can hope have any substance. . . . You've got more education already than you'll ever get in school, and you're getting more daily. Those certifications aren't worth the paper they're printed on. Get in the movement, stay in the movement, stick with it."

Fr. David Kirk, Jim Forest, and Tom Cornell (holding sign) at Foley Square, New York. Shortly afterward Tom surrendered to federal marshals to start serving a six-month prison term for burning his draft card.
Courtesy Catholic Peace Fellowship

I was by no means without replies, and deeply felt they were, as considering the lilies of the field sounded good but didn't seem a solid way to plan for the future. Also I was excited at the thought of four years of study at Berea, a unique academic institution that, since 1855, has provided all its students, black and white, with full-tuition scholarships, plus room and board for those who needed it. Berea's slogan is the declaration that "God has made of one blood all peoples of the earth." But Phil was not only determined but persuasive. My final consent to an open-ended commitment as CPF secretary resulted in considerable Berrigan joy, signaled by a solid whack on his leg and an exclamation of "That's the spirit, man!" Phil ordered another round of Irish whiskey.

While rarely lost for words, Phil had areas of shyness and silence. He was most noticeably mute regarding what he had done in World War II. It wasn't from Phil but Dan that I first learned of Phil's military past. Like so many who have been on battlefields, he bore hidden scars. But if there was a special, silencing pain about that zone of his life, it is only the most extreme example of his general reticence to enlist his own biography in explaining his convictions.

Phil and Dan were aware that CPF finances were precarious. Sixty-five dollars a week had been budgeted for the salaries of Tom Cornell and myself, but weeks went by when there wasn't enough in the CPF bank account for me to write Tom's check or Tom to write mine. In July, Dan and Phil Berrigan came to our homes for a meeting (we were living in adjacent apartments in the same building on Ridge Street on the Lower East Side). During deliberations about the poor state of CPF income, Phil discreetly looked into my refrigerator and Dan into the Cornells'. "In toto," Tom recalls, "they found two quarts of milk, a block of Velveeta cheese, and two half loaves of bread. Dan wrote a check. We were in business again."

# Saying No

As the 1960s unfolded, Dan and Phil each developed an expanding talent for saying no in word and action to both war and racism.

In the latter area, they flew to Alabama in mid-March 1965 to participate in the second Selma march. The first march had been stopped with extreme brutality. Six hundred black participants had assembled in Selma on Sunday, March 7, intending to cross the Edmund Pettus Bridge on their way to Montgomery, Alabama's capital. Just short of the bridge, their way was blocked by Alabama state troopers, local police, and deputized white

Protesters crossing the Edmund Pettus Bridge in Selma, Alabama.

vigilantes who ordered them to turn around. When the protesters refused, the gas-masked officers deployed police dogs, shot tear gas, and waded into the crowd, beating the nonviolent protesters with clubs, some wrapped with barbed wire. More than fifty marchers were hospitalized, among them organizer (now Congressman) John Lewis, whose skull was fractured. Images of "Bloody Sunday" were televised around the world. When Martin Luther King Jr. called for religious leaders from all over the nation to come to Selma for a second march, Dan and Phil were among the responders.

The atmosphere in Selma was grim, Dan wrote, charged not only with vivid memories of the recent police attack and several murders but with countless years of white violence directed at blacks:

*We came in, thirty-five strong from New York. . . . Selma was quiet as a millpond; but the quiet was ominous; the pin had been pulled, the depth charged dropped. Children wandered in the sun, the stores were open, the fresh tourist signs were out: WELCOME TO SELMA."*

—Consequences, Truth, and . . .

> It was in the air of Selma; the air bore it like a groan. . . . Through these town roads, the body of a black man, roped like venison to the sheriff's car, had been driven into the black area. Go slow—slow. Let them see who's in charge here. It was in the air. Fifteen years ago a black man, arrested on the word of a cranky white woman "for talkin' back," had been murdered in Selma jail. "An unknown policeman" had entered his cell and shot him. His body was dumped off on his family. No verdict, no investigation. But the town has not forgotten.
>
> It is still in the air. Jimmy Lee Jackson, shot in Marion for defending his mother against a trooper's club, died in Good Samaritan Hospital here [in Selma]. He had powder burns on the skin of his belly. The barrel had been pushed to its closest range and fired twice. The blacks remembered that night. When they tried to send hearses from Selma to Marion to pick up the wounded [from the first march], lying untended in the streets, their answer had come from the sheriff's office: "Come in here, you'll get what the rest got—I'll dump you in the river."[105]

But when the second march set off for Montgomery on March 21, police and state troopers didn't dare attack what was now an event sanctioned by a federal court order and protected by hundreds of federalized Alabama National Guardsmen. Five days later, twenty-five thousand marchers stood in front of the state capitol. Five months later, thanks in large measure to the recent events in Selma, Congress passed the Voting Rights Act of 1965.

Dan and Phil did not meet Dr. King in Selma, but their brother Jerry did. Dr. King spent an afternoon greeting pilgrims at the Greyhound bus station, and Jerry had a pleasant conversation with him. Decades later, John Dear asked Dan what he remembered about Dr. King's talk in Selma. "I remember his definition of the church," Dan said. "'The church is the place you go from,' Dr. King said. I loved that. Everyone thinks that the church is the place you go to, but Dr. King reversed that and said it was the place you go from, and then he demonstrated it on the march from Selma to Montgomery."

In the face of terrifying danger, Dan was deeply impressed by the leadership role being played not only by Martin Luther King Jr., as an individual, but by the black church as a whole. Dan wrote,

Whoever heard of a church, North or South, that has rung, day after day, week after week, with unending songs, prayers, sermons; a church that spilled into the streets; a people ready for whatever hell the troopers are ready to bring down on them: dogs, horses, whips, tear gas, billy clubs? What liturgy prepares men and women and children for [violent assault by white racists]? What faith arms them by forbidding them arms, tells them to march when they can, to kneel when they cannot, to face the oppressors—maybe even to convert them? The questions are fierce, and for the moment, for white Americans, unanswerable. But the point is clear: the questions

Martin Luther King Jr. Bob Fitch Photography Archive, © Department of Special Collections, Stanford University

*"Light by light, individual purpose was fused in the condensed air of black courage and black passion. Free-e-e-dom. Free-e-e-dom. They sang it together, the skilled and the ignorant, the neophyte and the victim. Some of them know what they sang. But the others were learning."*
—Consequences, Truth, and . . .

A B-52 on a bombing raid in Vietnam.

are real questions, as real as the broken bones and the blood, as real as the new hope.[106]

March 1965 also saw a major escalation of the war in Vietnam: the initiation of Operation Rolling Thunder, a campaign of sustained bombing of North Vietnam by the United States. Again acting together, Dan and Phil joined the first round of signatories to a "declaration of conscience" pledging "to encourage those who can conscientiously do so to refuse to serve in the Armed Forces." The declaration urged others "to refuse . . . to take part in the manufacture or transportation of military equipment, or to work in the fields of military research and weapons development."

One sentence hinted at the kind of action that would occur three years later at Catonsville: "We shall encourage the development of nonviolent acts, including acts which involve civil disobedience, in order to stop the flow of American soldiers and munitions to Vietnam." The text included the warning that whoever signed was at risk of imprisonment: the draconian conscription law passed by Congress had forbidden advising those subject to the draft to refuse service—the potential penalty

*"I began . . . as loudly as I could, to say 'no' to the war. I remember being afflicted with a sense that my life was being truly launched—for the first time— upon mortal and moral seas that might indeed overwhelm me, as the tidal violence of world events churned them into an even greater fury. . . . There would be simply no turning back upon the initial serious moves we were making at that time."*

—No Bars to Manhood

for doing so was up to five years in prison and a ten-thousand-dollar fine.

Published in various newspapers and journals, within weeks the declaration was signed by at least six thousand people, including Nobel laureate chemist Linus Pauling, historian Staughton Lynd, folksinger Pete Seeger, civil rights leader John Lewis, psychologist Erich Fromm, Bayard Rustin of the War Resisters League, and Dorothy Day. Dan and Phil had put themselves in the lions' den.

Dan explained his decision to sign the declaration at a rally in New York's Community Church the night of February 18. It served as a kind of manifesto:

> It is astonishing to reflect how in time of war, the word of God tends to become complicated and diffuse. Suddenly, his word has a thousand footnotes, refining, clarifying, explaining away. The powers of the state show a mysterious concern for the integrity of the word of God. They issue their own tracts and texts. Believers must see that the God of all has suddenly taken sides for and against. A universal Love has narrowed itself to accept hate and to command hate. The message of peace is interpreted in favor of nationalism, of the ideologies of the moment, of the frenzies of human causes. The purity and simplicity of the Bible are clouded; it becomes a complicated and even devious thing to be a believer. One must approach God through a thousand others who speak for God, who talk another language than his, who issue commands counter to his commands.
>
> So the question of where believers stand in wartime is of crucial moment, as it could never be in normal times. For in time of war, another god declares himself. His name is total war. He is determined to claim all men and everything that is in man. He claims conscience, consciousness, and community; he claims life and limb. He will have the

*"The ground was shifting under my feet. My conception of history and of moral action was being altered, even as I strove to act. The old, tidy, well-arranged box of the universe was flying open, and the seven plagues were loosed upon the world. There would be no closing that box again. There could only be an attempt to follow the course of evil and the death with whatever trail mercy and compassion might blaze."*
—No Bars to Manhood

Dorothy Day with A.J. Muste at a peace rally in New York.

world devastated, in the image of his own chaos and fury; the destruction of man is his universal and unassailable will.

For those who choose to reject this monstrous idol, there is small space in this world. Total war excommunicates the man of peace. It casts him out of his community, out of the human family, out of his future. It offers him a life of shame and, perhaps, death in disgrace.

Men of maturity and conscience are obliged to judge the actions of their society and to speak up. And where it is necessary, they are obliged to pay the price of their speech, to put their bodies where their words are, to stand in peaceable conflict with the powers of the state. . . .

Our community today is a gathering together of peacemakers. We pray that the God of peace may cleanse us of our will to war, that he may bestow on us some measure of his wisdom and steadfastness in the tasks of peace. We gather, we pray together, and we disperse again, knowing that the work of peace cannot be accomplished in the churches; it can only begin here. The making of peace implies the will to return to our world in love, to stand firm in public, to confront the powers and principalities, to assert in time of war that no government which makes war can govern well; that we ourselves will not submit before a governing hand that would thrust weapons into our hands and command us away from the paths of peace.

Dorothy Day, present at the meeting, asked if she might include Dan's speech in the *Catholic Worker* about to go to press. Giving her the text, Dan agreed, but two days later wrote me, "Probably it would be better if we killed the statement in *The Catholic Worker*. . . . There is every indication publication of this would only exacerbate things [with his superiors]. . . . I suppose there is no restriction on mimeo'ed stuff." (Merton used the mimeograph machine at his monastery in much the same way in circulating his otherwise forbidden reflections on war.) But his letter arrived too late; the speech was in print, and the exacerbations, if any, occurred. Dan's first antiwar speech was on page one of the March 1965 *Catholic Worker*.

In a note to me dated March 5, Dan wrote, "These are very mysterious and dark waters we are walking. The question is, what next? . . . But it seems sure now the order [the Society of Jesus] is not going to take an all-out fallout position, probably due to many modifying pressures."

Travels around the country and further writing were increasing Dan's visibility. In editorial attacks on the "declaration of conscience," with its support of nonviolent resistance, a number of pro-war writers called for the indictment and imprisonment of the signers. There were even those who thought such dissidents were traitors who deserved execution.

In a letter to me sent July 2, Dan reported that he was officially persona non grata in the Archdiocese of Los Angeles. "I am in New York today, which is to say, I am not in Los Angeles. Which is to say, I was banned from there last week, a call arriving from Sister Corita [Kent] on Saturday with the sad news that the chancery had called and made it evident that I was unwelcome. It seems to me, without undue personal chagrin (I hope I have gotten beyond all that), that there may be a small footnote here for the Catholic community at large. But I leave the decision to you." He listed details of the topics he had hoped to discuss at the eight-day seminar at Immaculate Heart College ("on liturgical renewal, on crisis and community, on the beatitudes, the Mystical Body [of Christ]—and necessarily on the moral consequences in race and peace questions"). He went on, "It seems to me that the day when such tactics of intervention can be used undercover ought to be ended, as soon as can be done. At least it may be a service to church renewal to give the public the facts."

*"The nonviolent person is the one who, within normal times, can save normal times from their idolatries—neglect of the poor, growing bourgeois selfishness, weapons of war, and the other realities around us. . . . The nonviolent person does not seek an impossible compromise with the times, nor a prior, intemperate synthesis for the times. The nonviolent person sees life in terms of a choice toward change, involving a re-ordering of life."*

—Talk from 1965,
Essential Writings

# Exile

David Miller of the Catholic Worker burns his draft card.

On October 16, 1965, David Miller, a former Le Moyne student of Dan's who had joined the New York Catholic Worker after graduation, decided to offer a symbolic act at a demonstration protesting the Vietnam War. Miller, in suit and tie, with close-cropped Nordic hair, stood on a truck in front of the Whitehall Street Induction Center in lower Manhattan, pulled out his draft card, and turned it to fire and ash. Such acts had occurred often enough before, frequently in Catholic Worker hands, but it had only been a few weeks since a furious congressman, seeing such card-burning in a *LIFE* magazine photo, had gotten the Congress specifically to outlaw the "willful mutilation or destruction" of draft cards. Imprisonment for up to five years was the penalty. President Lyndon Johnson signed the bill into law the next day.

Neither Dan nor his brother Phil hesitated in leaping forward in articulate defense of David's gesture and, for that matter, any form of nonviolent resistance to the ever-expanding war. As became increasingly clear in the months that followed, not all Jesuits were pleased that a

Jesuit was making common cause with those who were, for whatever reasons, lawbreakers.

During those same days a new interfaith peace group was in formation—Clergy Concerned about Vietnam (later Clergy and Laity Concerned about Vietnam)—with Dan, Rabbi Abraham Joshua Heschel, and Lutheran pastor Richard John Neuhaus serving as its cochairmen. Its first public meeting was scheduled to take place on November 30. Dan was to be one of the speakers.

On November 6, three weeks after Miller burned his draft card, Catholic Peace Fellowship cosecretary Tom Cornell plus four friends decided to replicate that action with the intention of arguing in court that such a gesture was a form of free speech, thus protected by the Constitution. Tom also reasoned the new law was a form of idolatry, treating as sacred a scrap of paper that in reality was simply an easily replicated government form of no intrinsic value.[107] The event took place on a stage at the north end of Union Square with a thousand people watching, including a small group of irate war supporters who, as the five draft cards were burning, chanted, "Burn yourselves, not your draft cards."

Among those in the crowd was twenty-one-year-old Roger LaPorte, a part-time student and newly arrived volunteer at the Catholic Worker. Four days later, before dawn on November 9, Roger sat down on First Avenue between the United Nations and the US Mission to the United Nations, doused himself with kerosene, and set himself on fire, an action similar to the self-immolation of several Vietnamese Buddhist monks. In the ambulance carrying him to Bellevue Hospital, he told an attendant, "I am a Catholic Worker. I did this as a religious action. I am against all war." Roger died the following day.

Many saw Roger's action as a suicide, the grave sin of self-murder, but those at the Catholic Worker who knew Roger had no sense he had been struggling with despair or mental illness. Their perception was that he

*"It was the proposal of Abraham Heschel that Neuhaus, himself, and I undertake to organize a response of the religious community against the war. To be named Clergy and Laity concerned. The announcement, among the Jesuits, was badly received. . . . Indeed, such troubles were brewing as would transform all former incidents, no matter how painful, into a species of child's play."*
—To Dwell in Peace

Dorothy Day speaks in support of draft card burners in Union Square.
Jim Forest

was trying to make others protect life, hoping that, in sharing voluntarily in the involuntary fate of so many Vietnamese who were being burned alive, the horrifying consequences of war might be made less abstract to Americans. His gesture was antiwar, not antilife. Though Dan had not known Roger personally, he saw what Roger had done as possibly "an act of misguided heroism."

Worried that Dan might make a statement that Roger's death was something other than suicide, Dan's provincial, John McGinty, quickly ordered Dan to make no declarations about Roger—"I was under no circumstances to issue a public statement regarding the young man's death."[108] But in what he judged a private context—a Mass for Catholic Workers in one of the rooms of the Nativity Mission parish around the corner from St. Joseph's House—Dan was invited to make some comments. "I aired my reflections before the stricken community," Dan wrote in his autobiography, "the question of suicide and the possibility of sacrifice, suggesting we leave the imponderables to God. It was the best I could do; it was also, I thought, the least."[109]

The text of Dan's sermon survived but was not published until 2009. Some extracts:

[Roger] came to the Catholic Worker family at a time of bitter and cruel war. He sought and moved closer to a community of mercy and peace. Long before the Vietnam War, the Worker had grown through the works of mercy into the works of peace. The members came to understand that the two are in fact one. They are joined by the single blessing conferred on them by the Savior in his Sermon on the Mount. It could not be thought strange that before most Catholics could see the juncture, the Catholic Worker saw it, and spoke of it, and explored it, with that prophetic charity which is granted in greatest measure to the merciful heart. So when the war was

Cornell University, Division of Rare and Manuscript Collections

unleashed, the peacemakers were ready. . . . They acted without fear and took the consequences. And they found themselves in possession of a kind of knowledge, a grasp of history, a sense of humor, a rightness of direction, which were explainable only in light of the lives they were leading. Which is to say, service of the poor—immediate, anonymous, authentic, and single-minded—had conferred on these a balance of spirit which made them ready for times most were powerless to discern and helpless to interpret. . . .

Let us therefore not be . . . dismayed by the death of Roger LaPorte. Beyond apparent violence, apparent tragedy, a great gift is offered to us. But the gift can be claimed only if our minds are open to it. The gift, I think, is this: an understanding that the death of a good man is always offered for the sake of life. More exactly, it is offered for the sake of the living. For those who understand, this horrendous final gesture of a young life means exactly this. His death says, in a voice louder even than his life, "No more death! Death never again!" . . . The word is one with the great command: "Love one another, as I have loved you." But when we refuse one another, death again has dominion over us. When we meet the crises of other lives with indifference or temporizing or double talk, when we grow thoughtless and cruel in our security, death's dominion is asserted once more. . . .

In the deepest sense, what we remember here together is not a death at all, neither a dead Christian nor a dead Christ. It is a resurrection; it is a new hope, new steadfastness, new vision, new resources of joy and peace. Indeed, if Christ died, it was in order to rise again. It was to assert that death does not have the last word, or the loudest word. It means that we have the power of denying all tribute, all validity, all respect to the forces of death. It means that

*"The message of the Cardinal was delivered to the New York public in due time. It spoke of suicide; it reminded Catholics that our moral theology in no way countenanced such an act.*

*I thought that a series of nagging questions was by no means resolved by this pronunciamento. Was the death of Laporte, in fact, a suicide? And even if it was, did the official judgment on the matter reflect the compassion of Christ?*

*And more: what if the death reflected not despair, but a self-offering attuned (however naively or mistakenly) to the sacrifice of Christ? Would not such a presumption show mercy toward the death, as well as honoring the grief of the living?"*
—To Dwell in Peace

we have the power of putting death itself to death, of declaring war on war, of offering to others the pure and uncorrupted waters of their love.[110]

A garbled report of Dan's compassionate remarks made its way to his provincial, who saw this as a violation of his order. Failing to contact Dan for his own account of what he had said and the fact that it had been in a closed circle, an outraged McGinty summoned a meeting of the province's four "consultors" (a panel of senior Jesuits who play a part in significant decisions), who in turn referred the matter to the general of the Jesuits in Rome, Pedro Arrupe. Arrupe was away, however, so the matter fell to one of his consultors, Paolo Dezza. Acting on the report that Dan had flagrantly violated an explicit order from his provincial, Dezza agreed that a punitive response was appropriate.

On November 16, six days after Roger had set himself on fire, McGinty phoned Dan's immediate superior, James Cotter, editor of *Jesuit Missions*, with the instruction that Dan was to be "out of the city within twenty-four hours." Reviewing various possibilities, Cotter decided to send Dan on a Latin American tour that he had intended to make himself. Cotter walked into Dan's room saying, "The fat's in the fire." Dan responded, "I haven't got much fat, and where's the fire?" "You've got to go on a trip." Dan was, Cotter said, being sent to Latin America, first stop Cuernavaca, itinerary beyond Mexico to be worked out. The date of his return? Uncertain, open-ended . . .

At the time Cotter formed the impression that Cardinal Francis Spellman, an outspoken supporter of the Vietnam War, had forced this move on the Jesuits. "After all," Cotter remarked to Dan, "we do have to get along with the cardinal." (It has often been written by Dan and many others that the Jesuits had been obliged by Spellman to send Dan out of the New York Archdiocese, but recent research done by Rodger Van Allen convincingly

*"The damned war! It was a creeping miasma, an irresistible current: it swept along, in its frothy wake, nearly everyone and everything. Our community was put on a war footing. And because I was objecting to the war, I must be treated like a deserter or an informer. The form of punishment narrowed: There was silence, then ostracism, scorn— and finally, exile."*

—To Dwell in Peace

Cardinal Francis Spellman, Archbishop of New York.

shows it was the Jesuit provincial, John McGinty, who made the decision.[111])

Dan called me at the Catholic Peace Fellowship office, voice choked, and asked me to come up immediately. When I arrived half an hour later, Dan told me there were but two options to consider: accept the departure order or refuse it. Were he to refuse, the Jesuits might expel him.

I urged Dan to obey. My view was that very little could be gained by resisting the order except controversy regarding the limits of authority. The issues that preoccupied Dan and the rest of us—nonviolent resistance to the war—would be largely ignored. Obeying while publicizing the situation, on the other hand, still allowed the issue of abuse of authority to be raised, and with it that of conscience, while keeping Dan from being expelled from the Jesuits. I pointed out to Dan that there might even be some providence in his going south for a while. When B'rer Fox hurled B'rer Rabbit into the briar patch, I reminded him, it was B'rer Rabbit who had the last laugh.

Dan fired off a letter with the unwelcome news to Merton, who also thought, however unfortunate the circumstances, a trip to Latin America might be providential: "If you go to Latin America it might be all to the good, in some long-range plan. I could perhaps put you in touch with some good people, depending where you go."[112]

No doubt Dan talked with others. His discipline was to do hard thinking in a communal context, making sure all the possibilities had been explored and his own leanings tested. Out of all this came his decision to take the one-way ticket. "It feels a bit like a shotgun divorce,"

Dan speaking at first Meal of Reconciliation in Manhattan, October 4, 1966. Jim Forest

*"I discovered, gradual as a dawn over the mind, the irony that is a most delicious form of knowledge. To wit: the act that was designed to break me in pieces was serving only to toughen my resolve. Who was it said, that which does not kill me only strengthens me?"*
—To Dwell in Peace

Cornell University, Division of Rare and Manuscript
Collections

Dan commented to me, "but somehow the divorce has become a trial separation." The question of expulsion from the society still lingered.

With McGinty's twenty-four-hour exodus order in mind, while travel details and visas were being arranged and tickets purchased, Cotter made urgent calls appealing for short-term hospitality for Dan outside the archdiocese. Remarkably his fellow Jesuits at Le Moyne had no room in the inn, but Georgetown University said yes.[113]

Word got out. In the days that followed, editorials criticizing the transfer action appeared in many periodicals. *Commonweal* wrote that Dan's banishment was "a shame and a scandal, a disgustingly blind totalitarian act, a travesty on Vatican II."

At the Clergy Concerned about Vietnam meeting November 30, a few days after Dan's flight to Mexico, an empty chair on the stage had a sign on it reading, "Father Daniel Berrigan, S.J." Photos of the vacant chair were widely published.

On December 5 the New York chancery office was picketed by hundreds of people carrying such signs as "St. Paul was a Rebel Too," "Jesus Was Arrested for Stirring Up the People," "Free the Church from Stalinism," and "Merry Christmas, Dan, Wherever You Are."

On December 7, Dan wrote me from the Centro de Investigaciones Culturales in Cuernavaca, Mexico, where he was taking a crash course in Spanish.

Letters coming in here, phone calls, and, yesterday, a copy of the *National Catholic Reporter* make it clear that great things are in the wind. And yet with their cost too. Phil wrote that Tom [Cornell] had been beaten after the Washington march. . . . This is a terrible cost to pay for being a peacemaker, and one never gets to the point of not being appalled by the violence against those he loves. . . . I am going along from day to day here, marveling at the strange ways of Providence. . . . There is nothing to be worried over on my score. According to present reports, I will be going south from here in a week or ten days. . . . Are people in good spirits? We have in a sense been through a lot since Roger's death, but what a time of strength and joy too! . . . Mucho love to all.

On December 12 an open letter to the Archdiocese of New York as well as to the New York Jesuit community occupied a full page of the *New York Times*. "The issue here is simply freedom of conscience," the signers declared, going on to ask if a priest could speak out on Vietnam only if he supports the war. "If a priest is controversial [and] takes a position different from that of conventional wisdom . . . [is he] as a result dangerous to the Church? The Roman Catholic manner of dealing with such a priest is not to debate him, not to offer alternative arguments, but simply to silence him and send him to another country where his attempt to give Christian witness will not offend. . . . Such a meaning is intolerable in the Roman Catholic Church [and] . . . denies what the Church has achieved. It must be eradicated." The text had a thousand signers, including many Jesuits.

By now McGinty must have been having second and third thoughts about his shoot-from-the-hip role in what had become known internationally as the "Berrigan Affair."

Meanwhile, however reluctant he was to be there, Dan was seeing a great deal of Latin America. In Rio de Janeiro he witnessed the consequences of a flash flood that had cascaded through some of the city's vulnerable *favellas*, creating "a stew of death," while in Lima he felt nauseated just breathing in the smoke of small fires lit in densely packed hovels not far away from the spacious homes of wealthy families whose comfort depended on the discomfort of others. He met fellow Jesuits, community organizers, social workers, nuns, priests, and others whose lives centered on assisting those who were struggling to survive but whose work, in many cases, was all but ignored by the hierarchy. "I encountered in almost every country . . . a church either internally colonized or virulently imperial, the two being perhaps the same thing, a church of, by and for the wealthy."[114]

In such oppressive conditions, in which few bishops said discomforting words to the social elite, Dan could sympathize with those who turned to violent methods of self-defense. "One hopes that the revolution [that seems inevitable] would be nonviolent," Dan later wrote for *Jesuit Missions*, "but I came back from Latin America much more tentative about the possibility of forging the needed changes apart from violence. . . . All the forces of Church and society seemed to be united against change."[115] It was a short-lived moment of shaken faith in what nonviolent methods could achieve even in a profoundly hostile environment.

As protests regarding Dan's exile continued, Dan wrote me from Chile February 17: "A letter from my Provincial assures me I will be welcome back to NY for my work—that was a great relief indeed. I think all the fuss has helped some anchorites come to a better mind and brought a breath of freedom to more priests and laymen. Is this so?"

After a four-month, ten-country journey south of the border, Dan returned to New York on March 8, the one-way ticket now made round-trip. Among those welcoming him with joy were many Jesuits.

Merton teased Dan that the controversy his exile had triggered had made him "one of the most popular priests in the US. . . . And you ask why you were shipped out?

*"I questioned my soul, had authorities been so fond as to assume that exposure to the realities of Latin America would turn the offender from his offense? The assumption seems naïve in the extreme. A far better plan would have seen me disposed of in mid-Sahara or some remote polar region, surrounded by ruminant camels or flocks of penguins. . . . With neither dromedaries nor spiffy birds for company, but surrounded by the infection of misery and injustice, even a slow learner like myself found his learning speeded up wonderfully. I came home, worse than ever."*

—To Dwell in Peace

Nothing but good can come to you from it. . . . You are news, man. Way it looks to me is this: you are going to be able to do a great deal of good simply stating facts quietly and telling the truth quietly and patiently."[116]

At a press conference in New York on March 11 occasioned by publication of *They Call Us Dead Men* (essays) and *No One Walks Wat*ers (poems), Dan made it clear that there would be no trimming of his sails regarding the sin of war. "Our presence in Southeast Asia," Dan said, "represents a contempt for the rights of innocent individuals and constitutes a continuing divergence for the purposes of destruction of resources that are badly needed in other parts of the world. . . . When I left in November, everything seemed so closed. Now the peace movement has grown in numbers and quality."

Wasting no time in putting his body where his words were, on March 30 Dan was in the front ranks of a New York peace procession, in company with sixty priests, nuns, rabbis, and ministers, walking from synagogue to Protestant church to Catholic cathedral, then on to the United Nations.

Thinking more and more about the ways the churches collaborate in war, the following day he wrote Tom and me suggesting that CPF give some thought to the issue of priest-chaplains in the military who never raised any questions about the morality of what the military was doing. "The traditional idea [is] that the state throws bombs with its right hand and with its left calls on priests to succor the troops. But what of [antiwar pronouncements of] Popes John and Paul and the Council?" Was it not time to challenge the Church to refuse the role of being a chaplain of war?

Something of Dan's mid-1966 mind-set comes through in his comments on my draft of a CPF fund-appeal letter: "The letter seems to me OK except I miss in it a note of urgency and push which the NY Times gives me each morning, the latest madness saying with a gargoyle grin, What are you going to do with this one,

*No One Walks Waters* (1965).

Pedro Arrupe, S.J., Father General of the Society of Jesus.

bud? The letter sounds a bit as though we were keeping house in normal times. Ha. Can't you give some hint of the wash of suffering the war is bringing home to our doorstep? Give us a bit of anguish, or why talk about hope?"

On the draft he penciled in such additions or changes as, "You can read the extent of our need in your daily paper. The noise of violence is louder each day. How to declare peace as loudly as our government declares war? . . . How to raise in the religious community the painful questions the war itself has brought on so urgently, a religious community which has in the past expended far more energy on its internal welfare than on the question of whether and how man is to survive."

The momentum continued with few breaks and little shift in the style of life, except Dan's longing to go to Vietnam and "get under the bombs." He made a brief trip to Paris, hoping friends there might assist him in obtaining a visa, but the effort proved futile.

In an effort to encourage the American Jesuit community to oppose the war and do more to impede violence and injustice, Dan wrote the Jesuits' father general Pedro Arrupe and then went to Rome to meet him. While there was no immediate result from their encounter, Arrupe must have been impressed by his visitor from America. Five years later he visited Dan in prison.[117]

# Pouring Blood

lose ties had developed between Dan and the Religious of the Sacred Heart of Mary, largely as a consequence of Dan's friendship with Sister Jogues Egan, president of Marymount Manhattan and later provincial of the order for that region.[118] In June 1967 Dan was invited by the community to lead their annual retreat at a Benedictine monastery, St. Paul's, near Newton, New Jersey.

On the retreat's last day, several of us from the Catholic Worker and the Catholic Peace Fellowship responded to an invitation to join in celebrating a child's baptism in a nearby lake and take part in the picnic that followed. Dan, in a bathing suit, wore an image of a silver fish as a medal. Afterward Dan proposed to drive with me back to the city. "Then we could talk, as the chorus girl said to the bishop, combining business with pleasure."

One of the things we discussed on our ride was whether Dan should accept an invitation to become an associate director of United Religious Work at Cornell University. The job would involve teaching, counseling, celebrating Mass, administering the other sacraments, and not least compelling, "promoting student activism." Cornell had become a major center of mid-sixties student protest. Also Dan would be close to home; Ithaca wasn't far from Syracuse. It was an attractive possibility. On the other hand Dan loved New York and was hesitant to

Dan enjoys a lakeside picnic following a baptism. Jim Forest

Top: Cornell University Campus.
Robert Ellsberg

Above: Dan at Cornell. Cornell University, Division of Rare and Manuscript Collections

leave. He also wondered if a job at Ivy League Cornell might be a sellout?

After several weeks of pondering, Dan said yes. Meanwhile, at the suggestion of Peace Corps director Sargent Shriver, he spent the mid-summer in Pueblo, Colorado, teaching Hispanic students who were participating in an Upward Bound program.

In that period Shriver, a brother-in-law of John and Robert Kennedy, repeatedly arranged for Dan to be a guest at the Kennedy compound in Hyannis Port, Massachusetts. "In those days," Dan told me, "I was still respectable because I hadn't broken the law yet."

On one occasion in 1966, soon after his return from Latin America, Dan was invited to dinner at Robert Kennedy's house and discovered that Secretary of Defense Robert McNamara was a guest as well. "Since we have both Father Berrigan and Secretary McNamara here," said Kennedy, "I suggest having a discussion of the war." Not hesitating, Dan turned to McNamara and said, "Well, you didn't end the war this morning, so how about ending it right now?" McNamara responded, "Let me just say this to Father Berrigan. Vietnam is like Mississippi. If they won't obey the law, you send the troops in."[119] The discussion went no further.

Dan arrived at Cornell in late August 1967. The first term he cotaught a course on the Gospel of John that he christened "The Imagination of God," as well as a noncredit course on nonviolence. He quickly developed a reputation for asking disturbing questions: What about the university's investment portfolio, segments of which connected Cornell to the military-industrial complex and the war in Vietnam? How did Cornell treat the seasonal migrant workers the university employed in its orchards?

He also raised challenging questions with students dismissive of nonviolent methods of social change. "The New Left suffers," Dan argued, "from American pragmatism. It fights violence with the tools of violence. I fight it with the Gandhian and Christian dimensions of nonviolence. They measure effectiveness by pragmatic results. I see it as immeasurable, as the impact of symbolic activity."[120]

Dan, as much pastor as preacher, became known for accompanying conscientious objectors to their draft board hearings as well as to induction refusals.

It was in the early months of his chaplaincy at Cornell that Dan had his first experience of being jailed, an unplanned five-day stay under lock-and-key in Washington. With a group of a hundred Cornell students, he was arrested at midnight, October 22, at the Pentagon. The Cornell contingent was one of many that had gathered there with the idea that the five-walled city of warfare needed exorcism. Dan recorded two reflections in his journal:

*1. Why was I so long retarded from so crucially formative a happening?*

*2. What's the big joke, You there?*

He also noted, "For the first time I put on the prison blue jeans and denim shirt, a clerical attire I highly recommend for the new church."

Dan was the first American Catholic priest to be jailed for antiwar protest. Five days later Phil became the second, in his case courting a much longer sentence.

On October 27 Phil and three others—David Eberhardt, Tom Lewis, and James Mengel—poured several bottles of their own blood on files kept in Baltimore's central draft board at the US Customs House. However superficial the harm done—a relatively small number of papers were stained—damage or destruction of government property was no small offense. "We shed our blood willingly and gratefully," a group statement declared, "in what we hope is a sacrificial and constructive act. We

Top: Antiwar protest at the Pentagon

Above: Phil Berrigan under arrest.
Cornell University, Division of Rare and
Manuscript Collections

*"My brother's action helped me realize, from the beginning of our republic, good men had said no, acted outside the law when conditions so demanded. And if a man did this time might vindicate him, show his act to be lawful, a gift to society, a gift to history and to the community."*
—The Trial of the Catonsville Nine

Drawing by Tom Lewis of Phil Berrigan in jail. Cornell University, Division of Rare and Manuscript Collections

pour it upon these files to illustrate that with them and with these offices begins the pitiful waste of American and Vietnamese blood 10,000 miles away."

Dan was released from jail the day Phil and his three collaborators entered. Dan noted in his journal entry for October 27: "This is the day of Phil's action in Baltimore. *Oremus pro fratribus in periculo*" (Let us pray for our brothers in peril).

Freed from jail, Dan was driven to the Washington Catholic Worker house for lunch. From the car radio he heard a report of Phil's arrest. Phoning his mother, he told her the news. There was a long pause before Frida responded, "Now let me understand. You are out of jail, but Phil is in jail? Okay." Frida was completely calm.

Phil's turn toward more costly acts of civil disobedience made both brothers think more critically about those whose antiwar protest followed a less confrontational route. Especially for Phil, the word "liberal" had come to mean cautious or even cowardly. All liberals opposed the war but, as Phil saw it, did nothing to block it, nor did the liberal critique of the United States go deep enough. In Phil's analysis, America, while using the rhetoric of morality and human rights to gift wrap its foreign policy, was applying its military might for imperialist goals.

No one had done more than Phil to keep the Catholic Peace Fellowship afloat during its first three years, but in the fall of 1967 Phil concluded that the CPF's main tasks—helping conscientious objectors and organizing demonstrations—were not adequate responses to the war in Vietnam. A long chain of events had led Phil to that conclusion, years punctuated with speeches all over the country; countless meetings with legislators, administration officials, generals, and bishops; peaceful invasions of military installations; vigils in front of the homes of members of the Joint Chiefs of Staff; and intense efforts to prod Congress to hold hearings on the illegality and immorality of the Vietnam War. The results convinced

Phil that "petitionary nonviolence" had been tried and, after the most sincere and concerted efforts, proved inadequate. The time had come for militant, nonviolent resistance. Phil began using the word "revolution" and to describe himself as a revolutionary.

On December 2 Phil wrote to Tom Cornell and myself to announce his withdrawal from both the Catholic Peace Fellowship and the Fellowship of Reconciliation, with which CPF was affiliated:

> [My criticism is] slowly and reluctantly spoken, mainly because I abhor hurting friends, sometimes to the point of cowardice. But . . . I had better say what I think.
>
> My impression has been, for well over a year, that the Fellowship of Reconciliation has moved steadily to the margin of the war-peace issue. Frankly, I no longer take it seriously; and I take the CPF seriously only because I love and respect my friends who are in it. Not because it is realistically facing Vietnam and/or the Cold War.
>
> Now it may be, and I'm ready to admit this, that people in both organizations are doing their utmost, and doing it conscientiously. That's their affair. But in face of what this war has become, with its contribution to probable nuclear war—they are out of it. Tom [Cornell] says that the movement must be orchestrated. Perhaps. But the term reminds me of white liberal jargon—jargon used by people who still will be building their broad base [of support in society] as the Bombs come in. I will refuse to indict anyone's conscience, but I don't have to cheer their work, which seems to me safe, unimaginative, staffish and devoid of risk or suffering. . . .
>
> [Dan and I] have been led to different roads, ones which seem to us more at grips with this awful war and the insanity of our country. To stop this war, I would give my life tomorrow, and I can't be blamed

*"We have been accused of arrogance. But what of the fantastic arrogance of our leaders? What of the crimes against the people, the poor and powerless? Still no court will try them, no jail will receive them. They live in righteousness. They will die in honor. For them we have one message, for those in whose manicured hands the power of the land lies. We say to them: Lead us. Lead us in justice, and there will be no need to break the laws."*

—Phil's testimony,
The Trial of the Catonsville Nine

if I have little time for those who want to run ads in the New York Times. . . . Both Dan and I are seriously dealing with clergymen and laymen, professionals and family people, who have come to the point of civil disobedience and the prospect of jail, and are even foundering with convictions beyond that point. As [President] Johnson continues to have his war, and that means the probability of invading North Vietnam, we will either witness from jail, or we will go ahead with social disruption, including nonviolent attacks against the machinery of this war. . . .

In a word, I believe in revolution, and I hope to continue a nonviolent contribution to it. In my view, we are not going to save this country and mankind without it. And I am centrally concerned with the Gospel view that the massive suffering of this war and American imperialism around the world will only be confronted by people who are willing to go with suffering as the first move to justice. . . .

I hope this clears up more than it obscures. Whatever the case, you will continue to mean much to me as a friend and teacher. Christ's love and peace. Phil.

CPF booklet, "Catholics and Conscientious Objection."

Dan was also beginning to see a new direction in peace work. While not withdrawing from CPF as Phil had done, Dan also felt it was time to step onto thinner ice. As he put it in a letter to me dated December 3, a day after Phil's, "The question is whether we are helping people get radical, [whether we are] content to stay small and do things and encourage actions which will be evangelical and identifiable as such. Or are we trying to present an opposite "power" in the image of the opposite number, or at least something "presentable" to large numbers of Catholics, and therefore morally neutral—or liberal—but not radical, [not] at the roots."

The two letters occasioned pain, bewilderment, and defensiveness for Tom and me. As I reminded both Dan and Phil, in fact what the Catholic Peace

Fellowship was doing really mattered. Tom and I had been speaking at rallies, conferences, and teach-ins all over the country as well as in churches and seminaries. There were half a dozen or so vigorous regional CPF groups. Not least, we were playing an effective role in encouraging potential soldiers not to fight. Before Vietnam, Catholic conscientious objectors had been a very rare breed; not so during the Vietnam War. In the course of the war, more than three hundred thousand copies of the CPF booklet I had written, *Catholics and Conscientious Objection*,[121] were sold or given away. A priest, Lyle Young of the Emmaus House community, had joined the CPF staff to assist us in counseling those—on average, fifty people a week—who were seeking draft-board recognition as conscientious objectors and, thanks in large measure to CPF assistance, in most cases obtaining such recognition.

But, especially for Phil, such activities fell short of the prison-risking resistance that, he was convinced, the times now demanded. That many refused to take part in war did not change the fact that, however reluctantly, most who received draft notices complied, put on uniforms, learned to kill, and did whatever they were ordered to do. The war moved forward on its merciless track. We who opposed the war were like firemen trying to put out a conflagration with a garden hose.

In fact, Dan was himself much less certain than Phil of what should come next and whether destruction of property was appropriate. In a letter dated October 6, two weeks after the blood-pouring action in Baltimore, Dan had written Merton "in strict confidence" that "good people are talking more and more violence" while dismissing Martin Luther King's nonviolence as naïve. "There is rage and discontent in the air," Dan noted, "which in many cases seems to be the seeding into us of the sins of the war makers themselves, and the loss of our own choices by the imposition of theirs."

Dan at Cornell. Cornell University, Division of Rare and Manuscript Collections (Bruce Anspach)

*"I feel very badly about the concerns I'm causing with you and other members of the Community . . . but as you know, I have little hope for man as long as this country pursues its insanity. And I have great hope for revolution, and the kind of witness the Gospel seems to suggest."*

—Letter from Phil to Dan, April 1968

Cornell University, Division of Rare and Manuscript Collections

Phil also, Dan told Merton, was thinking of strategies of violence, though against property, not people:

> The news is that Phil and a group who have been outstanding and courageous on civil disobedience in Baltimore are now seeking bigger action. They are going in for violence against military or government property.[122] . . . There is sure to be a huge howl from the two-headed [state and church] establishment, legal and religious [if an act of property destruction occurs]. . . . But will such an action communicate at all??? . . . We seem to be nearing the point where racism and war-making are pushing us in the direction of a more dangerous revaluation of the *violence-to-persons-through-inviolate-property* equation. Also the possibility of vindicating the truth of nonviolence toward persons by working violence on idolatrous things, thus removing, at least by way of prophecy, all the garbage which expensively keeps persons from being human toward persons. [The ever-worsening war in Vietnam is] inevitably pushing good people into very dangerous waters. Phil and the others are seeking light from me . . . [but] there is not a great deal of light I can shed.[123]

Dan begged Merton for what wisdom he could offer. "We need you as always and turn to you in hard times as the one most likely to shed light—a noble vocation indeed."

In his response Merton posed a range of reservations and hard questions. To what extent, he asked, "is the new revolutionism . . . simply irresponsible, capricious, idiotic, pointless, haphazard and inviting disaster? To what extent do these people realize they are so disoriented that at the moment all they can think of is systematic unreason and disaster—acceptable insofar as precipitated by themselves? . . . The obsession with being "with it" whatever "it" may turn out to be. It seems to me that the indif-

*"When Philip and his friends walked through the door of the draft board, there was no exit, not for years. They were seized by the great Seizer. They were trespassers on his turf, had dared muck up the exquisite order of his necrophiliac files, where the names of the soon to be killed, or the soon to kill, or both, were preserved against the Day of Great Summons."*

—To Dwell in Peace

ference with which the radicals and some liberals are now nonviolent, now flower power, now burn-baby[-burn], all sweetness on Tuesday and all hell-fire on Wednesday, reflects sheer mindlessness and hopelessness. . . ."[124]

Might it not be better, Merton asked, for the Catholic Peace Fellowship and the "Catholic left" to be "less naïve, try to go it more on our own, have a more or less firm and consistent position? [Would not] our best contribution to the whole mess [be] a kind of relative clarity and consistency and firmness that stays with a clearly recognizable Christian and Gospel position? Have we ever even begun to explore what real nonviolence is about? Is this just the testing that is essential before we even get sorted out enough to begin? Are we now ready for a novitiate? In my opinion the answer is to close ranks with people [committed to nonviolence] like [Martin Luther] King. . . . To become recognizable as committed to very clear limits on the violence thing? At least to take up enough of a basic position to be able to go on from there to decide whether yes or no we can be violent "against property." That is outside the Gandhian [path] right away. My opinion would be some of us ought to stay with Gandhi's end of it until we have at least gone deep into it and seen what was there (as King has). . . . We have to be able to define our limits. I don't say violence

Dan in his Cornell office. Cornell University, Division of Rare and Manuscript Collections

*"We have assumed the name of peacemakers, but we have been, by and large, unwilling to pay any significant price. And because we want peace with half a heart and half a life and will, the war, of course, continues, because the waging of war, by its nature, is total—but the waging of peace, by our own cowardice, is partial. So a whole will and a whole heart and a whole national life bent toward war prevail over the velleities of peace."*

—No Bars to Manhood

against property is off-limits. [But it] certainly seems to me that killing people is. But if it comes to burning buildings, then people are going to be in danger and whoever is involved is going to be partly responsible for people getting destroyed even on his own side in a way that the nonviolent resister would not be responsible. . . ."

Merton also questioned the group dynamics involved: "Politically are we just getting involved in a fake revolution of badly mixed-up, disaster-inviting people who are willing to do anything absurd and irrational simply to mess things up, and to mess them up especially for the well-meaning 'idealists' who want to run along proving that they are such real good hip people?"

Might there be a pathology involved, Merton asked, in a turn toward violence even if limited to property? "Psychologically how nuts is the whole damn business? In my opinion the job of the Christian is to try to give an example of sanity, independence, human integrity, good sense, as well as Christian love and wisdom, against all establishments and all mass movements and all current fashions which are merely mindless and hysterical. But of course are they? And do we get hung up in merely futile moral posturing? Well, somewhere we have to choose. The most popular and exciting thing at the moment is not necessarily the best choice."

Merton ended the letter by noting he was hampered in not knowing exactly what Phil was planning: "I don't say any of this comes anywhere near applying to the situation Phil speaks of. I have no real idea whether that is sane or nutty: I am just talking in terms of the whole situation judged by the smell of the smog that reaches me down here."

Dan felt, he told me later, "torn down the middle by the two people I most admired—Phil pulling in one direction, Merton the other."

# Night Flight to Hanoi

D an had long been haunted with the idea of going to Vietnam and experiencing the war where the bombs were falling. In 1967 he took an active part in a Catholic Peace Fellowship–Fellowship of Reconciliation project to raise medical relief for Vietnamese civilian war victims, both north and south. He then went a step further in seeking to be part of a CPF-FOR delegation that would personally deliver some of the medical supplies. Getting an export license that would allow shipment of such supplies not only to South but to North Vietnam was the major problem; even the donation of lifesaving material intended for civilian war victims was regarded as "trading with the enemy," a felony.

"A group of us," Dan recalled, "visited the State Department to demand relief from this inhuman decree."[125] A woman assigned to meet the delegation said no exceptions could be made, no matter what the nature of the gift. Any attempt to trade would incur the penalties of law. The encounter only stiffened Dan's resolve, even if that meant prosecution and imprisonment. "Does it not say in an old book that Christians read from time to time and claim to venerate," Dan asked me at the time, "'If your enemy hungers, feed him'?"[126]

At this point he turned to his provincial and sought his blessing to go to Hanoi "on a work of mercy." To Dan's astonishment the approval was refused. "My supe-

Dan in Vientiane, Laos, enroute to Hanoi. Courtesy Berrigan family

rior at the moment was a sterling upholder of the law. . . . It was he who later coined the marvelous distinction . . . to the effect that I was 'in the order but not of it.'" However, not wanting to make the decision without broader consultation, a meeting was arranged involving several other senior Jesuits. At this small gathering, one of the questions put to Dan was, "If you were not to go to Vietnam under such circumstances, would you judge yourself guilty of a mortal sin?"[127] Perhaps it was Dan's simple answer, "Yes," that convinced the provincial and his consulters to give permission.[128]

For all the efforts made by Dan and other Americans to move forward with the medical relief project, the remaining obstacles proved too many. In the end the supplies were delivered by the Geneva-based World Council of Churches. Yet it was at this juncture that Dan's yearning to go to Vietnam was fulfilled in an entirely unexpected way. The government of North Vietnam had decided to make a peace gesture—the release of three captured US bomber pilots imprisoned in Hanoi. Dave Dellinger, a prominent figure in the American antiwar movement, was contacted by the Hanoi regime and asked to choose two people to bring the flyers home. Dellinger phoned Dan and historian Howard Zinn, asking if they were willing; both agreed. Having himself been a bomber pilot during World War II, Zinn was a doubly apt choice.[129]

Packing little more than a toothbrush and a change of clothes, Dan left Ithaca January 30, hours after receiving the invitation. Riding a nighttime bus to New York, he found himself sitting next to a soldier who belonged to the honor guard that buried the dead—mainly young men killed in Vietnam—at Arlington National Cemetery: "We talked on and on: the volleys, the folding of the flag, the emotion and dread of accompanying the families, the small talk, the inadequate stumbling phrases. . . . He burst out, 'It's horrible! I'd rather be in Vietnam taking my chances.'"[130]

Last-minute ticketing put Dan and Zinn on a patchwork quilt of flights—from Kennedy Airport to Copenhagen and on from there to Frankfurt, Rome, Teheran, Karachi, Calcutta, Bangkok. . . . They arrived at their last stop in Vientiane, Laos, twenty-eight hours later only to discover the cancellation of the Friday night flight to Hanoi that they had gone sleepless to catch. After a one-week wait in Vientiane they finally boarded an aged Boeing 707—one of three such planes still in service anywhere in the world—and arrived at night in Hanoi.

In his account of the mission, Dan struggled to find words for what Hanoi was like: "How to convey the at-

*"How long have I wished to share the common life, to be compassionate with men and women, within the same fear, the same skin, the same trembling and fire and ice, to mourn with the men and women who die and do not wish to die; to weep for the children."*

—Night Flight to Hanoi

mosphere, that long and dolorous entrance into the destroyed city; the endless pontoons of the bridges replacing the bombed spans; the desolation and patience and cold; the convoys, the endless lines of military vehicles and cars. [Yet] the loveliest fact of all was the most elusive and insignificant; we had been received with flowers."[131]

A night of uninterrupted sleep was rare in Hanoi—air-raid sirens repeatedly punctuated the dark hours. The first four nights the howl of sirens proved to be false alarms. It was only on the fifth that bombs were dropped on the city. Dan wrote in his journal, "We went to sleep

Dan Berrigan and Howard Zinn meet with North Vietnamese officials.
Courtesy Berrigan family

*"I have always believed that the peace movement must not merely say no to the war. It must also say yes to life, yes to the possibility of a human future. We must go beyond frontiers, frontiers declared by our country or by the enemy. So I thought it would be important to show Americans that we were ready to risk our lives to bring back American prisoners. . . . And so we went."*
—The Trial of the Catonsville Nine

like children and awakened like adults to the boom! boom! . . . Howard appeared at my door, disheveled in the half light, like a runner awaiting the shot, without his socks. . . . In a few moments we had crossed the garden and ducked into the shelter."

"We wondered later about the priorities of the American government," Zinn wrote. "They knew we were in Hanoi to pick up three fliers; did it not occur to them as at least a slim possibility that to bomb Hanoi at exactly that time might endanger the release? Granted that the military objectives of the bombing were more important to the United States than any consideration for the lives of the Vietnamese (with hundreds of schools, hospitals, churches destroyed, with whole villages razed, with anti-personnel bombs dropped in huge quantities, this was clear); were those military objects also more important to the United States government than the freedom of three American fliers, who themselves had been engaged in that same military action?"[132]

Yet, like grass growing through cracks in asphalt, in the daytime life continued even as the city suffered: "Throughout the week," Dan noted, "I could hear the chambermaids in the corridor singing; the plaintive atonal music with which the meek of heart console themselves for life in the cave of ravening lions."

After several days of being shown the damaged city and taken to its sandbagged museums, at last Dan and Zinn met the three men they were bringing home. "We drove through dark streets to the prison," Zinn wrote, "an old French villa adapted to the new exigencies. Inside, there was the usual introductory tea session. The prison commandant read to us his data on the three fliers: Major Norris Overly, thirty-nine, flying out of a base in South Vietnam, wife and two children in Detroit; Captain John Black, thirty, flying out of Udom airfield in Thailand, wife and three kids in Tennessee; Lieutenant (Junior Grade) David Methany, flying from an aircraft carrier, twenty-four, single."

At the end of the week, in time for the weekly flight to Vientiane, the pilots were turned over to their antiwar escorts and brought part of the way home. Under orders from Washington that the pilots should travel no farther with Dan and Zinn than Laos, Ambassador William Sullivan took charge of the ex-captives.

For Dan, in contrast with Phil, this had been his first experience of war up close. "Being an American under American bombs was an education without parallel," he said after his return. "It was as though the heavens had erupted and poured out the contempt of the gods."

What haunted Dan most not only in the days but years that followed were the faces of Vietnamese children, wide-eyed, terrified, sitting motionless in bomb shelters, innocent of war yet among its primary victims. One of his Hanoi poems, "Children in the Shelter," focuses on their silent gaze:

*"In any case we brought the flyers home. I think as a result of the trip to Hanoi I understood the limits of what I had done before and the next step that must come."*
—The Trial of the Catonsville Nine

Imagine; three of them.

As though survival
were a rat's word,
and a rat's death
waited there at the end

and I must have
in the century's boneyard
heft of flesh and bone in my arms

I picked up the littlest
a boy, his face
breaded with rice (his sister calmly feeding him
as we climbed down)

In my arms fathered
in a moment's grace, the messiah
of all my tears. I bore, reborn
a Hiroshima child from hell.[133]

# "Don't just do something, stand there. . . ."

The Baltimore Four. *Ramparts*

In April came the trial of the Baltimore Four. The judge, Edward Northrop, was determined that the one and only issue to be tried in his courtroom was whether the defendants had poured blood on government files, period. No discussion of morality. No international law.

Listening to Judge Northrop "droning on, angry and fretful," Dan recalled how, during the Second World War, he had been safely "tucked away in a seminary in the Maryland hills" keeping track of a distant war with maps and pins while Phil was risking his life on actual battlefields, "a soldier's soldier, decorated and commissioned in the European theater." Now Dan, too, had seen war with his own eyes and felt the earth shake as bombs exploded.

The jury quickly decided on a guilty verdict. Pending appeal, the four were free on bail. Though the damage caused had been superficial, the sentences Northrop handed down a month later were harsh: six years for Phil Berrigan and Tom Lewis and three for David Eberhardt; in the case of Jim Mengel, Northrop ordered a psychiatric examination.

At his sentencing Phil declared, "Our country now stands at the pinnacle of world power. We are history's most powerful empire, and perhaps its most dangerous one. We are richer than all the rest of mankind, and our military power surpasses that of all the rest of mankind.

The equation between the two, wealth and military power, is not an idle one. As President Johnson has said, 'The rest of the world wants what we have and we're not going to let them take it.'"

There was also, for Phil, censure from Baltimore's archbishop, Cardinal Lawrence Sheehan. "I cannot condone," he said, "the damaging of property or the intimidation of government employees." He briefly barred Phil from saying Mass publicly as well as from preaching or hearing confessions.

Even before the Baltimore trial began, the idea of burning the principal records at the Catonsville draft office was already on its tracks, but Dan, though in awe of his brother's courage and determination, was not yet a passenger. First he had to work his way through a few difficult questions. Did such an action blur the line between violence and nonviolence? However appropriate such an act of resistance might be, might it be counterproductive, alienating more people than it activated? Was there not some positive value in one brother serving as an unimprisoned voice for the other? What about the value of the work he was doing at Cornell and so many other places? But his relative physical fragility, he later insisted, had not been a worry. When one writer suggested that Dan hesitated because he realized he "lacked physical stamina" and was "prone to pneumonia," Dan huffily responded, "I really have a good deal of stamina; this makes me sound like *La Boheme*."

With bulldog determination, Phil set out to pull his brother across the border. On the evening of May 12, Dan sat down with Phil until four the following morning. There is no transcript, but whatever Phil said finally tipped the scale. I know from my own parallel conversations with Phil in those days that the word "serious" would have been used by Phil more than once, as in, "Isn't it time for you to do something *serious*?" "Serious" meant risking jail time that would likely be more than a year.

*"I went to Catonsville because I had gone to Hanoi, because my brother was a man and I must be a man and because I knew at length I could not announce the gospel from a pedestal. I must act as a Christian, sharing the risks and burdens and anguish of those whose lives were placed in the breach by us. . . . Although I was too old to carry a draft card, there were other ways of getting in trouble with a state that seemed determined upon multiplying the dead. . . . I went to Hanoi, and then to Catonsville, and that is why I am here."*
—The Trial of the Catonsville Nine

Shortly before dawn May 13, at the end of their all-night exchange, Phil announced to the others who were already committed, "Dan's in."

"I saw suddenly, and it struck with the force of lightning, that my position was false, that I was threatened with verbalizing my moral substance out of existence," Dan testified at the Catonsville trial. "I was placing upon young shoulders a filthy burden, the original sin of war. I was asking them to enter a ceremony of death. Although I was too old to carry a draft card, there were other ways of getting in trouble with a state that seemed determined

The Catonsville Nine burning draft files.

upon multiplying the dead. . . . So I went to Hanoi, and then to Catonsville, and that is why I am here." At the trial Dan also said, "I went to Catonsville because my brother was a man and I must be a man."

Four days later, on May 17, the nine stood around a small blaze in a Maryland parking lot, the event described in this book's opening pages. The lives of the nine and many others would never be the same.

The nine had chosen to act in daylight and wait for arrest. "Don't just do something, *stand* there," as Dan put it. An action with similar results could easily have been done under cover of night with those responsible disappearing into the shadows. Anonymity could have been

*"We believe that some property has no right to exist. Hitler's gas ovens, Stalin's concentration camps, atomic-bacteriological-chemical weaponry, files of conscription, and slum properties have no right to exist. When people starve for bread and lack of decent housing, it is usually because the rich debase themselves with abuse of property, causing extravagance on their part and oppression and misery in others."*
—Statement of the Catonsville Nine

achieved even by amateurs. But the action was meant not only to destroy papers but to take personal responsibility for what they had done and then to put the war on trial. More important than the files burned was the personal accountability for their destruction by those who had struck the match. At the first session of the Catonsville Nine Defense Committee in New York, I recall Dan saying, "Our defense is simply this: we did it, we are glad we did it, and this is why we did it."

Immediate reaction was mainly negative.

Catholic novelist Walker Percy was reminded of the sort of actions carried out by the Ku Klux Klan. In a letter to *Commonweal* he noted that Klan members might also claim to be following conscience: "they [do what they do, church and cross-burning] for God and country. I would be hard-pressed to tell a Klansman why he should be put in jail and the Berrigans set free."

In an editorial headlined "Shrill Symbol," the *National Catholic Reporter* said the Catonsville Nine action "comes through . . . as an offensive sort of prank." Another Catholic publication, *Ave Maria*, said the methods used by the nine failed to get their message across: "Blood and napalm, although they dramatize certain values, tend to raise other questions that obscure the point [the nine] are trying to make."

Countless rank-and-file Catholics, for whom patriotism meant "my country right or wrong," were scandalized that two priests would place themselves at odds with their own nation in time of war. In their view the Berrigans and other war-resisting priests were neglecting their real work and perhaps being unwittingly "used by the Communists."

The nonadmirers included two of the older Berrigan brothers. "I don't go along with all this destroying draft records and all the stuff that they've done," said John Berrigan. "When they started out, they were conscientious priests. We were all proud of them." "Dan and Phil," said their oldest brother, Thomas, "only talk of the

*"I think of the good, decent, peace-loving people I have known by the thousands, and I wonder. How many of them are so afflicted with the wasting disease of normalcy? . . . 'Of course, let us have the peace,' we cry, 'but at the same time let us have normalcy.' . . . There is no peace because the making of peace is at least as costly as the making of war—at least as exigent, at least as disruptive, at least as liable to bring disgrace and prison and death in its wake."*

—No Bars to Manhood

Dan and Phil under arrest. Cornell
University, Division of Rare and Manuscript Collections

terrible things they claim the government has done. . . . Never a word about the treachery and brutality of the Communists."[134] Brother Jerry, on the other hand, took great pride in what Phil and Dan had done at Catonsville.

One of the sharper rebukes came from theologian Rosemary Radford Ruether in an open letter to Dan published in the *National Catholic Reporter*. Had she been invited to take part in the action, she said, she would have declined, not for lack of sympathy but because it contributed to a sectarian ethos, rejecting those whose antiwar efforts did not result in lengthy prison sentences. "You don't believe change is possible either by revolution or by progressive change," Ruether charged. "The alternative then becomes apocalypse, the counsel of despair."

In his reply, Dan described the Catonsville witness not as a declaration of despair but as "a substantial act of hope," opening one more door of resistance to "a war which seemed, so short a time ago, a cloud no bigger than a man's hand [but which now] all but engulfs us."[135]

Response was not all negative. Many saw the action of the nine as prophetic and timely, including a number of Jesuits, among them Robert Drinan, professor of law at Boston College. "The destruction of draft files by the Catonsville Nine," he wrote, "may be a dramatic 'homily' against the evils of militarism. . . . The sincerity and heroism of those who participate . . . is beyond dispute." A group of Jesuit seminarians at Woodstock sent a letter praising the nine for their "integrity and moral commitment."[136]

Among those who sympathized with the action and

its goals but questioned the methodology were Dorothy Day and Thomas Merton, two of Dan's principal mentors.

Initially Dorothy Day was enthusiastic but then had second thoughts, seeing property destruction as a step toward violence. Phil's rough handling of the Catonsville draft board clerks disturbed her. (In an article for *Liberation* magazine, Phil wrote dismissively of clerk Mary Murphy, describing her as "a portly, middle-aged Irish matron" who had tried to protect her files "with furious dogged tenacity." Despite his efforts at calming her, in the end "Mrs. Murphy had to be manhandled repeatedly."[137])

"These [Catonsville-type actions] are not ours," Dorothy said repeatedly.[138] Those committed to nonviolent methods, she declared, "must hang onto our pacifism n the face of violence." She recommended afresh the examples of nonviolent action given by Gandhi and Martin Luther King Jr. Yet she was deeply moved by the readiness of the Catonsville Nine to go to prison as witnesses against a hellish war. "These men—priests and laymen—have offered themselves," she wrote, "as a living sacrifice, as hostages. They have offered the most precious gift apart from life itself, their freedom, as well as the prayer and fasting they have done behind bars, for these others, both Vietnamese and young Americans, being enslaved in our immoral wars."[139]

Merton's views were more critical. "I don't agree with their methods of action," he said in a letter to one correspondent, "but I can understand the desperation which prompts them. They believe they have to witness *in jail* to the injustice of the war."[140]

In an article for *Ave Maria* (one of his last pieces to be published before his death), Merton said protests like Catonsville needed to be considered with care as they present "a new borderline situation . . . as if the peace movement too were standing at the very edge of violence [and as if] this were a sort of 'last chance' at straight nonviolence and

*"The trouble with our state was not civil disobedience which in any case was hesitant and rare . . .
—our trouble
the trouble with our state
with our state of soul
our state of siege—
was*

*Civil Obedience."*
— And the Risen Bread

a first step toward violent resistance. Well, we live in a world of escalation in which no one seems to know how to de-escalate, and it does pose a problem. The peace movement may be escalating beyond peaceful protest, in which case it may also be escalating into self-contradiction. But let me make it clear that I do not think the Catonsville Nine have done this. What happened in Maryland bordered on violence but was in fact violent only to the extent that it meant pushing some good ladies around."

But Merton questioned the usefulness of such an action—a "prophetic nonviolent provocation"—in so traumatized a society. "The country is in a very edgy psychological state. Americans feel terribly threatened, on grounds which are partly rational, partly irrational, but in any case very real. The rites of assassination recur at more and more frequent intervals, and there is less and less of a catharsis each time." Merton's sense was that the participants' action had "frightened more than it edified."

Behind the Catonsville Nine action, Merton glimpsed a "jail mystique . . . a way of saying dumbly to the rest of the country that in our society nobody is really free anyway, that we are all prisoners of a machinery that takes us inevitably where we don't want to go. Presumably everyone in the country wants peace in one way or other. But most Americans have prior commitments—or attachments—to other things which make peace impossible. . . . We speak peace with our lips but the answer in the heart is war, and war only."[141]

Despite his criticisms, Merton's friendship with Dan and Phil remained intact. *Faith and Violence*, the last book Merton prepared for publication before his death, was dedicated to Phil and me.[142] "Hope you enjoy your new Trappist vocation [as a prisoner]," he wrote to Phil in September. "But don't get too much of it. Enough is enough."[143]

A few weeks after the Catonsville trial, on December 10, Merton died while attending a Benedictine-Trappist

Thomas Merton's grave. Jim Forest

monastic conference in Thailand. Dan was left in speechless grief: "I could not talk or write about him for ten years," he told fellow Jesuit John Dear in 1980. "Merton was with me when I was shipped out of the country to Latin America and he was with me in jail."

In his autobiography, written two decades after the event, Dan evaluated what had been done at Catonsville in the light of Pentecost:

> The act was pitiful, a tiny flare amid the consuming fires of war. But Catonsville was like a firebreak, a small fire lit, to contain and conquer a greater. The time, the place, were weirdly right. They spoke for passion, symbol, reprisal. Catonsville seemed to light up the dark places of the heart, where courage and risk and hope were awaiting a signal, a dawn. For the remainder of our lives, the fires would burn and burn, in hearts and minds, in draft boards, in prisons and courts. A new fire, new as a Pentecost, flared up in eyes deadened and hopeless, the noble powers of soul given over to the "powers of the upper air." "Nothing can be done!" How often we had heard that gasp: the last of the human, of soul, of freedom. Indeed, something could be done; and was. And would be.[144]

*"Merton has put in his time, not as a time server, but simply as a patient, hard-wrung, gracious monk, a kind of long-distance runner in place, a master of hangman's humor. And to me, a friend peerless among friends, a gift given once or twice in a lifetime."* —Portraits

# Souls on Trial

*"My intention on that day was to save the innocent from death by fire. . . . If my way of putting the facts is inadmissible, then so be it. But I was trying to be concrete about the existence of God, who is not an abstraction, but is someone before me, for whom I am responsible."*
—The Trial of the Catonsville Nine

When the trial of the Catonsville Nine began on October 7, 1968, the defendants were in good spirits, in part because, just two weeks before, their action had been replicated—and on a bigger scale by a larger group. The Milwaukee 14, of whom I was one, had taken thousands of the principal files of the city's nine draft boards and burned them with homemade napalm in a small downtown square.[145] There was also the impressive fact that Baltimore was crowded with thousands of supporters, including ten busloads from Cornell.

Every night during the trial, about a thousand supporters gathered at St. Ignatius Church in downtown Baltimore to hear reports of what had happened in the courtroom that day and to listen to speakers.

Lawyer and theologian William Stringfellow, one of Dan's closest friends, stood up one evening and said, "With this action, we say, death does not get the last word. Death has no dominion over us. . . . Remember, now, that the State has only one power it can use against human beings: death. The State can persecute you, prosecute you, imprison you, exile you, execute you. All of these mean the same thing. The State can consign you to death. The grace of Jesus Christ in this life is that death fails. There is nothing the State can do to you, or to me, which we need fear."

The Milwaukee 14, burning draft files.

Then Dorothy Day spoke. "We need," she said, "to fill the jails to stop this war! Fill the jails!"

Each morning Phil Berrigan and Tom Lewis, both in handcuffs, were delivered from the county jail to the courtroom by federal marshals, while the other seven, free on bail, filed in via another entrance. All nine sat at a long table with their four lawyers: William Kunstler (well-known defender of dissidents), Harrup Freeman (from the Cornell Law School), Harold Buchman (a Baltimore attorney), and William Cunningham (a Jesuit professor of law from Loyola University). US Attorney Stephen Sachs was in charge of the prosecution, while the day-to-day heavy lifting was done by two federal prosecutors, Arthur Murphy and Barney Skolnik.

The judge was Roszel Thomsen, sixty-six, a patient, affable Methodist, respected in liberal and conservative circles, who had earlier in life been president of the Baltimore School Board, in the course of which he had helped end school segregation. Once seated, each day he greeted everyone present with a "good morning." Though he was no more willing than Judge Northrop had been to have the legality or morality of the Vietnam War tested in his courtroom, he allowed much greater

*"If then I must go to prison . . . I shall go neither in a spirit of alienation, of bitterness, nor of despair. But simply in the hope that has sustained me in better and worse days up to now. May this offering open other alternatives to official and sanctioned murder, as a method of social change. May men of power come to a change of heart, confronting the evidence and quality of the lives we offer on behalf of our brothers."*

—No Bars to Manhood

125

leeway for the defense to present the issues that had motivated the nine.

Thomsen questioned thirty-six prospective jurors before selecting twelve, seven men and five women, including three housewives, an engineer, a saleswoman, a building inspector, a retired nurse, a truck driver, a steelworker, and an insurance agent. The average age of the all-white jury was fifty-six. Studying their faces, Francine du Plessix Gray, covering the trial for the *New Yorker*, saw "little hope of a hung jury."[146]

While not denying their responsibility for the actions they were charged with committing, the nine pled not guilty and attempted to launch a "justification defense": the argument that certain acts, while normally illegal, are not criminal in special contexts. Thus, a driver who goes through a red light in order to get a wounded person to a hospital is justified in doing so and will be neither fined nor jailed. As David Darst explained, "If I see a person trapped in a burning car and break the windows in order to save him, I am not committing a crime by breaking the window." "We were merely doing," said Dan Berrigan, "what we wish Germans had done in Hitler's Germany."

The nine were attempting, they insisted, to impede a criminal war. In support of their accusation, the defendants' first submission to the court, Exhibit "A," was a book, *Vietnam and International Law*, in which twelve lawyers argued that US military intervention in Vietnam violated the United Nations Charter, the Geneva Accords of 1954, and the US Constitution. Thomsen decided the book and its arguments were inadmissible, having no bearing on the charges the nine stood accused of: destroying government property and interfering with the operation of the Selective Service System.

On the prosecution's side not a word was said in defense of the Vietnam War. Sticking to narrow borders, their project was simply to present evidence that these nine people had burned certain Selective Service records and

*"At the outset, we decided that the trial should be extremely brief.... We would have been satisfied and happy with a single day in court. We were trying to wave aside as irrelevant ... all those legal devices by which one equivocates about what he actually has done or said."* —No Bars to Manhood

hindered the work of a government agency. The two wire baskets in which the papers had been ignited were presented along with some of the charred files and the can from which napalm had been poured. A news film of the action was screened, audio on, despite a prosecution effort to show the footage without sound; thus the jury was permitted to hear what was said

Attorney William Kuntsler with Dan to his left and George Mische to his right. AP photo

at the time by the nine and their praying the Our Father.

The two women working in the draft board gave testimony. Clerk Mary Murphy said, "I have never been treated with such bad manners in my whole life, and with such disrespect and uncharity."

None of the evidence was disputed. "We agree with the government on the facts, up to a point," said Dan. "But the end of theirs is only the beginning of ours."

"No defendant is going to dispute that the facts occurred as the government says they occurred," said defense attorney Kunstler. "They're proud of it and they think it is one of the shining moments of their personal lives."

Repeatedly the defendants were asked if they had been aware they were breaking the law. "Yes, we violated the law," Phil responded, "but the law is not absolute to us. I must say that our intention was to destroy the files, but our motive was to illustrate genocide in Vietnam and corruption at home. The real issue is: how can men serve [both] love and war? The fact is, they can't. Most Americans have great difficulty seeing the I, the self, as being the *we*, humanity. We cannot feel the effects of our actions as others see us. We think we can rape a people

Vietnam.
AP Photo/Huynh Thanh My

*"I wasn't concerned with the law. I wasn't even thinking about the law. I was thinking of what those records meant. . . . I was concerned with the lives of innocent people. I went in there with the intent of stopping what the files justify. . . . My intent in going there was to save lives. A person may break the law to save lives."*

—Tom Lewis,
The Trial of the Catonsville Nine

and have them love us. We cannot ravage the ecology of Indochina, kill ten civilians for every soldier, and expect anything but do-or-die opposition. We cannot fight the abstraction of Communism by killing the people who believe in it. We cannot talk peace while our deeds give the lie to our words. We can't have it both ways."

Accused of being arrogant, Phil responded that the real arrogance lay with the national leaders. "What of their crimes against the people, the poor and the powerless? Still no court will try them, no jail will receive them."

But what if some group of war supporters, one of the prosecutors asked, broke into a peace action center and destroyed their files? Would you not feel they had violated the law and should pay the price? "Certainly," said Phil. "Those who violate the law should be prosecuted. Their views ought to be exposed through testing by the community . . . just as ours are being tested." Should such people be convicted? Phil was asked. "I think that is your problem," Phil replied.

David Darst compared the Catonsville raid with an event described in all four Gospels, pointing out that Jesus, when he chased the moneychangers out of the temple in Jerusalem overturning their tables, could have been found "guilty of assault and battery." But with that action Jesus endangered no one's life but his own.

The most moving segment of the trial occurred when each of the nine gave testimony about what had led them to risk imprisonment by taking part in a collective act of civil disobedience. But each time one of the nine spoke about events in his or her life that had been major steps on the road to Catonsville—demonstrations protesting the war, attempts at dialogue with administration officials, witnessing the killing of peasant farmers in Guatemala, seeing US bombs falling on Ugandan villages—the stories were cut short by Judge Thomsen with the phrase "We are not trying" the war in Vietnam, the series of Guatemalan revolutions, American foreign policy, the problems of racism. . . . Even so, fragment by fragment, those in the courtroom understood that each of the nine had tried in various ways to relieve or end great suffering that had, in significant measure, been caused by the United States' priorities and polices and its imperial role in the world.

In his final statement, prosecutor Arthur Murphy argued against civil disobedience as a method of social change:

> I want it clearly understood that the government is not about to put itself in the position . . . of conducting its policies at the end of a string tied to the consciences of these nine defendants. This trial does not include the issues of the Vietnam conflict. It does not include the issue of whether the United States ought to be in that conflict or out of it. The government [prosecution team] quite candidly admits that the position these defendants took is reasonable—as to the fact that the war is illegal, that it is immoral, that it is against religious principles, that any reasonable man could take that view. We do not even say that a person has to be insane to have the views that they have. No, we don't say that. But this prosecution is the government's response, the law's response, the

*"If there were a group of children walking along the street, returning home from school, and a car came down the street out of control, even though there was a driver in that car. If I could divert the car from crashing into those children, I would feel an obligation to turn the car from its path. . . . I would be thinking ten times more of those children than of the driver of that car."*

—John Hogan,
The Trial of the Catonsville Nine

*"Our lives are part of a vast social paradox; the affluent are often eaten by secret despair, yet those who place their lives and good names in jeopardy are lit by an inextinguishable joy and hope. Indeed, we have such strong hope in the power of life, and in the vitality of our society, as to test our lives rigorously at the hands of power. We wish indeed to discover whether or not our society is dying in its main parts, or whether some mysterious new man is being born."*

—No Bars to Manhood

people's response, to what the defendants did. And what they did was to take government property and throw flammable material on it and burn it beyond recognition. And that is what this case is about.

Suppose you were to acquit these people on the only basis possible, in view of everything they have conceded? Acquit them, that is, although they did those acts with the intention of hindering the Selective Service System and of burning the files and records. Suppose that because of their sincerity, their conscience, their religious convictions, they were entitled to be acquitted in this courtroom? If these people were entitled to be acquitted by virtue of their sincerity and religion and conviction, then, according to the same logic, should not the man who commits any other crime feel also entitled to acquittal?

We also heard about unpleasant things happening, or about to happen, in other areas of the world. Among these nine defendants, there are four or five justifications floating around. One defendant is upset about one ill in the world, and that justifies his going to Catonsville. Another is upset about another ill in the world, and that justifies his going to Catonsville. And so on. The possibilities are infinite. There could in fact be fifty defendants, each upset about fifty different supposed ills in the world. And each one of them could say: this is why I violated the law.

Ladies and gentlemen of the jury, the government has never contended that this country is perfect, that it is without flaw, without ills and problems and failings. To assert that would be absurd. But I would suggest to you that, to the extent that this country has problems, those problems will be solved. We will progress. We will get better. The country will get better. But our problems are not going to be solved by people who deliberately violate our laws, the foundation and support for an ordered and just and civilized society.

In response, lead defense attorney William Kunstler reminded the jury that the actions for which the nine were charged were intended "to throw a roadblock into a system which they considered murderous, which was grinding young men, many thousands of them, to death in Vietnam." The papers they burned were not ordinary property but were intended to assist the government in deciding who would become the cannon fodder of war. "We are not talking about driving licenses.... No [other forms] so directly affect life and death on a mass scale as do these." Yes, Kunstler continued, there are legal methods of protesting war but the defendants had spent years using those means with no impact on what America was doing in Vietnam. "All the words, writing, marches, fasting, demonstrating—all the peaceable actions of the defendants over a period of some years—had failed to change a single American decision in Vietnam . . . [or] prevent a single innocent death, failed to end the anguish of napalm on human flesh, failed even momentarily to slow . . . the senseless destruction of men, women, and children." Kunstler appealed to the jury not just to decide whether the nine had burned papers and hampered the work of a government agency but to consider the reasons why they had done so and make a judgment based on their own consciences.

The Catonsville Nine.

Thomsen instructed the jury that they were obligated to decide guilt on the basis of the charges, not on the motivation of those on trial. Then during the interval provided by the jury's absence, a remarkable dialogue occurred between the defendants and Judge Thomsen. Thomsen initiated the exchange by asking both prosecution and defense if they were satisfied with the way the trial had been conducted.

"Your Honor," Dan declared, "we are having great difficulty in trying to adjust to the atmosphere of a court from which the world is excluded, and the events that brought us here are excluded deliberately by the charge to the jury."

*"So be it. We have tried to underscore with our tears, and if necessary with our blood, the hope that change is still possible, that Americans may still be human, that death may not be inevitable, that a unified and compassionate society may still be possible. On that hope we rest our case."*

—No Bars to Manhood

*"We see no evidence that the institutions of this country, including our own churches, are able to provide the type of change that justice calls for, not only in this country, but around the world. We believe that this has occurred because law is no longer serving the needs of the people; which is a pretty good definition of morality."*
—Phil Berrigan,
The Trial of the Catonsville Nine

"They were not excluded," Thomsen replied.

"They were," said Dan. "Our moral passion was excluded. It is as though we were subjects of an autopsy, were being dismembered by people who wondered whether or not we had a soul. We are sure that we have a soul. It is our soul that brought us here. It is our soul that got us in trouble. It is our conception of man. But our moral passion is banished from this court. It is as though the legal process were an autopsy."

"Well, I cannot match your poetic language," Thomsen answered. "You made your points on the stand very persuasively, Father Berrigan. I admire you as a poet. But I think you simply do not understand the function of a court."

"I am sure that is true, Your Honor."

"You admitted that you went to Catonsville with a purpose which requires your conviction. You wrote your purpose down in advance. Now I happen to have a job in which I am bound by an oath of office. Not only by an oath of office but by a long tradition of law, of which we are very proud in this country. We are proud of the Constitution of the United States. We are proud of the rights that people have under it. If you had done this thing in many countries of the world, you would not be standing here. You would have been in your coffins long ago. Now, nobody is going to draw and quarter you."

"Your Honor," Dan responded, "you speak very movingly of your understanding of what it is to be a judge. I wish to ask whether or not reverence for the law does not also require a judge to interpret and adjust the law to the needs of the people here and now. I believe that no tradition can remain a mere dead inheritance. It is a living inheritance which we must continue to offer to the living. Isn't it possible then to include in the law certain important questions of conscience, to include them nonetheless, and thereby to bring the tradition to life again for the sake of the people?"

"Well, I think there are two answers to that. You

speak to me as a man and as a judge. As a man, I would be a very funny sort if I were not moved by your sincerity on the stand and by your views. I agree with you completely, as a person. We can never accomplish what we would like to accomplish, or give a better life to people, if we are going to keep on spending so much money for war. But it is very unfortunate, the issue of the war cannot be presented as sharply as you would like. The basic principle of our law is that we do things in an orderly fashion. People cannot take the law into their own hands."

At this point David Darst joined the exchange: "Your Honor, does that include the president of the United States?"

"Of course, the president must obey the law."

"He hasn't," said Tom Lewis.

"Well, if the president has not obeyed the law, there is very little that can be done."

To which George Mische added, "And that is one of the things this trial is all about."

As the trial came its end, Dan rose once more to address the court. "We want to thank you, Your Honor. I speak for the others. But we do not want the edge taken off what we have tried to say by any implication that we are seeking mercy in this court. We welcome the rigors of this court. Our intention in appearing here after Catonsville was to be useful to the poor of the world, to the black people of the world and of our own country, and to those in our prisons who have no voice. We do not wish that primary blade of intention to be honed down to no edge at all by a gentlemen's agreement, whereby you agree with us and we with you. We do not agree with you, and we thank you."

"All right," said Thomsen.

"Could we," Dan then proposed, "finish with a prayer? Would that be against your wishes? We would like to recite the Our Father with our friends."

Thomsen was silent for a moment, then turned to-

Dan Berrigan flashes a peace sign.
Bob Fitch Photography Archive, © Department of Special Collections, Stanford University

*"We want to thank you, your honor . . . but we do not want the edge taken off what we have tried to say, by any implication that we are seeking mercy in this court. . . . We do not wish that primary blade of intention to be honed down to no edge at all by a gentleman's agreement, where you agree with us and we with you. We do not agree with you, and we thank you."* —Dan in The Trial of the Catonsville Nine

ward the prosecution. "I will be glad to hear from the government's counsel as to his advice."

"The government has no objection," said US Attorney Stephen Sachs, "and, in fact, rather welcomes the idea."

The defendants and their lawyers formed a semicircle. Everyone in court rose and, as far as one could tell, everyone joined in reciting the prayer:

"Our Father, who art in heaven, Hallowed be thy name. Thy kingdom come, thy will be done on earth as it is in heaven. Give us this day our daily bread, and forgive us our trespasses as we forgive those who trespass against us. And lead us not into temptation, but deliver us from evil, for thine is the kingdom and the power and the glory forever. Amen."

It was an amazing moment. No one could recall another instance of court-authorized prayer during a federal trial.

Returning to court after an eighty-minute absence, the jury found each of the nine guilty as charged.

"Now," asked Thomsen, "is there anything further that the government or the defendants wish brought to the attention of the Court?"

Dan responded, "We would simply like to thank the court and the prosecution. We agree that this is the greatest day of our lives."

The anticlimax of sentencing the nine occurred a month later. Far more lenient than Judge Northrop had been with the Baltimore Four, Thomsen sentenced Phil Berrigan and Tom Lewis to three-and-a-half years in prison, time to be done concurrently rather than added to the six-year sentence they had already begun. Dan Berrigan, George Mische, and Tom Melville were given three years. The other four—Mary Moylan, Marjorie Melville, John Hogan, and David Darst—were sentenced to two years. All but Phil and Lewis were freed on bail pending appeal, but they were also released six weeks later.

David Levine drawing of Daniel Berrigan on the cover of a special edition of *Holy Cross Quarterly*.

# Pilgrim of the Underground

ree on bail, Dan returned to Ithaca. For many on the Cornell campus, he had become a superstar. A petition had been signed by fourteen hundred students calling for Dan's reinstatement, and the administration, reversing an earlier decision, had given way, announcing that what had happened in Maryland had not involved the school.

One spring day half-a-year after the trial, a friend and I drove upstate from Manhattan and made our way to Dan's apartment. We found the door ajar but no Dan in sight. When we tracked him down and mentioned the unlocked door, he said it was always open. "But," I asked, "don't you worry someone might steal your things?" To which Dan very Dan-ishly replied, "If they do that, I suppose they need them." He busied himself cooking—the main course was a stuffed flank steak—and pouring drinks. The ulcer he had during the months before Catonsville, he reported, had healed. "If it starts up again I am going to send the doctor bills to the White House. It is their ulcer, not mine."

My journal entry of the day records, above a drawing of bread crumbs, an empty chalice, and a copy of an old war resisters' book, *Prison Etiquette*, "Tales of smoke and drink and friends. 'It's not the end, it's the beginning and the middle I find difficult,' Dan says."

On the following journal page there is a drawing of

Drawing by Jim Forest.

Cornell University, Division of Rare and
Manuscript Collections

Dan's campus office—a US flag hanging from the ceiling, with "CHILDREN NOT FOR BURNING" written in large letters across the white stripes. Behind a lamp, against a field of bright red felt, toy handcuffs and a plastic billy club are hanging, as well as several buttons—the largest one white on blue, proclaiming simply, JESUIT.

It happened that this latter item was a label once again in jeopardy. Dan told me there were rumors that a decision had been reached in the Jesuit leadership that he had become, through conviction for a felony, intolerable cargo.

On my return to New York, Dan had arranged for me to meet his new provincial, Robert Mitchell, to present reasons why he ought not to become an ex-Jesuit. I recall an afternoon meeting with Mitchell in his office at Fordham at which I worked through a list Dan and I had drawn up of unfortunate consequences were Dan given "the Jonah option," Dan's term for being "tossed overboard as a morsel for whales." I stressed the negative impact his dismissal would have on many young people whose connection with the Church was fraying by the day. It would be a matter of concern not only for Catholics but for many others if war-supporting Jesuits were regarded as nonproblematic while war-resisting Jesuits, like Dan Berrigan, were expelled. Such an act, I argued, "would confirm the old accusation that the Catholic Church had little tolerance for dissident conscience." Dan's expulsion "would be like revising the Gospel, removing 'Blessed are the peacemakers' and replacing it with 'Blessed are the warmakers.'" While Mitchell gave me no assurances—"the decision," he said, "is not mine alone to make"—he warmly thanked me for the visit and assured me it had been helpful. (In a letter sent to Phil years later, Dan recalled, "They [the Jesuits] almost kicked me into outer darkness after Catonsville, [but I] was saved strangely by so political an animal as [Provincial Robert] Mitchell, who flew to Rome to stop the show."[147])

In fact the coming attractions proved far less grim,

but that wasn't to be learned for several weeks. The executioner's axe was transformed into a butter knife. Though various Jesuit doors had closed to him, a Jesuit Committee of Conscience sprang into being. Using the theme "Our Brother Is in Need," many Jesuits joined in efforts to stand by Dan and help with the financial burden of the defense, now in the appeal stage. Where complete rejection had been feared, the final consequence was the most significant sign of Jesuit support—albeit a minority—since Dan's first entry into the peace movement.

It must have helped that a new book, *No Bars to Manhood*, was published at that time and was well received. The book's central theme was the Christian obligation to resist war, even if resistance is costly: "We have assumed the name of peacemakers, but we have been, by and large, unwilling to pay any significant price. And because we want the peace with half a heart and half a life and will, the war, of course, continues, because the waging of war, by its nature, is total—but the waging of peace, by our own cowardice, is partial. . . . There is no peace because there are no peacemakers. There are no makers of peace because the making of peace is at least as costly as the making of war—at least as exigent, at least as disruptive, at least as liable to bring disgrace and prison and death in its wake."[148]

Among the items I had noticed on Dan's desk in Ithaca during that spring 1969 visit was a substantial pile of paper that, on close inspection, proved to be the Catonsville trial transcript. "Light reading?" I asked. "Heavy reading," Dan replied, "but I have the idea of becoming a latter-day Sophocles and boiling it down into a play, something on the lines of *Antigone*. A play about conscience, a play about saying no to the king. What do you think?" "I'm up for a new *Antigone*," I answered.

How long the work of compression took, I cannot bear witness. I was in a Wisconsin prison soon after that visit and out of circulation for just over a year, but by the

*"I had just returned from answering one of my frequent summonses on law and order at Jesuit headquarters. As usual, things were not good. I went to a Jesuit friend and told him so, in mournful numbers. He answered laconically: 'Do you want to know why you're in trouble so frequently? . . . It's because you and some others show us what Jesuits can be. And that's why we can't stand you.'"*

—No Bars to Manhood

No Bars to Manhood
by Daniel Berrigan, S.J.
The burning personal statement by the dedicated priest who became an outlaw for his political beliefs

time I was free, *The Trial of the Catonsville Nine* was finished, the text in print, and productions being prepared in New York and Los Angeles. One of the first things I did after my release was to meet with the New York cast to answer questions they had about the people they were playing.

It may be mainly thanks to the play, performed again and again, year after year to the present day, that the Catonsville Nine have carved a place in history. The play in turn became a movie produced by Gregory Peck, a project in which Peck took particular pride. "It's a film," he told me when we met at a peace conference in Moscow in 1987, "that has so far paid back very few of the pennies that went into making it, but I predict it will be remembered long after I'm gone as one of the genuinely important films of its time." He recalled the anxiety he felt when Dan, then recently out of prison, saw the film for the first time. "It was being shown at the Cannes Film Festival, and Dan was invited to be present by the French Association of Film Critics. I would have been terribly embarrassed had he not liked it! Happily all went well."

In fact, Dan was ecstatic about the Cannes premiere. "The movie showing," he said in a letter to Phil, "was a mob scene followed by the largest (and longest) press conference in the history of the festival. The most excitement over any film of the year. I was on French TV for 5 minutes during news—quite unusual. Over 200 newsmen and movie people from around the world were at the showing and press conference."[149]

During that 1969 visit at Ithaca, the galley proofs of a new book of poetry were lying on a small table next to a reading chair. In its title poem, "False Gods, Real Men," Dan saw Phil and himself as barely upright windbreakers being battered by an apocalyptic gale:

My brother and I stand like the fences
of abandoned farms, changed times

too loosely webbed against
deicide homicide.
A really powerful blow
would bring us down like scarecrows.
Nature, knowing this, finding us mildly useful
indulging also
her backhanded love of freakishness
allows us to stand.[150]

I mentioned to Dan how impressed I was by signs of support for him that I had noticed hanging on various walls on campus. "In fact," Dan responded, "you could just as easily encounter my critics. Some of the more militant students who traveled to Baltimore for the trial now regard me as out of date, a grandfather clock that has stopped ticking. Nonviolence is becoming unfashionable. There are those who look back on [Martin Luther] King as an Uncle Tom. Their heroes have guns. Attend an SDS [Students for a Democratic Society] meeting and there is the smell of gunpowder in the air—which is to say the smell of burned-out hope."

On April 9, 1970, their appeal having been denied, the eight surviving members of the group (David Darst had died in an auto accident five months earlier) were due to begin serving their prison sentences, but only John Hogan and Tom Lewis turned themselves in that day. Tom and Marjorie Melville were given ten extra days in order to do their master's degree exams at American University. The remaining four were no-shows. They had decided to go underground to continue in active war resistance as best they could.

Phil Berrigan and David Eberhardt (of the Baltimore Four) were picked up after just ten days in hiding; FBI agents found them inside a rectory closet at a Catholic parish in Manhattan, St. Gregory's, where they had hoped to speak that night. George Mische managed to evade the FBI's radar six months before being arrested at gunpoint at the Chicago home of friends. Mary Moylan

Bob Fitch Photography Archive, © Department of Special Collections, Stanford University

*"In the name of the Gospel, I condemn today the speech of power politics, the speech of military murder, the language of religious mystification, all language that indicates the death of the mind, the studied obscenity, the speech that pretends to human dignity and truth while in fact it brings down the world. And I recommend in the name of the Gospel, modesty and loyalty, the springs in the desert; all the hidden efforts of men to live with human difference, to bear with crisis, … to bind up wounds, to be patient and long-suffering."*
　　　　　—No Bars to Manhood

proved best at achieving invisibility; she disappeared and remained out of sight until turning herself in nine exhausting years later.

One of the eight made being underground into a kind of public playhouse. Dan Berrigan, sheltered in a Sherwood Forest of friends and friends of friends, led the FBI on a Robin Hood–like chase that lasted four months. Dan, a threat to no one, was placed on the FBI's Ten Most Wanted list. Notorious consecrator of bread and wine at large! Disturber of wars and felonious paper burner! The fugitive has been known to carry the New Testament and should be approached with extreme caution! Disarmed and dangerous! *Wanted!*

Dan's game of hide-and-seek began at Cornell. It was an improvisational pilgrimage from the start. On the day he was due to turn himself in, he dropped his office keys on the desk of a colleague and went missing, with the idea that he would remain out of sight until the following weekend when a festival was planned at which Dan hoped to make a speech before being arrested by the FBI agents who were certain to be present. This would fit within the classical model of civil disobedience exemplified by Gandhi and Martin Luther King Jr.: you break a law, take responsibility for doing so, stand trial, get sentenced, then go to prison voluntarily. But Dan had been wondering if that final step was essential. Dan had been reading a new book by Howard Zinn, *Disobedience and Democracy*, which argued that "the sportsman-like acceptance of jail as the terminus of civil disobedience is fine for a society determined to limit reform to tokens [but] does not suit a society which wants to eliminate long-festering wrongs.... How potent an effect can protest have if it stops dead in its tracks as soon as the very government it is criticizing decides against it?"[151]

Perhaps more decisive than any theory was Dan's acute sense of what made good theater. Might basic questions the nine had brought to the trial be put back on center stage if a few of the participants ignored the classic

Speaking at Cornell. Bob Fitch Photography Archive, © Department of Special Collections, Stanford University

script, did the unexpected, and attempted, as Dan put it, "an extended leave of absence"?

The weekend event at Cornell took its name from one of Dan's poems, "America Is Hard to Find." Its final lines:

P.S. Dear friends
    I choose to be a jail bird
    (one species is flourishing)
    in a kingdom of fowlers
    Like strawberries good bread
    swans herons Great Lakes
      I shall shortly be
        hard to find
    an exotic uneasy inmate of the

NATIONALLY ENDOWED
ELECTRONICALLY
    INESCAPABLE ZOO
        remember me I am
free at large
untamable not nearly
as hard to find as America[152]

The possibility of evading arrest at the festival was as thin as a frayed thread. It was easy to spot the many FBI agents—most of them close to the stage—scattered in the crowd of ten thousand people who had packed in the university gymnasium. Wearing a heavy sweater and motorcycle helmet, Dan arrived and, once the many greetings and embraces had subsided, took the microphone and appealed to all present to find appropriate ways to resist the war. Explaining the delay in turning himself in, he said, "It is no more logical that a war resister obey a government order to surrender to American justice than that an American youth appear for induction into the military. I hope that I can, by example, encourage people to do what we did—to break the law in a way that

Dan and Phil are reunited underground. Bob Fitch Photography Archive, © Department of Special Collections, Stanford University

is politically significant." He then asked the crowd a rhetorical question: "Should I surrender?" Many responded with fervor, "Never! Never!"[153]

Surrendering would not have been necessary. FBI agents were poised to arrest him at the first opportune moment. But then events took an unanticipated turn. As the lights were dimmed, a troupe of performers from the Bread and Puppet Theater filled the stage. Wearing towering costumes, they commenced to mime a reenactment of the Last Supper. A member of the cast invited Dan to slip into one of the apostle costumes, a structure of burlap sacking topped with a papier-mâché head. Revested, Dan was led out of the gym and loaded into a waiting van that brought him to a cabin half-an-hour's drive away. The next morning he was taken to a farmhouse. Not only was America hard to find—so was Dan Berrigan. He was like that child in the French film *The Red Balloon*, who, after the stoning of his cherished balloon by several envious boys, was lifted into the sky by all the balloons of Paris.

Photographer Bob Fitch was with Dan the first days of his journey. "In his frumpy jacket, with a knit sailor cap flapping on top of his head, Dan was the most suspicious-looking fugitive," Fitch recalled. Noticing that Dan's shoes were badly worn around the toes, he traded his own. One of Dan's tattered shoes became a candleholder in Fitch's home.

The day after his disappearance at Cornell, Dan wrote an open letter to his fellow Jesuits explaining why he had not turned himself in: "The courts [by forbidding any argument about the legality of the Vietnam War] have become more and more the instruments of the warmakers. Can Christians, therefore, unthinkingly submit before such powers? We judge not. The powers and dominations remain subject to Christ, our consciences are in his keeping and no other."[154]

In the weeks that followed, Dan seemed available to nearly everyone but J. Edgar Hoover and his repre-

Bob Fitch Photography Archive, © Department of Special Collections, Stanford University

sentatives. Moving about like a leaf in an autumn wind, his itinerary was worked out by Paul Mayer, Howard Zinn, and a few others. Press and television interviews were arranged. He appeared at an alumni reunion.

He also popped up in a church pulpit in which he raised the question, "How do we translate in our lives the bombing of helpless cities. . . . How do we translate the 50,000 children napalmed? How do we translate into our lives the 50,000 Americans dead? . . . There are a hundred ways of nonviolent resistance up to now untried or half tried or badly tried. . . . Peace will not be won without . . . the loss and suffering and separation that the war itself is exacting. . . . I believe we are in such times as make it increasingly impossible for Christians to obey the law of the land and to remain true to Christ."

He finished with a request: "I ask your prayers for all those who are in deep trouble with the law, who have had to face separation from families and friends and to forge new lives for themselves in such times—a very small price indeed to prevent the death of a single child."[155]

There was at least one occasion when Dan met with friends. I recall getting a call from Paul Mayer. "By any chance," he asked, "would you be free tonight? We're having a get-together. You would be missed." He gave me an address in Manhattan's East 60s. There was no mention of Dan, but I had no doubt who was behind this last-minute invitation.

The apartment was quickly filling up when I arrived. Dan was seated on a couch sipping a glass of white wine. During the several hours the gathering lasted, topics ranged from weight loss ("Everyone feeds me well, but I keep thinning out," Dan complained) to the delight he took in recent draft board raids that were inspired by Catonsville.[156] "Maybe twenty draft board raids so far," Dan

Performers from the Bread and Puppet Theater help Dan evade arrest by the FBI. Bob Fitch Photography Archive, © Department of Special Collections, Stanford University

*"The first month is over, the future is charged with surprise, Come, Holy Spirit. The time will shortly be upon us, if it is not already here, when the pursuit of contemplation becomes a strictly subversive activity. This is the deepest and at the same time, I think, the most sensible way of expressing the trouble into which my brother and I have fallen. . . . We have been trying to remember humanity."*

—America Is Hard to Find

Top: Dan incognito.
Bob Fitch Photography Archive, © Department of
Special Collections, Stanford University

Above: Paul Mayer, who helped
organize Dan's underground
appearances.

exulted, "and dozens of draft boards missing their most vital papers." I reminded
Dan of how astonished I was, shortly after
the Catonsville blaze, when he told me he
hoped others would see it as a model and
take similar actions. "I had thought Catonsville was a one-off," I said. Dan laughed.
"Your face went white. For a minute I was
worried you had stopped breathing."

"What is it like living underground?"
someone asked. "It has been a strange and
often lonely time," Dan responded. "Most
of my hosts are people I've never met before.
Good, brave people, each of them putting
their heads on the chopping block." One
of those present pointed out that we were
not far from the chopping block—the nearby Manhattan
office of the FBI.

Certainly the FBI would have been happy to drop by.
Hundreds of agents were involved in the search. Under
the Freedom of Information Act, Peter Francis Shawn,
author of *The Catonsville Nine*, obtained boxes of FBI
files relating to Dan Berrigan. The papers document FBI
director J. Edgar Hoover's personal obsession with catch-
ing the elusive Jesuit priest.

I reminded Dan of Queen Elizabeth's pursuit of
Catholic priests, many of them Jesuits, in sixteenth-century England. "I expect the chase will not be a long one in
my case," Dan responded. "I'm glad that drawing-and-
quartering is not currently in vogue."

The following week Dan spent many hours in intense
conversation with his next host, Robert Coles, child psy-
chiatrist associated with Harvard University Health Services and author of a series of books on children of crisis.
Meeting each other for the first time, the two discussed a
wide range of questions: What is health? What is the future of the family? In times of crisis, how do professionals
relate to social movements for peace and human rights?

Their dialogue was taped and an edited transcript published as a book, *The Geography of Faith*, in 1973.

Coles, by no means a radical, was impressed by Dan's eagerness to listen and not simply proclaim. "Daniel Berrigan is a strong-minded but not particularly a self-centered person," Coles wrote in the book's introduction. "He wants to talk *with* people rather than *at* them. He wants to persuade, even exhort, but he keeps a sharp eye upon his listener and seems to desire (even invite) a measure of disagreement. I found little of the ideologue in him, little of the wordy theorist." He considered Dan "a tough, knowing, complicated, lively, passionate man . . . [He] had none of the self-righteous 'leader' in him."[157]

One of Dan's remarks to Coles made clear that he regarded his days underground as quite temporary: "I *have* to get caught, you see. If I never got caught that would mean I was hiding too much. The whole point of all these weeks underground is to stand witness all over—here and there and, God willing, everywhere possible."[158]

While still in the wild, another of Dan's projects was writing an open letter to those active in the Weather Underground,[159] appealing to them to renounce bombs and embrace nonviolence. The letter's opening sentence was a challenge not only to young dissidents who had turned to bombing as a means of protesting war but to anyone who regards deadly methods as a necessary means to achieve praiseworthy goals:

Bob Fitch Photography Archive, © Department of Special Collections, Stanford University

No principle is worth the sacrifice of a single human being. . . . When madness is the acceptable public state of mind, we're all in danger, for madness is an infection in the air. And I submit that we all breathe the infection and that the movement has at times been sickened by it, too. . . . The madness has to do with the disposition of human conflict by forms of violence. In or out of the military, in or out of the movement, it seems to me that we had best call things by their name, and the name of this thing, it seems to me, is the death

*"I wanted to do something foolish, in a bad time. . . . I want above all to avoid offering merely a new kind of captivity, a stasis, food for romantic fascination with what I had done. I want to help others come over into freedom, in the very effort to free myself."*
—The Dark Night of Resistance

Dan's friend, lay theologian William Stringfellow. Skip Schiel

*"How shall we live our lives today? It is scarcely possible, it will be less and less possible, to live them at the center of the web, without being cursed in our humanity, metamorphosed finally into the beast whose activity we take up as our own. The beast who eats human beings."*

—The Dark Night of Resistance

game, no matter where it appears. And as for myself, I would as soon be under the heel of former masters as under the heel of new ones. . . . A revolution is interesting insofar as it avoids like the plague the plague it promised to heal. Ultimately if we want to define the plague as death (a good definition), a pro-human movement will not put people to death.[160]

The hideout at which Dan had hoped to stay longest was the home of his friends William Stringfellow and Anthony Towne on Block Island, off the coast of Rhode Island. While in their care he started work on a new book, *The Dark Night of Resistance*,[161] whose theme was inspired by the spiritual classic *The Dark Night of the Soul* by St. John of the Cross. The war-driven nighttime we live in, Dan wrote, requires our saying "no": "Everything begins with that no, spoken with the heart's full energies, a suffering and prophetic word, a word issuing from the nature and direction of things. *No.* A time to tear and pull down and root out. A time for burning out the accumulated debris of history, the dark noisome corners of our shrines, a universal spring-cleaning."[162]

Pastor and writer Bill Wylie-Kellermann, a mutual friend, tells me that one of the topics Dan and Stringfellow discussed "was the prospect of starting an 'underground' seminary after the fashion of Dietrich Bonhoeffer's Confessing Church school at Finkenwald in Germany of the 1930s. Dan had gone underground on the anniversary of Bonhoeffer's execution by Hitler and had begun that same day a review of Bonhoeffer's biography. Stringfellow suggested housing the seminary on Block Island using one of the local hotels, as these were populated only in the summer."

It was on Block Island that the FBI at last found the elusive Jesuit. Ironically the breakthrough was thanks to a letter Sister Elizabeth McAlister (a nun who taught art history at a Catholic girls' school in Manhattan) had smuggled to Phil Berrigan, now an inmate at Lewisburg Federal Prison in Pennsylvania. Phil and Liz had recently fallen in love and desperately sought unaudited contact. Boyd Douglas, a fellow prisoner who had been allowed to attend classes at a nearby college, had offered to act as postman for Phil but in fact was turning over photocopies of the letters to the FBI. One of Liz's letters provided the tip-off that Dan was now Stringfellow's guest: "Stringfellow still plans on trying to get to you, I think, but he's now or soon will be somehow mixed up with bruv [brother]. . . ."[163] Dan had been located thanks to a love letter.

It was August 12, 1970. This time no chances were taken that Dan might slip away. A Coast Guard cutter took position off Block Island while seventy—yes, seventy—FBI agents, some disguising themselves as birdwatchers, surrounded the Stringfellow house. Dan was slicing apples while watching the weather turn stormy.[164] Leaving the fruit behind, he rose to greet his captors. "I suppose you're wondering who I am. I am Daniel Berrigan." One of the agents, his Jesuit education on parade, whispered, "*Ad majorem Dei gloriam.*" This was the Jesuit motto: "To the greater glory of God."

A photo of a handcuffed Dan Berrigan being escorted off the Coast Guard cutter, a grim FBI agent on either side while Dan smiled as if he had won the lottery, quickly made its way around the world.

The day after Dan's arrest was marked far less by mourning than by celebrations hurriedly arranged by local peace groups all over America. I called folksinger Pete Seeger, told him of Dan's arrest, and asked if he would sing at a demonstration near the federal courthouse on Foley Square in New York. "With the greatest pleasure," Seeger replied. At Emmaus House in East Harlem, the community I had joined after leaving prison, we made a handout featuring the day-old photo of radiant Dan in handcuffs. Beneath it was the headline "DAN BERRIGAN IS FREE." "Would that more of us," the text declared, "were as free as Daniel Berrigan."

*"I suppose my roundup will appear in literary annals somewhere between epic and farce."*
—To Dwell in Peace

Dan apprehended by the FBI on Block Island. Cornell University, Division of Rare and Manuscript Collections

# Dan in Danbury, Prisoner #23742-145

Prisoner #23742-145. Cornell University, Division of Rare and Manuscript Collections

Dan was assigned to one of the better federal penitentiaries, Danbury, about an hour's drive northeast of New York City in Connecticut. "I'm not sure," Dan joked when I visited him in prison, "if Danbury is named after me or I'm named after Danbury, but clearly we were destined for each other. But, inmate that I am, perhaps you should drop 'Dan' and address me as 'prisoner 23742-145.' It's a number packed with mystical significance."

Soon after arrival, Dan wrote to relatives and friends, "No point in mourning. Though I did myself, at first. It is dreadful that good friends suffer. But how else will anything get accomplished? We have had years and years trying to find just that other way. And then it came to this. Now my feeling is that, if we entertain any regrets, it will be because we did not take it in the neck earlier. But better late than not at all. Of course [Phil and I] miss you. But in war people are always separated—and unarmed and killed, and we learn to bear with it. The worst has by no means happened to us—we are clothed and fed and have books, time, freedom to pray. The little we are asked to endure would be considered good fortune by millions of the world's poor. It is in that spirit we try to go forward, to hearten our friends. Certainly for priests and nuns to be jailed is an honor in such days—it will be one of the few honors the Church can point to in years ahead."

Dan began a diary, later published as *Lights On in the House of the Dead*. An early entry revealed how bleak he felt:

There is no answer I know of except to live by faith day after day and leave the future in the hands of God. It is hard in middle age to be crushed between the two millstones of days and nights in captivity. Is it too hard to bear, or not yet hard enough to be human? It would be easier if one could see some light on the horizon, some larger horizon opening before one which would allow the year to act as a mere interlude, a chastening of self toward a "normal" future in a civilized society. But the truth is something darker and more ominous. No dawn is in sight—in fact the night itself is deepening, to the point where one is constantly being pushed further to the edge of personal extinction, as the price of bringing any change at all.[165]

Happily—remarkably—a few weeks after Dan's arrival, Phil was transferred to Danbury. Did it signal a brief flash of compassion in the Federal Bureau of Prisons? Probably not. But the brothers were at the same address for the first time since boyhood. Dan was assigned to work as assistant to the prison dentist, Phil given a job in Danbury's business office. They saw each other daily, discussed the issues for which they were serving time, heard each other's confessions, read the Bible together, occasionally celebrated a simple unauthorized Mass, and rediscovered each other.

Being at the same place, enduring similar woes, made it possible to renew their bonds with each other and also to talk through areas of tension between them. Phil had developed a quiet resentment, even jealousy, about Dan's celebrity status, and this needed airing, while Dan at times felt bullied by Phil.

In his prison journal, *Widen the Prison Gates*, Phil

Top: Dan and Phil visited by their mother, Frida. Courtesy Berrigan family

Above: Dan and Phil visited by brother Jerry and his wife Carol. Courtesy Berrigan family

described the resentments that strained his relations with Dan: "I confess to harboring hobgoblins concerning Dan. As he put it, I had a 'younger brother' difficulty with him. . . . I had been used to running my own show, used to my own independence and even arrogance. I became adolescently envious and jealous, began to fabricate ambitions and injustices on his part that were quite nonexistent. I accused him of liberalism . . . egotism . . . and center-staging. . . . We had it out, very painfully and sorrowfully."[166]

They had—and continued to have—their differences. "Dan is a superior propagandist," Phil wrote in a letter to Liz McAlister, "and does it incomparably well, but I have different views about priorities."[167] (It was at Danbury that Phil revealed to Dan his secret marriage to Liz.)

The two were closely watched by prison staff as well as by the FBI, the latter doing checks on all those who came to visit. Besides family, the list included Howard Zinn; John Deedy (an editor of *Commonweal*); Bob Hoyt (editor of the *National Catholic Reporter*); various Jesuit and Josephite priests; Dan's editor at Macmillan, Betty Bartelme; myself; and many others.

Among the visitors, the headliner for Dan was Pedro Arrupe, the Jesuits' superior general, who had come all the way from Rome. The two had much in common. Arrupe, a survivor of the atom bomb dropped on Hiroshima, knew firsthand the special horrors of modern war. He described that event as "a permanent experience outside of history, engraved on my memory."[168]

It has to be taken for granted that Dan's and Phil's incoming and outgoing letters were not only read but photocopied and carefully studied. The FBI sought glimpses of what friends on the outside might be planning while the warden worried that the two might be making plans to escape. Several letters Dan had hidden in his shoes were discovered in the course of a strip search after meeting with visitors, for which Dan lost a week of "good time"—his eligibility for early release.

*"There is no answer I know of, except to live by faith day after day and leave the future in the hands of God. It is hard in middle age to be crushed between the two millstones of days and nights in captivity. Is it too hard to bear, or not yet hard enough to be human? . . . No dawn is in sight—in fact the night itself is deepening, to the point where one is constantly being pushed further to the edge of personal extinction, as the price of bringing any change at all."*
—Lights On in the House of the Dead

The brothers were allowed to co-teach a "Great Books" course that met twice weekly for ninety minutes. The group started with one of the most subversive books of all time, *The Gospel According to Saint Matthew*. From there they went on to *Gulliver's Travels*, modern poetry and novels, and such Greek tragedies as *Antigone*, the first drama centering on conscientious objection and civil disobedience.

All the while the Vietnam War was busily consuming lives. "It was the corpses that called the shots," Dan reflected in the prison section of his autobiography.

> Not the Vietnamese corpses, but the American dead, arriving home in great mountains of boxes, closed against the horrified, grieving gaze of families and friends. Home at length, dead as cordwood. And yet, to political intent, the dead were living indeed, on their feet, and vociferous as Dantean souls in purgatory. . . . The dead manifestly had a purpose: to multiply their number. So many had died, should we now conclude that they had died in vain? And how were we to stifle the outcry of the protesters and troublemakers, except by multiplying our dead, manufacturing more dead, making of them the indisputable proof of our resolve?[169]

One bizarre episode at Danbury was the failed effort of a Vietnamese couple to have Dan baptize their recently born baby. "But they were never able to get the message through to me," Dan later recalled in a conversation with his friend, the Vietnamese Buddhist monk Thich Nhat Hanh. "All of this was settled without anybody—the chaplain or anybody—telling me of it. Later I

Phil in the prison yard. Cornell University, Division of Rare and Manuscript Collections

learned the story and the chaplain's role in it. He was the sort of man who always tried to avoid issues . . . to have things settled elsewhere—by the bishop or by the prison authorities. . . . So he asked the bishop about this request, but with a recommendation that it be refused. Then he could always say that the bishop decided it." Finally Dan heard what had happened and confronted the chaplain, who admitted his role, justifying what he had done by saying prison was no place for a baptism. "I grew angry," Dan said, "and told him, 'You're the type of priest who would have thought the Mass should not be celebrated on Calvary.'"[170]

One of Dan's fellow prisoners at Danbury, war resister John Bach (now a chaplain at Harvard), appreciated Dan's talent for challenging the gray climate of the prison environment, his refusal "to be beaten into the somber, sullen, dreary, colorless existence of confinement. It's the suggestion of a meaningless death itself which prison reinforces at every rote step. To stay upbeat is profoundly political and one of the strongest blows against the empire. Laughter was Dan's antidote, his strategy for affirming life. One example—during a strip search after a visit, as Dan and I were standing next to each other and performing the syncopated, comical dance of opening our mouths and sticking out our tongues, running our fingers through our hair, lifting our balls, turning around, bending over and spreading our cheeks, Dan says to me, 'Keep smiling. When they've gotten your smile, they've gotten too much.'"

While Phil was less a court jester than Dan, he also played tag with the prison system. "Once in the visiting room," John Bach relates, "Phil came over to me with a can of soda, which could be purchased from a vending machine, and says, 'Have a sip of my Coke.' I replied, 'Nah, thanks anyway, I don't drink that crap.' And Phil says, 'No, have a sip of *my* Coke.' I did and nearly gagged on the contents—bourbon! I'd love to think it was Leonard Bernstein who smuggled it in and trans-

*"If jail is the great seizure of humanity by the death force of the state, then every assertion of life, goodness, cheerfulness, friendship is glue in the locks. No key may enter and claim. If the state is a death mechanism, it is up to us to live here, and to give life, and to measure the passage of days, as well as our failure and growth, by the life we lead."*

—Lights On in the House of the Dead

ferred it into the Coke can, but probably it was one of the lawyers."

Dan was popular among his fellow inmates. "No other prisoner in Danbury," Bach writes, "could fill the other three seats at the tables in the chow hall as readily as Dan."

While at Danbury, Dan wrote some of his finest poems. "I should have gone to prison sooner," Dan told me. "It's a pressure cooker of poetry." My favorite of his prison poems is "The Risen Tin Can." Its inspiration came from Dan's discovery of a noisy machine behind the prison whose function was to flatten tins that, once emptied, had gone into the kitchen trash. Dan found in this device the perfect metaphor for what prisons attempt to do to those whom they confine:

> We prisoners are, so to speak, tin cans
> emptied of surprise, color, seed, heartbeat, pity,
>     pitch, frenzy
> molasses, nails, ecstasy, etc., etc.
> destined to be whiffed and tumbled into elements of
>     flatland
> recycled, dead men's bones, dead souls

In polar opposition to the soul-crushing mechanisms of society, for Dan, is the resurrection, referring not only to the desertion of all graves at the end of time but the obtaining of a here-and-now inner freedom animated by love. The tin can—that is, each of us—is capable of undoing its flattened condition and taking wing:

> This is the year of the RISEN TIN CAN, in the
>     Vietnamese sense.
> REVOLUTION REFUSAL REBUTTAL
>     POETRY.
> When I was a tin can I thought like a tin can I
>     looked like a tin can
> I spoke like a tin can

*"There is no guarantee of political or personal success. There is rather a sense of 'rightness,' of standing within history, in a way that confers health and creates spiritual continuity."*
—Lights On in the House of the Dead

153

now that I am a man I have put away the things of a
    tin can
NEMPE
tin armaments tin hearts tin bells rin-tin-tin gross
    national tin
American tin . . .

The unforgivable sin against the unholy spirit, Dan
continues, is the conversion of tin back into human flesh,
one instance of which is the act of writing a poem:

Shaking of foundations! It is not to be borne
that sounding and tinkling tin
unzipped, emptied of its regal redoubtable guts
    brains gore
should arise to the phoenix form of the twice
    born. . . .

The can flattener's great commandment, "the First
Command of the Lost Way," is "bc like me":

But
Let a blade of grass intervene, a vagrant lustful
    loving frenetic stammer arise in one; let him
    remember his lost friends, the cords of Adam,
    let a single bird cross his starved sight—
Let a single countervailing voice, color, feeling,
    sound—
All is undone . . .

The can flattener is in fact the demonic voice that
converts the living into the dead:

He parts his face like a dead sea
into: benevolence or murder.
When he looks benevolent he means murder
When he looks murderous he means business
Business is good; you or someone else; viz—

*"It remains important that prison be regarded as a boot camp for spiritual change, at least on the part of some. For prisoners to get reborn (for anyone to get reborn), someone must pay. The payment for birth is blood; the cost of rebirth cannot be cheap. The question is not how to evade payment, but how to pay up like a human being."*
    —Lights On in the
    House of the Dead

He freezes your rent, he is burning someone's hut
He cures your cancer, he is filling his germ bottles
He worships on Sunday, Buddhists die for it.

. . .

Now it is a matter of imperial indifference whether
you and I, cits, dimwits, midges, near zeroes, non
      heroes, whether we exist or no. But one thing
      is clear; in our regard the myth of Genesis has
      been turned around. Henceforth to read:
In the beginning was Skinner's labyrinth. The furry
      humanoids, deloused, decorticated, lobotomized,
      housed, fed, schooled by the state
totally environmentalized
a synthesis of formally partial structures (university,
      madhouse, prison, cinema, food trough, sex bed,
      church) these scamperers and scavengers by dint
      of expertise and electrode have learned
when to fear when to love when to piss when to feed
when to praise when to—

. . .

In our flattened state, the poem continues, the vital
ingredients of actual life are missing:

    . . . a certain
light in the eyes ("like shining from shook foil"), a
      plumbless interiority, a tease and come on,
      something funky in youth, wrinkles as of
      laughter about aged brows, a sip in your eye
      look of fire and ice
OR at the least a glimpse of Edens lost, a look of
      scarce contained grief, as for other shores
      horizons estuaries, "blue remembered hills,"
      yes—outraged love.

The poem, written in the last days of December 1971,
ends in a celebration of Christ's birth:

> *"In a true sense it can be said of Philip and me that we have nothing to do but stand firm in these months: to survive, to act as a silent prick to the consciousness of those outside—whether of friend or opponent, church or state. 'Here we stand.' On the other hand—there are the prisoners, the task of understanding, the discipline required to be men for the men, to grow in love, to use time as though time were indeed 'tinged with the blood of Christ.'"*
> —Lights On in the
> House of the Dead

It is Christmas
the pride of peacocks
the birth of a child
his many forms
rising swaying around him
like eyes in feathers
dances harvests brides
resurrections
and underside
his shadowed
befallings
Pray; those eyes
touching our eyes
make us that man.[171]

*"What more fitting place to celebrate my fiftieth birthday. Ha! . . . I want to start all over. I want to write one immortal line. I want to perform one good nonviolent act. I want to reactivate all the dead cells that cling to my skull like last year's honeycomb, sweet and musty. I want America to get reborn into gentleness. . . . I want to walk in the woods and kneel down in a sodden place and stretch out on pine needles and never get up. . . for a few years in which the above may be seen occurring."*
—Lights On in the House of the Dead

Unflattened by prison Dan might be, but prison was nearly the death of him. His health was far from excellent. For years he struggled with back pain, often severe, and a herniated esophagus. On June 9, 1971, he suffered a severe allergic reaction to Novocain injected by the prison dentist. In *Widen the Prison Gates*, Phil describes what happened:

After lunch, one or two friends relate a vague story about Dan getting sick in the dentist's chair. "They're taking care of him now," one guy tells me. The news doesn't sound too urgent, but I hurry to the hospital nonetheless. The entire hospital staff is gathered around him. The doctor is taking a cardiogram, three technicians apply oxygen, another drains a bottle of glucose into his arm. He is conscious, but laboring hard to breathe, while his pulse races at a tremendous, shallow pace. I look at the faces hovering around him, trying to read a sign of reassurance, or relief, or hope. . . . I slowly grasp that this is no spell of weakness, no fainting fit. It is something immensely more serious, serious perhaps to death. I stand by in utter helplessness until it occurs to me that I can pray. So I pray, and watch him struggle for breath, his fingers blue with cold, twitching as if in protest. And I dumbly realize that he is beating back dark oblivion. . . . I had simply never imagined life without him. . . .

The doctor leaves to phone a specialist [and summon an ambulance], and I follow. . . . [And then] an inmate bursts in. "Dan wants you!" I rush back. The oxygen mask is off his face, and he's chatting with everyone. Weak as he is, and still in shock, he nonetheless worries about his friends and the anxiety they feel, especially me, I lean over him to talk and he seizes my head and kisses me resoundingly on the cheek. He gives me another lesson in the love that binds us.[172]

Friends greet Dan on his release from prison. Jim Forest is to Dan's right.
John C. Goodwin

Dan was rushed to a local hospital and pulled through "by the skin of my not-very-good teeth," as he later told me. Friends aware of his seriously weakened condition petitioned the Federal Bureau of Prisons for early release; several ex-prosecutors joined the appeal. When the US Parole Board in Washington nonetheless decided to continue Dan's incarceration, more than twenty of his fellow prisoners, John Bach among them, decided to protest with a work and hunger strike; they also called for a shortening of Phil's six-year sentence. Part of the administration response was to move Phil and other strikers out of Danbury. Phil ended up at Allenwood Prison Camp in Pennsylvania. His removal served as a double punishment—Dan and Phil were cut off from each other.

Before his transfer to Allenwood, Phil gave his Bible to Dan, for whom it became ever after one of his most prized possessions. When Dan showed it to me, I was astonished at how battered a book it was—page after page filled with marginal notations in Phil's hand, countless lines and paragraphs underlined, exclamation marks here and there, the occasional coffee stain. "You would be hard-pressed," said Dan, "to find anyone in any church who has read the Bible more attentively than Phil. Phil's real crime is reading the Bible."

Now in separate prisons, their correspondence resumed. In one of his letters to Phil, Dan confessed his inner struggles:

A supporter embraces Dan on the day of his release. Jim Forest is to Dan's right. John C. Goodwin

For me the hardest thing is patience, beyond doubt. I have concluded after 50 years of trying vainly to synchronize with other people's planets, it is simply no go. I shall have to lose, win or at least run the race on my own. Does that sound foolish? In any case your months here [at Danbury] gave me the best run for my money yet. I had not realized how complementary we were—which meant different edges, as well as nicely joined ones. The years apart, the very different lives we led, had made a difference at least I had not reckoned on. That plus the really bitter adjustments I was called on to make in coming to prison at all—made for quite a time. But as far as putting a stone on a string and lowering it into the psyche, I think there was nothing quite so wholesome as our sessions *tete-a-tete*. I came out often feeling birched and steamed clean. And with more respect + love for you, even though I sometimes may have gotten to your apotheosis prematurely; so much of living and suffering still lying ahead for both of us. I hope at times you may warm your hands at the fire of others' love for you.

You hit it on the head; we've got to make it, at least for another while yet. I've tried a few people at times half jokingly; I think last June 9 [the Novocain incident] confirmed me in certain zen tendencies, as regards even death. I needed your "right on!" and sometimes wonder if you had not been there, whether I would have wanted to survive badly enough to make it. Well, dear bruv, this lil review of conscience is meant only to share the present, in view of a future He knoweth. Someday all of us will sit to the board + crack walnuts + quaff mulled wine in the Kingdom.[173]

John C. Goodwin

At last, on February 24, 1972, after eighteen months

John C. Goodwin

under lock and key, Dan was set free—early release, the Parole Board decided after all, in light of health factors. One guesses that Parole Board members were terrified that Dan might die while in their care. Hundreds waited in knee-deep snow to cheer as the Danbury gate closed behind him. A ribbon of supporters stood atop a low stone wall holding a long banner that read, "Our apologies, good friends, for the fracture of good order, the burning of paper instead of children."

# Free at Last

Dan speaks at the Catholic Worker.
Marquette University Archives

Dan left Danbury for Manhattan, where he spent the first few days with several family members celebrating his freedom in the temporarily vacant apartment of composer-conductor Leonard Bernstein. Bernstein had once invited Dan to spend a day working with him on the text of an oratorio, *Mass*.[174] Friendship took root. "Bernstein's apartment was in the Dakota," Dan told me, "a palace! Look out any window and there was Central Park. Quite a contrast to Danbury."

Dan's first significant act was to celebrate a Mass of thanksgiving at the Catholic Worker. He prefaced the liturgy with the presentation to Dorothy Day of the fifty dollars routinely given to inmates as they returned to the unwalled world. Dorothy took it, turned to a coworker, and said, "Go to my room and get the jar of holy water." The jar produced, Dorothy dipped the fifty dollars in holy water, held up the dripping cash, and said with a smile, "Now we can use this!"

Mass was celebrated in the dining room–kitchen area of St. Joseph's House on First Street. The congregation was mainly Catholic Worker volunteers and the down-and-out who ate meals there plus some of Dan's friends. I was pleased to see Dan still had the dark purple ceramic chalice and paten that had been given him, in my care, by a Benedictine potter several years before. A print of one of Van Gogh's sunflower paintings graced a nearby wall.

"How we have missed you!" Dorothy exclaimed.

Dan moved into a Jesuit residence at Fordham University in the Bronx, but not all his fellow Jesuits living there were pleased to have the notorious, embarrassing, prison-stained Daniel Berrigan in their midst—"Such arrogance!" said a Jesuit elder. One day, returning from a lecture trip, Dan came home to find the building locked, the lock changed, and his meager possessions in several boxes outside the entrance. Hurt and upset, he called the Jesuit provincial and told him what had happened. The provincial replied, "Well, Dan, go find yourself a nice apartment in Manhattan and send me the bill." Dan never learned why he was kicked out of the house and rarely spoke of the event, but he was impressed by how, with his provincial's support, it led to a better arrangement.

Dan with Dorothy Day. Jon Erickson

Dan's first postprison assignment was with the Woodstock College faculty,[175] linked to Union Theological Seminary. The school was next to Riverside Church.[176] "It took a Rockefeller to bury God standing up," Dan remarked to one of his students, Bill Wylie-Kellermann, as they gazed up at the church's skyscraperlike tower. Dan rented an apartment at McGiffert Hall on the same block.

In a recent letter, Bill told me what it was like to be in Dan's classroom:

> At Union I was one of the students taking Dan's year-long course on John's Apocalypse, or Revelation. His reading of Revelation in those days was laced with

Handing out leaflets in front of St. Patrick's Cathedral. Cornell University, Division of Rare and Manuscript Collections

T. S. Eliot's *Four Quartets*—such bits as "in the end is our beginning." He reported having memorized the *Quartets* while at Danbury, a discipline he undertook to survive the deadly homilies of the prison chaplain. While the chaplain droned on, Dan explained, he applied himself to Eliot's poetry. Dan's lectures were nearly oracular and ecstatic utterances. We'd be scrambling to keep up in our notebooks. More than once I recall one of us saying, "Wait. What did you just say?" and he'd look up, as if coming out of a trance, to shrug and confess, "I dunno." Dan's little book *The Nightmare of God* comes close to being a transcription of that post-prison class. He wasn't so much teaching us to put more politics into our poetry and scripture study as he was urging us to put more poetry into our politics. His life and witness provided the authority for reading scripture as a life-and-death matter.[177]

One of the classes Dan taught at Woodstock-Union was about pastoral care of the dying. Mel Hollander, a friend of mine, signed up for it not because he expected to become a pastor of any kind but because he was dying of cancer and thought the class might help him cope with his severe depression. The cancer was in an advanced state; Mel's pale, waxy skin and the bruised areas around his eyes could not be ignored. During the period of Quaker-like silence with which Dan started his classes, his eye fell on Mel and stayed there for what seemed to Mel an eternity. At last Dan broke the silence with a question to Mel: "What's the matter?" Mel considered for a moment giving an evasive answer but decided instead to reveal his calamity: "I'm dying. I'm dying of cancer." Without batting an eye, Dan replied, "That must be very exciting."

Mel told me afterward that no medication he was taking, no book he had read, had done so much good for him as those five words. They were a kind of lightning flash. In the light of that flash, Mel said, "was the resurrection of Jesus, as real as the streets of New York." He knew at once that he was in the midst of the most remarkable experience of his life. Nose to nose with death, suddenly he felt intensely alive.

Perhaps it was that flash of lightning that somehow pushed the cancer back. In any event, Mel, who had come into Dan's class expecting to die within months, lived another seven years, finally dying in a fire. In what Mel called his "extra years," he devoted himself to work with Vietnamese refugees.

I knew of no one who had ever received a fund appeal from Dan, but Dan received, by letter or whisper, quite a few requests for aid and always tried to help. Nearly all his income from writing and giving retreats was given away. But need outstripped income until Dan at last held out a beggar's cup. "Maybe a year or two after he got out of Danbury," onetime fellow prisoner John Bach recalls, "Dan wrote a letter to his many friends saying that he had been able to modestly spread money around to sustain others as well as various causes and now he was raising money for further sharing. He called the appeal 'Radical Cheek'—a reference to Tom Wolfe's phrase 'Radical Chic.' He even made an offer. Give a small donation and you get a signed poster. Make a five-hundred-dollar donation and he would come to your house and write a poem on your wall. All you had to do was provide the ladder. Dan knew this wouldn't be an earth-shaking success, but it was a great idea and a sign of hope during woeful times. He came to our house in Hartford, and in his distinctive and wonderful calligraphy wrote his version of the 126th Psalm, later published in his book *Uncommon Prayer*, on our wall:

Cornell University, Division of Rare and Manuscript Collections

When the spirit struck us free
we could scarce believe it.
Were we free
were we wrapped
in a dream of freedom?
Our mouths filled with laughter
our tongues with pure joy. . . .

At the bottom of the eight-foot poem, all its readers were invited to write names of political prisoners."[178]

The fact that Dan had been a political prisoner himself sometimes created obstacles for him. I recall a trip with Dan to a Student Christian Movement (SCM) conference in Sheffield, England, in 1973. Getting to the conference had not been easy for Dan. There had been several calls from our British hosts—they had been tipped off that Dan was on a list of people barred from entering the United Kingdom. Dan and I had been staying in Paris the days before with our mutual friend, the Vietnamese monk Thich Nhat Hanh. It was agreed that I would fly to London's Heathrow Airport, arriving an hour before Dan's flight touched down, so that I might speak with the press if Dan were stopped. More significantly, SCM staff had arranged with the Archbishop of Canterbury, Michael Ramsey, to be standing by at his residence, Lambeth Palace, ready to call the British Home Secretary if need be. The warning was well grounded. On landing, Dan's plane was boarded by two police officers, who, with a photo in hand, slowly walked down the aisle studying faces. Dan gazed up at the policemen expecting to be led off the plane, but neither he nor anyone was removed. "It seems the photo they had of Dan was an old one in which he was much younger and still wearing a Roman collar," the SCM secretary commented. "The fact that he was wearing an old Irish fisherman's sweater threw them off!"

*""Slowly, fitfully, during these years I am coming to understand what my life can offer—in word, act, attitude. I must obey rhythms which neither America nor I can set in motion or cancel out. . . . Call it a tradition, a discipline of prayer, sacrament, the old words and realities worn smooth as David's pebbles. Palm them, press them, fling them. They will save your life, your sanity."*
—Ten Commandments for the
Long Haul

# Harrisburg

hile Dan was on the run, FBI director J. Edgar Hoover was closely following the correspondence of Liz McAlister and Phil Berrigan—an exchange Phil had entrusted to a fellow prisoner, Boyd Douglas. Ignoring warnings from other prisoners that Douglas was not to be trusted, Phil was convinced that the one Lewisburg inmate who had easy access to the outside world was a reliable courier. In fact, Douglas photocopied the letters and passed the copies on to his FBI handlers.[179]

The most important fact about the letters Douglas photocopied for the FBI is that they were an attempt at private communication between two people, Liz McAlister and Phil Berrigan, who now regarded themselves as married, albeit unofficially and without having informed their respective religious communities or even close friends.

The letters in many respects were like all personal letters: unpremeditated, enjoying the freedom that letters give to overstate or be rude, to blow off steam, to tell the truth without polish, to impress, to confess, to admit needs and fears, to play with ideas, and to bear important news. From Liz's point of view, a top priority of the letters was to reassure Phil that the resistance community he had founded wasn't disintegrating in his absence. Toward this end Liz made much more of what their circle

Sister Elizabeth McAlister at a peace rally in 1967. Cornell University, Division of Rare and Manuscript Collections (John C. Goodwin)

Phil in prison.

of friends were up to than was in reality the case. To raise Phil's morale, she was inventive—as she later put it, "I was guilty of over-statements, presenting undeveloped ideas as being a *fait accompli*."

The first letter to land in FBI files was begun by Phil on May 22, 1970, and was finished two days later. It begins with gratitude for Liz's first visit to Lewisburg (she had presented herself as Phil's cousin, a deception that worked only once) and goes on to celebrate the news she brought that day that she had decided to be part of an action group that was preparing to destroy draft files in Delaware: "And the news—glorious! First of all, that you were so clear in your own mind and so confident. And I knew implicitly that you were a vast help to the others—sense of history, human philosophy and tactics, courage, discipline. . . . And then the sense of humor that refused to remain quiet, indicative of a balance of spirit, and a resolution during the dark night period."

Then Phil thinks aloud about ways of relating the forthcoming draft board action to the killing by National Guard troops of four students at Kent State University on May 4.[180] He next proposes several people who could sort out who is, and who isn't, ready to take part in the upcoming resistance action in Delaware. There is a paragraph given over to concern about their correspondence difficulties—no single theme, save resistance, so preoccupies both Phil and Liz. He takes note of a few gray hairs on Liz's head and sees her becoming "a striking pepper and salt." Suggesting the sort of marriage he and Liz would have, he envisions the possibility of relationships that are open to resistance activity and the priority of peacemaking, "an entirely new definition" of marriage, something "transcending anything I've seen around." He adds that, like Liz, he is really a "very old-line Christian," and at the same time, again like Liz, "very much of the next century."

The first letter from Liz was mainly an account of the difficulties they were up against in the Delaware draft board action. After mentioning others in the group, she says teasingly of herself, "Then there's this [nun] who's a real so & so—very difficult to get along with." She goes on to note the prison administration now regards her as "an undesirable correspondent" and has returned her recent letters to Phil so marked. She asks whether she should come and see the warden to protest her removal. She curses the judge who had just refused to reduce Phil's six-year sentence for the blood-pouring action in the Baltimore Customs House. She worries about a professor's speculations that the US administration is contemplating the use of nuclear weapons in Indochina.

And so, day by day, the letters continue.

One of Phil's recurrent themes was his frustration with the sympathetic but noncommitted, those who see Vietnam on fire and whose only response was a resolution to vote for a different president next time. As he said to Liz in one letter, "To a sobering degree, there is nothing [of significance happening] save what our people do." If Phil was at war with war, he was hardly less in combat with those whom he regarded as fainthearted.

It is an irony of providence that the same correspondence that gave the FBI Dan's address in hiding, the Stringfellow house on Block Island, created the event that planted the seed of the most explosive charge in the Harrisburg indictment, "a scheme," as J. Edgar Hoover would later put it, "to kidnap a highly placed government official."

It is possible that Douglas would never have become an FBI agent were it not for the desperation of the FBI's search for Dan. The conversations that occasioned the most controversial letters of the exchange between Liz and Phil would not have occurred had it not been for the jolt of Dan's capture.

And it is certain that, like so many ideas tossed around in the search to "make it a little more difficult for them to murder," as Liz put it, this idea got no further than its freewheeling conversational moment. Indeed,

Liz McAlister.

Henry Kissinger.

the conversation would have had no memorial had Liz not made it the subject of a letter to Phil.

In a letter dated August 17, Liz wrote to Phil to report on a gathering the previous day hosted by Julie Diamond and her husband, Eqbal Ahmad:

Eq[bal] called us up to Connecticut last night. . . . [At the meeting] Eq outlined a plan for an action which, would say—escalated seriousness—& we discussed pros & cons for several hours. It needs much more thought & careful selection of personnel. To kidnap—in our terminology to make a citizen's arrest of—someone like [President Nixon's national security adviser Henry] Kissinger. Him because of his influences as policy maker yet sans cabinet status, he would therefore not be so much protected as one of the bigger wigs; he is a bachelor which would mean if he were so guarded, he would be anxious to have unguarded moments where he could carry on his private affairs—literally & figuratively. To issue a set of demands, e.g. cessation of use of B-52s over N. Vietnam, Laos, Cambodia & release of political prisoners. Hold him for about a week during which time big wigs of the liberal ilk would be brought to him—also kidnapped if necessary (which, for the most part, it would be)—& hold a trial or grand jury affair out of which an indictment would be brought. There is no pretense of the demands being met & he that would be released after this time with a word that we're nonviolent as opposed to you who would let a man be killed—one of your own—so that you can go on killing. The liberals would also be released as would a film of the whole proceedings in which, hopefully, he would be more honest than he is on his own territory. The impact of such a thing would be phenomenal. Reasons for wanting to do it: it will ultimately be done by someone here [in the US] & end in fiasco or violence & killing. Eq wants to do it

& do it well & I believe he has the know how to direct such an escapade. The major problem, as I see it, is the severe consequences for something that is largely "drama" with little lasting effect. . . . Think about it & maybe when I see you in Danbury [where Phil was about to be transferred] I can get your thoughts as well as fill you in on where the plan lies.

Liz went on to mention meetings with various friends (among them myself) to work on "more projects & possibilities." She added, "I say [all this] to you for two reasons. The first obviously is to get your thinking on it, the second is *to give you some confidence that people are thinking seriously of escalated resistance*" (emphasis added).

One of the most basic responsibilities that comes with loving another person is trying to respond constructively to the other's depressions. Dan's arrest, though hardly surprising for Phil, was nonetheless a heavy blow. Phil had such a reputation for toughness that few were aware of how fragile he could be or how much he depended on Dan for encouragement and validation. One gets a glimpse of the intensity of the commitment these two very different brothers had formed with each other in the inscription Phil wrote inside the cover of his first book, *No More Strangers*: "To Dan, the first copy, with gratitude that defies my expression since I do not yet know what I owe you, with hope also that Christ's will come more to fruit in both of us. And with a brother's love."

The "citizen's arrest" letter was the last report Liz sent to Phil care of Boyd Douglas. There was just time for Phil to write his own final letter via the same route. Three days before his August 25 transfer to join Dan at Danbury, he entrusted Douglas with his reply, a letter more disturbing than the one he had received from Liz.

"About the plan—the first time opens the door to murder. . . . When I refer to murder, it is not to prohibit it absolutely (violence against nonviolence bag); it is merely

Liz McAlister, 1972. Cornell University, Division of Rare and Manuscript Collections

*"The war is still the first fact of life for the living—as it was when I went to prison, as it was when I went underground, as it was when I went to Hanoi and Catonsville, as it was when I went into exile. There is no issue comparable to the deaths of innocent children. . . . We will never rest until sanity has been restored to the mighty and power to the powerless. This is our pledge of allegiance, to God and to humanity."*

—Essential Writings

to observe that one has set the precedent, and that later on, when government resistance to this sort of thing stiffens, men will be killed."

No portion of Phil's correspondence with Liz was so dear to the prosecutor during the trial that these letters eventually generated than these few sentences. Like so many other war resisters at that time of exhausted frustration with peaceful protest, Phil was putting an exploratory toe across the border that separates nonviolence from violence.

Phil told Liz that he found the Kissinger idea "brilliant but grandiose," then cautiously added, "I've found, with bitter experience, that when people opt for too much, they're either stupid or egotistical. . . . Which is to say that grabbing the gentleman will take a force of perhaps 10 of your best people—guarding him, getting communications out, perhaps moving him 2 or 3 times within the week. Now in addition, to grab a prosecution of liberals would take a dozen more, making the network too wide. But even if that were possible, how can it be guaranteed that they would indict him in any sort of real fashion? . . . Nonetheless, I like the plan and am just trying to weave elements of modesty into it."

But what actually happened at the gathering Liz had reported to Phil? Those who were present included Sister Jogues Egan (provincial of the Religious of the Sacred Heart of Mary, the order to which Liz belonged), writer Ann Morrisett Davidon and her husband William Davidon (a physicist), Julie Diamond (teacher and writer), Eqbal Ahmad (a political scientist who was then a Fellow at the University of Chicago's Center for International Studies), and Liz McAlister. There had been an excellent meal and no shortage of wine for washing it down. It was, said William Davidon, "a freewheeling, speculative conversation."[181] All those present were friends of Dan's who had helped in one way or another during his four months underground. Topic A was a shared concern to find out how the project of preserving Dan's freedom had finally unraveled. Had anyone been careless? Had anyone any ideas how Dan was found? Liz said nothing of her letters to Phil. The guessing got nowhere and was abandoned, as there were more pressing questions at hand: Were there any possibilities of freeing Phil while he was en route from Lewisburg to Danbury? What else was possible? More action around draft boards? Or something new?

It took little time to conclude that a nonviolent jailbreak was, as Eqbal put it, "ridiculous." Nor did another round of draft-board action seem an adequate response to this new event.

The word "kidnap" was never used in the discussion. Eqbal raised the possibility of a "citizen's arrest" of Kissinger. The phrase had haunted him since he had read a *Village Voice* report of a speech by David McReynolds, a staff member of the War Resisters League. The idea had also been mentioned at the April 21 rally at St. Gregory's Church, when Eqbal spoke in Phil's place after the FBI arrests.

Speculating on the practicalities of citizens arresting war criminals, Eqbal proposed, if an arrest were made, it could involve a subsequent meeting of the apprehended official with antiwar scholars and activists who would then release a statement on war crimes and propose that his release be contingent on the end of US B-52 bomb raids on North Vietnam.

"But more serious objections were raised," Eqbal recalled. "What would one do if there were resistance? Did this not imply the threat of violence? I took the position that philosophically that was not important. What would be important would be releasing the officials unharmed, and doing so at a press conference. That fact would dramatize our care for human life and contrast it with the carelessness toward human life of the United States government. Of course I knew the United States would not for a moment consider stopping its bombing operations. It was similarly obvious that it would be a

Phil Berrigan. Bob Fitch Photography Archive, © Department of Special Collections, Stanford University

Eqbal Ahmed, Pakistani scholar and one of the Harrisburg defendants.

disaster to antiwar work should the official be harmed in any way."

Two of those present, Sister Jogues Egan and Ann Davidon, were appalled with the proposal, judging it completely unacceptable as a pacifist tactic. Others thought the idea deserved discussion, but eventually agreed that, while the theory was fascinating, the reality was far too risky.

When it was obvious that the idea was out of the question, talk turned to other notions. The one and only consequence of that night's discussion—the letter about the conversation that Liz sent to Phil—wasn't known by those who were present until the following spring, when an indictment of the defendants published a portion of the exchange.

"The problem was," Eqbal later explained to me, "as we all essentially agreed, that once you begin asking very hard questions about making a citizen's arrest of a man like Dr. Kissinger, you come to the inescapable conclusion that you cannot accomplish your goal without some force or coercion, and that even if by some miracle you could, then he would not talk. And if he doesn't talk, what the hell are you going to do with him?" Eqbal laughed, recalling a time in his childhood when he imagined he might catch dinosaurs in large paper bags.

What completely killed the idea for Liz came not many days later when she received a note from Boyd Douglas. He had read the two letters and, no doubt under instructions from his FBI handlers, expressed enthusiasm for the proposal and volunteered to get her a gun. "I read the note and felt like throwing up," Liz told me. She destroyed Boyd's note almost immediately. The idea was done with.

In his random thoughts about the possibility of arresting Kissinger, Phil had responded to Liz, "Why not coordinate it with the one against capital utilities?" This referred to an idea that had intrigued Phil—the possibility of disabling a recently installed bank of Navy computers in the Forrestal Building in Washington. Earlier in the year, in late February or early March, Phil and Baltimore priest Joe Wenderoth—Joe with an officious clipboard in hand—went into the Forrestal Building incognito, walking past a guard with Phil saying, "Yes, the measurements seem to be right, but we'll just have to check 'em out." The guard nodded a hello. Finally, with the help of an engineer, they found their way to a tunnel entrance, asked one of the workers on a loading ramp to make sure no one locked it, and entered into a tunnel thick with dust and lined with steam pipes that carried heat to thousands of government offices. On the way out they walked by another guard, who accosted them with a sudden heart-stopping, "Hey!" They went over to the guard, already feeling a handcuff chill on their wrists, and found he wanted to bum a cigarette.

Yet even in this moment of playing with an idea rather than planning anything, Phil questioned its value: "There'd be a massive manhunt—it would mean [a] life [sentence]. And this is a factor to be considered."

Liz made a hand copy of Phil's response and sent it to two Baltimore priests who had worked closely with Phil, Neil McLaughlin and Joe Wenderoth.[182] Both were appalled and burned it. When Joe heard Sister Jogues and Liz were going to Danbury to see Phil, Joe's only request was to ask Sister Jogues, "Please hit him in the mouth for me." The words were said without a smile. Jogues gave Joe a nod that said, "With pleasure."

On November 27, 1970, with most members of Congress away for the Thanksgiving holiday, J. Edgar Hoover appeared before the Senate Supplemental and Deficiencies Committee to seek support for a $14 million supplement for expansion of FBI staff. Those present—committee staff plus two senators—were jolted into a more attentive state when Hoover, justifying the need for more special agents, announced that "an anarchist group . . . led by Daniel and Philip Berrigan" was "concocting a scheme to kidnap a highly placed government

*"Mr. Hoover of the FBI was at the time redundantly extant. More: he sat in the saddle of a steed presumably fit for the course. The renowned jockey, somewhat overweight by now, somewhat muzzy in the head, still rankled greatly within. But the fact was, he no longer rode a winning horse. . . . Nonetheless, Hoover's fury carried the day. The indictment came down."*
—To Dwell in Peace

J. Edgar Hoover, Director of the FBI.

Cover of *Time* magazine.

*"Those were terrible days.
I have learned since, but was
unaware then, of a favored way
of disposing of dissidents. It is to
level a kind of legal first strike,
a killing blow. The aim is to
traumatize, to raise a public noise
of such volume that the spirit of
the accused is crushed, friends
demoralized. It is the shock that
kills; or is meant to."*

—To Dwell in Peace

official" as well as destroy conduits and steam pipes in Washington." Headline writers suddenly had a page-one story.

But oddly enough, in the days and weeks that followed, no charges were filed, no arrests were made. Neither Dan nor Phil, as prisoners, were available to journalists to refute Hoover, though Dan told me during a visit at Danbury that it was a pity Hoover had "failed to reveal the actual plans—to blow up Kissinger and kidnap heating tunnels." We laughed. Neither he nor I were yet aware of the letters on the topic that Phil and Liz had exchanged.

One member of Congress, former nuclear submarine captain William Anderson, decided to challenge Hoover: "Knowing the Berrigan brothers and being reasonably well acquainted with their careers as priests, theologians, scholars, and their dedication to Christian principles, and having read much of their writings, I find it impossible to believe such allegations are true."

Shortly after Hoover made his charges, I received a letter from Phil that was in part confessional:

The evening was cold and snowy—like our hearts. For purposes of security, we [Dan and Phil] walked in the [Danbury] handball courts to discuss Hoover's bombshell. The best reasons we could find for his statement were the FBI's incapacity to prosecute the recent draft board raids, Dan's impudent and effective underground, and Hoover's sagging reputation. . . . I dared not conclude, at that point, that [Boyd] Douglas had betrayed us. [Dan knew nothing about the letters or their contents.] A ponderous gloom invaded us. I remember fighting to reconcile myself to the idea of life imprisonment. . . . [I asked] what will God ask one to do? How many prison years will be required? . . . I remember thinking too, with astonishment, "Wow! They've finally got me!" Finally I thought of the others. Thanks to me, they were now in deep trouble. However I might excuse myself; however they might excuse me; however people might rally to our defense, the fact is I had been guilty of imprudence and shallow judgment, asking for concern and services that few would have the arrogance to expect—information on the movement, requests for advice and speculation etc., etc. I had no rational or justifiable right to risk myself, let alone them.

On January 12, 1971, three months after Hoover had made his charges, the first indictment was issued. Phil, Liz, and Eqbal plus three priests who had worked closely with Phil in Baltimore—Joseph Wenderoth, Neil McLaughlin, and Anthony Scoblick—were charged with conspiring to kidnap Kissinger and destroy heating pipes serving government buildings in Washington, DC. The maximum sentence was one stop short of execution: life imprisonment. Though Dan had originally been named by Hoover as coarchitect of the alleged crimes, he was not charged but merely listed as an "unindicted co-conspirator" along with Sister Jogues Egan, Sister Beverly Bell, Paul Mayer, William Davidon, Tom Davidson, and Marjorie Shuman. There was some comfort in the realization that the indictment was very shaky: how would the prosecutors show that the supposed felonies had ever become a plan of action when in fact there had never been a plan?

The dramatic charges resulted in intensive press coverage. In its issue dated January 25, 1971, the faces of Daniel and Philip Berrigan gazed out of the cover of *Time* magazine next to a headline that read "Rebel Priests: The Curious Case of the Berrigans." Dan remarked to me, "When I saw the cover, for

Six of the Harrisburg Seven; Phil was in prison. Courtesy Ted Glick

the blink of an eye I wondered if we had won the Nobel Prize for Peace."

Three months after the first indictment was issued, it was replaced by a second: conspiracy to destroy draft files was added to the charges. Attorneys at the Department of Justice must have thought that, at the very least, they could win convictions on the draft files charge. At the same time, two other names were added to those indicted: draft resister Ted Glick and Tony Scoblick's wife, Mary Cain Scoblick. (In press reports those indicted were named as "Daniel and Philip Berrigan plus six others." The Scoblicks began introducing themselves as Tony and Mary Other.) Another change was the removal of Dan's name, along with several others, from the list of unindicted co-conspirators.

The trial venue was set by the Justice Department for Harrisburg, Pennsylvania. As none of the defendants had any link with Harrisburg nor were any of the charges Harrisburg-connected, it seemed an odd choice, but it was a city whose voting record was heavily Republican and thus was regarded as reliably pro-war. Clearly the prosecution assumed it would be easier in Harrisburg to empanel a jury that could be counted on to deliver a guilty verdict.

After four weeks of jury selection, the trial of the Harrisburg Seven[183] finally began on February 21, 1972, with an opening statement by US Assistant Attorney General William Lynch, who declared the government would prove that Philip Berrigan was the leader of a group that "meticulously considered and carefully planned" a conspiracy to kidnap presidential adviser Henry Kissinger, blow up heating tunnels under government buildings in Washington, and vandalize draft boards in several cities.[184]

The defense was led by Lynch's onetime boss, former US attorney general Ramsey Clark, who had volunteered his services. The eight other lawyers included Leonard Boudin, Paul O'Dwyer, Terry Lenzer, and William Cunningham, S.J.

*"Steam was gathering, under considerable pressure. There were unprecedented elements in the case; one could imagine the media licking their chops. There were nuns and priests, their mutualities and friendship—and who knew what more. . . There were young and old, black and white, the newly converted and the old pacifists. Folklore, fantasy, rumor: the recipe would sell.*

—To Dwell in Peace

Days after his release from prison, Dan began attending the trial, arriving just in time to watch Boyd Douglas begin his testimony.

The government's case relied chiefly on Douglas's testimony. He was on the stand fourteen days, the first seven being examined by Lynch, who also read aloud, with the-

Liz McAlister and other defendants in the Harrisburg Conspiracy trial.

atrical emphasis, major extracts from the letters. Under cross-examination, it became clearer and clearer that telling the truth was not one of Douglas's strong points and also that the FBI had both arranged his release from prison and paid him a great deal of money for his services. Douglas was a witness for hire.

While the prosecution's presentation of witnesses went on another six days, the discrediting of Douglas proved a deathblow to the prosecution's case.

At last it was the turn of the defense to present its case.

"Of the Harrisburg defendants," Dan recalled at Phil's funeral in 2002, "all but Philip voted against his taking the stand. [Phil being Phil,] of course he would welcome cross-examination—'Let the truth be told, no matter the price.' He was an icon of impatience at white heat. Finally, he yielded to the others at the strong urging of defense attorneys."[185] Dan was among those who counseled the seven not to present a defense. Dan especially opposed Phil giving testimony because he anticipated that cross-examination would be withering and that Phil would respond to hostile questions like a bull charging a red flag. Dan was worried that, if convicted, Phil might

Dan Berrigan. Cornell University, Division of
Rare and Manuscript Collections (Michael Fager)

be sentenced to life in prison. Reluctantly, Phil gave in to Dan's advice.

To everyone's astonishment the case for the defense was extremely brief. Ramsey Clark stood up and declared, "Your honor, these defendants shall always seek peace, and they proclaim their innocence of these charges. The defense rests."

It seemed the trial was providentially linked to the church calendar; the jury was out all through Holy Week and Easter weekend. On Easter Monday the jurors returned to the courtroom to announce that they were stalemated: ten of them were for acquittal, two for conviction, with no chance of any of the twelve changing their views. With a hung jury heavily weighted for a not-guilty verdict, Judge R. Dixon Herman observed that a retrial was unlikely to result in conviction.[186] For the defendants, their lawyers, and their supporters, the trial of the Harrisburg Seven ended on a note of Easter joy.

On May 1, 1972, four weeks after the trial's end, its chief instigator, J. Edgar Hoover, died. When asked for comment, Dan responded, "I hope Hoover receives the mercy he never afforded others."

One of the oddest moments in the Harrisburg case was a meeting between several people who had been named as unindicted co-conspirators—William Davidon, Sister Beverly Bell, and Tom Davidson—and Henry Kissinger at the White House in March 1971, a year before the trial. William Davidon had proposed the meeting "so that we can meet and think of each other as individual persons and not stereotypes, and also so that we can discuss some foreign policy issues." As a memento, Kissinger cheerfully accepted several buttons issued by the Harrisburg Defense Committee that bore the interrogative text "Kidnap Kissinger?" The off-the-record exchange was friendly but occasioned no breakthroughs. "We agreed to disagree," said Davidon. "The scary thing is that [Kissinger] really is a nice man."[187]

# Outraged Love

"Rejoice with me," Dan wrote to friends in August 1973, "that the ape of federal prison is off my back at last." Facing no charges and the Harrisburg trial over, Dan accepted a teaching position with the theological faculty for the fall term at the University of Manitoba in Winnipeg, Canada.

Dan soon found his approach to talking about God—the root meaning of the word "theology"—was not aligned with that of his colleagues. He later confessed, "I am often at odds with the religious departments of universities; likewise with seminaries. I find the incumbents ordinarily far removed from the realities of life, fervently bent on extrapolating favorite theories, fervently attached to perquisites, marvelously ignorant or indifferent to the plight of people. . . . [In Manitoba] I found myself in the company of nine or ten world experts in world religions. These eminent divines, gathered from the four corners of the globe, held forth on the convergence and branching of world symbols, ecstatic writings, moral codes, mimes and stories, historic and mystic developments that comprise the rich legacy of the world tribe. . . . As time passed, I grew less impressed with my peers and I became clear that the sentiment was heartily mutual. . . . As Luke's gospel puts it, 'Thoughts of many hearts stood revealed.'"[188]

Wherever he went, Dan quickly found himself en-

*"Walking the morgue, where dead minds aped the ways of the living, I strengthened my resolve to live before I died."*
—Ten Commandments for the Long Haul

Cornell University, Division of Rare and
Manuscript Collections (Mark Morris)

gaged with local protests, on this occasion acting in solidarity with striking maintenance staff, men and women who were poorly paid. "Workers here," Dan wrote, "five hundred of them, are being screwed by a set of bureaucrats that would make Job weep."[189] Refusing to cross picket lines, Dan taught his classes and also lived off-campus. One class focused on prison literature.

Among the lecture invitations that Dan received while in Canada was one from his friend Eqbal Ahmad that was to trigger one of the most painful episodes of his adult life. Writing on behalf of the Association of Arab University Graduates, Eqbal asked if Dan would deliver the keynote address at a conference in Washington, DC, on October 19. The topic would be Israel and its Arab neighbors. Dan toyed with the idea of "begging off"—he had never been to Israel or anywhere else in the Middle East—but "then a better, second thought occurred. . . . If it was important to speak up while the peace, at least a relative peace, held—then why not when war broke out?" The Yom Kippur War, fought against Israel by a coalition of Arab states, had begun on October 6 and was still in progress while the conference was occurring.

"Indeed," Dan added, "did not the need for dispassionate and reasonable courage increase while the guns were cutting down whatever rational exchange remained alive? If the first casualty of war was the truth, might it not be important to prevent, at least on one scene, that mortal casualty from occurring?"

Whatever adjectives one might apply in describing Dan's lecture, "dispassionate" would land at the bottom of the list. Before an audience mainly composed of those allied with the Arab side of a war in progress, Dan devoted most of his lecture to a fierce critique of the other side, Israel.

In concentrating on Israel Dan saw himself as "paying an old debt . . . a debt of love . . . a debt of outraged love."[190] Unfortunately little of that love was evident in his words on this occasion while his outrage hit with tsunami strength.

Jewish survivors, Dan charged, had arisen from the dark night of the Holocaust only to turn into "warriors, armed to the teeth. They took possession of a land [Palestine], they exiled and destroyed old Arab communities, they . . . made outsiders of those who were, in fact, the majority of citizens. Then they flexed their muscles; like the *goyim*, the idolaters, the 'inhabitants of this earth,' like Babylon and Egypt and Assyria; like those kingdoms which Israel's own prophets summoned to judgment, Israel entered the imperial adventure. [Israel] took up the imperial weapons, she spread abroad the imperial deceptions. . . . The wandering Jew became the settler Jew; the settler ethos became the imperial adventure. . . . The slave became master and created slaves. . . . The price of [Israel's] emergence was bitter and heavy . . . some one and a half million refugees, whom Israel has created in the process of creating herself."

Dan accused Israel of having turned a deaf ear to Judaism's sacred books: "Her prophets shed no light upon her politics. . . . She has not passed from a dispossessed people to a democratic state, as she would claim; she has passed from a dispossessed people to an imperial entity."

"It is a tragedy beyond calculating," Dan continued, "that the State of Israel should become the repository, and finally the tomb, of the Jewish soul. That in place of Jewish compassion, Israel should legislate armaments and yet more armaments. That in place of Jewish passion for the poor and forgotten, Israel should legislate evictions, uprootings, destruction of goods, imprisonment, terrorism. That in place of Jewish peaceableness, Israel should legislate a law of expanding violence. That in place of Jewish prophetic wisdom, Israel should launch an Orwellian nightmare of double talk, racism, fifth-rate

*"According to my critics, I had been guilty of every conceivable delict in 'that speech.' My tone was abrasive, my criticism of Israel was insufferably presumptuous. The audience of Arab students was ill chosen; the timing, if not malicious, was at least maladroit. I was, in fact, either a dimwit or an anti-Semite."*
—To Dwell in Peace

*"Meanwhile, with a vision of my own, and with my friends, and step by step, and without encouragement and guidance, I went on repeating, in many tongues and symbolic acts, a simple and central command: 'Thou shall not kill.'"*
—Ten Commandments for the Long Haul

sociological jargon, aimed at proving its racial superiority to the people it has crushed."

Dan's indictment was unrelenting: "Israel has not abolished poverty and misery; rather, she manufactures human waste, the byproducts of her entrepreneurs, her military-industrial complex. Israel has not written justice into law; she has turned the law of nature to a mockery, creating ghettoes, disenfranchised peoples, exiles, hopeless minorities, cheap labor forces, Palestinian migrant workers. Israel has not freed the captives; she has expanded the prison system, perfected her espionage, exported on the world market that expensive blood-ridden commodity, the savage triumph of the technologized West: violence and the tools of violence. In Israel, military might is increasingly both the method and the goal of political existence. Her absurd generals, her military junk, are paraded on national holidays before the narcoticized public. The model is not the kingdom of peace, it is an Orwellian transplant, taken bodily from Big Brother's bloody heart. In Israel, the democratic formula is twisted out of all recognition; the citizens exist for the wellbeing of the state; it follows, as the imperialist corollary, that that measure of terrorism and violence and murder is applied to dissidents, as shall guarantee the "well-being of the state," as the ominous phrase is understood by those in power."

Dan's slash-and-burn critique did not exclude the Arab states: "We must take into account [the capacity of the Arab states] for deception, which is remarkable even for our world . . . their contempt for their own poor . . . their willingness to oil the war machinery of the superpowers . . . their cupidity masked only by their monumental indifference to the facts of their world. No, I offer no *apologia* tonight for the Arab states any more than I do for Israel." All that said, it was a teaspoon of condemnation for the Arab states compared to his gallon of criticism of Israel.

At the heart of Dan's lecture was his rejection of all war:

I do not believe it is the destiny of human flesh to burn. . . . I do not believe that a violin concerto, however immortal in execution, is the proper comfort to offer a napalmed child. I believe that the fiddler should come down from the roof, put his violin aside, take up an extinguisher, raise a cry of alarm, break down the intervening door. I believe that he should on occasion of crisis destroy property in favor of human life. You see, I am a heretic in a consuming and killing culture, as well as in a complicit church.

Dan made several suggestions that would, he argued, contribute to peace in the Middle East: a declaration by Arab states to respect Israel's 1967 borders, the return by Israel to its 1967 borders, formal recognition by the surrounding states of the right of Israel to live in peace and security, and assistance from all sides for the displaced Palestinian people.

As reports of the lecture spread, a tempest spread with it, "a storm as exceeded all previous tornadoes, hurricanes, landslides [and] tidal waves," Dan recalled fourteen years later in his autobiography.[191] Many Jews who had once regarded Dan with respect now judged him guilty of "old-fashioned theological anti-Semitism," as Rabbi Arthur Hertzberg put it. Dan's portrait of Israel, Hertzberg noted, excluded all positive elements: "There is [for Berrigan] no redeeming feature in Israel's internal life, no honor, no compassion, no social justice, only unrelieved wickedness. What leads him to bear such false witness against a neighbor he has never seen in the flesh?"[192] In the months that followed, similar articles and editorials were published in numerous journals both Jewish and Christian, many of the authors more furious than Hertzberg.

I recall taking part in a conversation at the time with a rabbi who knew Dan well and regarded him as a friend. "What a pity," he said, "that Dan didn't show his lecture to a few Jewish friends beforehand! Many Jews are critical of Israel's refusal to recognize the Palestinians as a people and are trying to promote peaceful solutions and defend human rights! We could have helped Dan better understand both Israel and the Jewish community. And how could he think it would be helpful to lash Israel in front of people who seek Israel's destruction! Sadly now he has made peacemaking more difficult."

I told Dan of the exchange. Though hurt and defensive, Dan agreed that it was a mistake not to have first shared the draft text with some of his many Jewish friends. "Would that [Rabbi Abraham Joshua] Heschel[193] had still been alive to give me counsel," Dan said. He also recognized that whatever criticisms he had of Israel should not have been aired before an audience hostile to Israel. "But whatever my failings," he told me, "I am no more an anti-Semite than I am an anti-Catholic!"

In a televised conversation with Hans Morgenthau, a professor of political science at the City University of New York, Morgenthau asked Dan if he were to make his speech again, would he change it? "Well," Dan responded, "I've learned a great deal, not merely about myself, but about the American Jewish community, and that has made me very sober about the whole question. I would think of nothing essential I would want to retract; [but] I would want to add something. . . . I don't think I conveyed my sense of love for Israel and for the Jewish people, which is very deep in me. I said at one point that this was an act of love, but it was outraged love. I should have developed that more."[194]

In the many letters I wrote at the time in defense of Dan, I freely admitted that his lecture was flawed and unbalanced and was given before the wrong audience, yet the core issues he raised were valid and his voice in the tradition of the prophets of Israel. I often quoted from the first chapter of Rabbi Abraham Joshua Heschel's book *The Prophets*:

"To us, a single set of injustices—cheating in business, exploitation of the poor—is slight; to the prophets

Abraham Heschel.

disaster. To us injustice is injurious to the welfare of the people; to the prophets it is a deathblow to existence; to us, an episode; to them a catastrophe, a threat to the world. . . . To the prophets even a minor injustice assumes cosmic proportions."[195]

Having resolved to look for an opportunity to visit Israel, in late April Dan set off with his friend Paul Mayer on a flight to Tel Aviv. The plan was to tape conversations with a wide range of people—Zionists, Israeli dissidents, Palestinian refugees, religious and political leaders, and others whom they met by providence—and make a book of the edited transcripts. At the same time, the trip would be a pilgrimage to sites sacred to Christians, Jews, and Muslims. Dan wanted to see the places "the prophets and kings and sinners who have shaped and misshaped us actually lived."[196]

They started off in Jerusalem with Paul's own Israeli family. Paul's father was a passionate Zionist who earlier in life had worked with Martin Buber. Paul's uncle had been dean of the Hebrew University medical faculty. In the days that followed, they met rabbis, academics, writers, Knesset members, and Palestinians. They had lunch at a kibbutz and were given a tour. In the Israeli-occupied West Bank, they visited Palestinian refugee camps.

It was, for Dan, a crash course in the labyrinth of competing claims and conflicting readings of history in what three religious traditions regarded as the Holy Land. Whatever thoughts Dan had previously held about Israel, Palestine, and the Middle East became more complicated by the hour.

There were many poignant moments, as when Dan witnessed a poor Palestinian offer an orange to an Israeli bus driver—a gesture of human solidarity—while the alarmed driver recoiled, terrified that the orange might contain a bomb.

It impressed Dan that nearly everyone on both sides was in mourning. In the recent Yom Kippur War, three

*"No nation state is entitled today to anything more than skepticism. In the case of the Israelis, there is no need to invoke the past in order to arrive at a sane attitude. Let's only say that today, the Israelis are entitled to more compassion than ever. Their leadership, on the other hand, whether religious, military, or political, is entitled only to ever more contempt. So are their patsies, Jews, Christians, whoever, in the United States. We must, in short, resolve to save the Israeli people by making it impossible for present policies to continue."*
—To Dwell in Peace

thousand Israelis had died, equivalent to roughly three hundred thousand had a similar percentage of Americans been killed in war. "Everyone has lost someone," Dan wrote, "almost a new whiff of holocaust." He guessed the losses were similar if not greater on the Arab side. And on every side the killing was justified as an act of divine obedience.

The days in Israel, the many long encounters, the experiences of heartfelt welcome from one and all, deeply moved Dan, as did "the golden light, the pilgrim places worn by centuries of pilgrims, the three faiths holding tight on three beginnings, nurtured and bled for." But, with the exception of a Melkite bishop whom they met in Haifa, Dan and Paul found no one of any faith—Muslim, Jewish, or Christian—who saw a way forward that didn't involve more killing.

Dan grieved as much as ever for the stateless Palestinians he met in refugee camps, but he could no longer regard the Jews of Israel collectively as the only guilty party. The Jews of Israel were haunted by the Holocaust and were "still mourning the dead, [and] still furious over . . . [acts of] Palestinian terrorism." Yet he now knew that many Jews as well as Palestinians were searching for solutions that could benefit both peoples.

Their next stop was Lebanon, where once again they met a wide range of people, including Yasser Arafat of the Palestine Liberation Organization, and both George Habash and Nayef Hawatmeh of the Popular Democratic Front for the Liberation of Palestine. Each assured their guests that their organizations had renounced terrorism. They seemed sincere; Dan dared to hope what they said was true. But he glimpsed a harsher reality when a young Palestinian displayed his weapon, boasting that the gun, not the Lebanese card he carried, was his true identity, and that one day, with Israel defeated, his weapon would bring him home to Palestine. There was also a poster on Hawatmeh's wall rejoicing in the killing of several Israeli Jews a few weeks earlier.

**The Great Berrigan Debate**

The Committee on New Alternatives in the Middle East

A booklet produced by the Committee for New Alternatives in the Middle East following Dan's controversial lecture.

From Beirut they flew to Cyprus where they thought it would be safe to mail back to New York the recordings they had made. The box, however, disappeared en route, so the book that would have emerged from their conversations perished. Dan wondered which intelligence agency had intercepted and taken charge of the tapes.

Back in Jerusalem, after dinner at the Mayer family home, they heard the news that Palestinian terrorists had killed twenty-two Jewish children and wounded sixty-eight others in Ma'alot, a town in northern Galilee.[197] Hawatmeh's group claimed responsibility. Dan felt betrayed; Hawatmeh's renunciation of terrorism had been a lie that Dan, in his innocence, had dared to believe.

One day after the massacre, Israel bombed several refugee camps in Lebanon in retaliation for the attack on Ma'alot, killing twenty-seven people and injuring many more. One of the targets was the very camp Dan and Paul had visited ten days before. No doubt the dead included some of the children whose eager faces they had seen.

A press conference was arranged for May 19 at which Dan asked both Palestinian and Israeli leaders by what authority they dared decide "who shall live and who shall die?" In a joint statement, Dan and Paul stressed the importance of a solution to the Palestinian question that takes into account "the right of this people to a homeland," for without a homeland "the next generation in Israel, as in the camps, will be condemned to the same cycle of violence, bloodshed and reprisal."[198]

It distressed Dan, he told me after his return to New York, that the most closed people he had met during his Israeli sojourn, the people most accepting of violence, were the most religious, while the most open people, the people most eager to break the cycle of violence, were often antireligious.

Dan added, "The God who said 'thou shalt not kill' would have pleased us more had the commandment been 'thou shalt not kill except in war.' How fervent we are in worshipping the god of bloodshed."

*"But always, it must be insisted, someone dies. And invariably, those who die have no vote in whether they live or die. And invariably, those who bear responsibility in such matters do not themselves die. They live on, to decree the deaths of others."*
    —Ten Commandments for the
    Long Haul

# Small "c" christian, Small "b" buddhist

One of Dan's most significant friendships took root late in 1968, the night of November 12, when both he and Thich Nhat Hanh were among twenty-three poets reading from their work at Town Hall on West 43rd Street in Manhattan. Other readers included Galway Kinnell, Arthur Miller, Anaïs Nin, Mark Van Doren, and Robert Lowell. Organized by the Fellowship of Reconciliation, the Poets for Peace project was a quiet but not insignificant protest against both the Vietnam War and war in general.

Thich Nhat Hanh, a brown-robed monk who has since become one of the most renowned teachers of Buddhism and the practice of mindfulness, was the only Vietnamese person on the stage. At the invitation of the Fellowship of Reconciliation he had come to America to meet with national leaders and journalists, university students, and religious congregations. His purpose was to describe the devastating impact of the war on ordinary people in his homeland, mainly peasant farmers. He bore witness that the main victims of the war were those who were the most defenseless—infants, children, mothers, the ill, the aged. In the talks he gave, he often read from his poetry. I no longer recall which one he recited that night, but it might well have been "Recommendation," a poem originally written for young volunteers doing social service in Vietnamese villages:

Promise me,
promise me this day,
promise me now,
while the sun is overhead
exactly at the zenith,
promise me:

Even as they
strike you down
with a mountain of hatred and violence;
even as they step on you and crush you
like a worm,
even as they dismember and disembowel you,
remember, brother,
remember:
man is not our enemy.

The only thing worthy of you is compassion —
invincible, limitless, unconditional.
Hatred will never let you face
the beast in man.

One day, when you face this beast alone,
with your courage intact, your eyes kind,
untroubled
(even as no one sees them),
out of your smile
will bloom a flower.
And those who love you
will behold you
across ten thousand worlds of birth and dying.

Alone again,
I will go on with bent head,
knowing that love has become eternal.
On the long, rough road,
the sun and the moon
will continue to shine.[199]

Dan (seated) with other "Poets for Peace" at
a reading in 1968.

Thomas Merton and Thich Nhat Hanh.
Cornell University, Division of Rare and Manuscript
Collections

I am similarly uncertain which poem Dan read that night, but it may have been "The Face of Christ":

The tragic beauty of the face of Christ
shines in our faces;
the abandoned old live on
in shabby rooms, far from comfort.
Outside,
din and purpose, the world, a fiery animal
reined in by youth. Within
a pallid tiring heart
shuffles about its dwelling.
Nothing, so little, comes of life's promise.
Of broken, despised minds
what does one make—
a roadside show, a graveyard of the heart?
Christ, fowler of street and hedgerow
cripples, the distempered old
—eyes blind as woodknots,
tongues right as immigrants' —all
taken in His gospel net,
the hue and cry of existence.

Heaven, of such imperfection,
wary, ravaged, wild?

Yes. Compel them in.[200]

After the reading, Nhat Hanh and Dan sat together talking as if there was no one else backstage. Each felt an immediate affinity for the other. As Nhat Hanh later explained to me when I was accompanying him on his lecture trips, "There are small 'b' buddhists and big 'B' Buddhists as well as small 'c' christians and big 'C' Christians. The small 'b' buddhists and the small 'c' christians can easily talk to each other. The big 'B' Buddhists and big 'C' Christians cannot. I am a small 'b' buddhist, and Dan Berrigan and Thomas Merton are small 'c' christians."[201]

One of the threads of connection was their shared friendship with Thomas Merton. Earlier that year Nhat Hanh had been Merton's guest for two days at his monastery in Kentucky. The two had spent many hours discussing the war and also monastic formation and practice in their two traditions. Soon afterward Merton had written the introduction to Nhat Hanh's first English-language book, *Vietnam: Lotus in a Sea of Fire*.[202] The text began with the deeply felt words, "Thich Nhat Hanh is my brother. He is more my brother than many who are nearer to me in race and nationality, because he and I see things exactly the same way." Dan felt a similar bond with Nhat Hanh.

Not allowed to return to Vietnam, Nhat Hanh made France his base. With an ocean in the way, Dan and Nhat Hanh had little opportunity to see each other, but during Lent and Easter 1974 Dan flew to Paris for a prolonged stay with the small community led by Nhat Hanh. The visit was interrupted by Dan's trip to Israel but resumed immediately afterward.

In *Ten Commandments for the Long Haul*, Dan wrote of his stay within this war-free outpost of Vietnam:

I see a small room in which I studied and meditated. . . . I was being healed. I was being healed of America, of the Western Church, of the Jesuits, of the wounds of war, of prison, of the disease of making it, of my race in time against time. I kept my old New York horarium, *orarium*, late nights of reading and prayer, late mornings, afternoon walks, evening conversations with Nhat Hanh. In the park of Sceaux [in the south of Paris, close to Nhat Hanh's apartment], I sought out a remote corner and sat amid the flowering trees to consider my lot, my life, my foolish and steady heart, steady in the foolishness of peacemaking, determined in the manner of that organ to pursue its own beat.[203]

Cornell University, Division of Rare and Manuscript Collections

Thich Nhat Hanh. Jim Forest

Dan recorded and then edited his more formal conversations with Nhat Hanh. The following year a book resulted: *The Raft Is Not the Shore*.

Their exchange began with the subject of memory and moved on to the Eucharist and death. As the days passed, they discussed religion in the world, life in exile, priesthood, imprisonment, self-immolation, economics, communities of resistance, and Jesus and the Buddha. Dan reached deeply into Christian sources, Nhat Hanh into sutras and other Buddhist writings, while both shared stories of decisive moments in their lives.

Memory, Dan ventured in their first taped dialogue, was a creative faculty that reunited—literally *re-membered*—a broken body, a broken soul. It re-membered not just what was and is but what could be. Thus, a man like Martin Luther King could "remember" and describe, as he did in his "I Have a Dream" speech, a future without anyone in bondage. Dan's vision of what *could* be inspired two liberating questions: "How do we cease being slaves? How do we cease being slave masters?"

Nhat Hanh was reminded of memory in another sense, as suggested by the French word *recueillement*—recollection—the attitude of someone trying to be himself, not to be fragmented: "One tries to become whole again." This was the beginning of awakening, of enlightenment, an event that can happen suddenly, in the blink of an eye. Nhat Hanh recalled the time he had meditated on the Christian Eucharist and suddenly understood the action of Jesus in identifying himself with bread and wine. With this act came "a drastic awakening"; the disciples of Jesus experienced enlightenment. They no longer lived in a phantom world.

Dan replied that the Eucharist, linked as it is to the Last Supper before Christ's arrest, brought to mind the death of Jesus. After the meal, during which bread was broken and wine shared, Jesus experienced a blood-sweating agony in the garden of Gethsemane. Finally, having accepted his own death, he walked freely to his captors.

In each life, Dan said, every person has experiences that prepare him for death, as for example Dan's own close encounter with death while in prison. "Suddenly knowing I was dying," he told Nhat Hanh, "was a very quiet and simple moment, and there was no fear."[204]

Nhat Hanh suggested that Dan's calm contact with death while at Danbury was due to his letting go of what he had earlier thought of as death and simultaneously his discovery that life and death are interconnected. One cannot exist apart from the other; they are as joined together as two sides of a coin. "That is why," said Nhat Hanh, "when one has seen the real nature of things, he will acquire a kind of fearlessness—an attitude of calm—because he knows his death will bring no end to life. . . . His existing does not depend on his 'being alive' now."

Nhat Hanh's insight reminded Dan of his last visit with Thomas Merton not long before his death. In a talk with the novices about death, Merton spoke "with joy" as if anticipating his own. "He said the only thing that relieved the life of a monk from absolute absurdity was that his life was a joyful conquest of death. . . . [The monk] was living apart from a world which paid death such tribute—racist, violent, militaristic—a kind of taxation exacted on people by death itself." Dan learned from his friendship with Merton, he told Nhat Hanh, what a great privilege it was "to live a life of faith in which the possibility of the conquest of death is in our midst every day."[205] But most of us, Dan went on, are driven by fear-centered idolatries. "Our real shrines are nuclear installations and the Pentagon and war research installations. This is where we worship, allowing ourselves to hear the command that we kill or be killed, a command which seems to me is anti-Christ."[206]

Dan and Nhat Hanh had both been educators yet both agreed that classrooms are rarely the ideal environment for deep learning. One may earn a doctorate on a certain topic but fail to be transformed. Dan had been reading Dietrich Bonhoeffer and told Nhat Hanh how Bonhoeffer's real conversion began when "he was on trial [in Nazi Germany] and in prison [awaiting execution] and realized there was a deep difference between a theologian and a Christian."[207]

A few days later, returning to this topic, Dan recalled a distinguished seminary professor who traveled widely to give a lecture titled "The Idea of Love in the New Testament." "I thought," said Dan, "that was a strange thing to talk about—the *idea* of love. I thought he might talk about love in the New Testament . . . instead of the *idea* of love, the *idea* of God, the *idea* of this, the *idea* of that. . . . One reason for the deep trouble at the seminary was that there was no atmosphere around them inviting them to become Christians. Rather the atmosphere was inviting them to become experts on Christianity."[208]

Their conversation turned to the experience of separation and exile. Nhat Hanh had last been in Vietnam in 1968. When he left he had assured his coworkers he would be back in two weeks, three at the most. The Saigon government, however, had refused to allow his return—weeks of absence became years of exile. Occasionally dreams brought him back to a green hill he had played on as a child. Dreams provided his only visa.

Dan saw himself as a different sort of exile, the person who is never fully at home no matter where he is.

I've been trying to figure out for a long time what possible circumstances would help me, as they say,

*"Gandhi often spoken of making the means equivalent to the end, so that one would not do anything today that would disperse or distract or corrupt what onc is trying to move toward. That is perhaps one way of putting the greatness of the saints and of those we admire, that their lives contain the end in the very movement toward it."*
—The Raft Is Not the Shore

"fit in." I think this is a big anxiety in my order. I just don't seem to settle into any kind of regime. And, of course, in a sense they are right. On the other hand, what one is trying for these days is not a sort of arbitrary rebellion, without foundation or reason. One is trying to defend human life, and you can't do that by fitting into a regime. But at the same time, I think one has the responsibility to do one's best to help people understand. Perplexing questions come up. People say to me, "Where's your community?" I simply can't say, "Well, I live in such and such a street and I have these groups and all this,' because every year it changes. One year I'm in Canada, next year I'm in Europe. I'm here or there. And this doesn't easily admit of acceptance. All the while one feels in exile.[209]

Dan Berrigan and Thich Nhat Hanh.
Jim Forest

Dan's colleagues told him, "Now that the sixties are over, is it not time to live a normal life? You did what you had to do, but that's over. It was an episode. Now it's time to settle down." But Dan found that the killing that required his response in the sixties was still going on in the seventies. It was still necessary to say, "No one should die!"

Nhat Hanh recalled a story told by Albert Camus of a priest visiting a prisoner on the eve of his execution. The priest seeks a last-minute conversion, but the prisoner refuses. "The prisoner refuses," said Nhat Hanh, "not because he wants to refuse Christianity" but "because the prisoner knows the priest understands neither himself nor the man he wants to save."

"It's intolerable," Dan commented, "for a priest to lead people to the guillotine, and to have the same keys that the guards and the warden have. I used to visit prisoners when I was in Canada, and it always struck me when I saw the chaplain take out his keys. . . . He unlocks the door—he dramatizes his own freedom and the unfreedom of prisoners. A terrible thing to do!"[210]

One day Dan asked, "How do you look into the eyes of Jesus or the Buddha?" Nhat Hanh replied there is no way, no method. The real question is how attentively do you look at anything: "How do I look at a branch of a tree? The problem is not how, but the subject who does the looking." Nhat Hanh told the story of someone who traveled a long distance to see the Buddha but, having failed to stop and help a woman in need whom he passed along the way, saw nothing special when at last he was face-to-face with the Buddha. "So I say that whether you can see the Buddha or not," Nhat Hanh concluded, "depends very much on you."

Dan was reminded of what Jesus said about the Last Judgment as recorded in Matthew's Gospel: "What you do to the least person you do to me."[211] But how does one become capable of such attentiveness? "If people could breathe with the silence of Jesus," Dan continued, "something would happen. He spent a lot of his life silently. If only one could go into the desert with Jesus or be in prison with him during Holy Week or penetrate to his silence before Pilate and Herod, when he refused to answer as another way of answering."

One of the witnesses to Dan's stay with Nhat Hanh was Mobi Warren, an American volunteer who was assisting the work of the Vietnamese Buddhist Peace Delegation in France. She recalled in a recent letter:

The months Dan spent in Paris with the delegation, were centered, of course, around the conversations that became *The Raft Is Not the Shore*. I had the privilege of sitting in on several of those conversations. They took place in Thay's small room. ["Thay," pronounced "tie," is the Vietnamese word for "teacher."] The only furniture was a desk and Thay's bed, a

Thich Nhat Hanh. Jim Forest

thin mattress on the floor. Thay and Dan sat on the floor for their conversations with Sister Chan Khong in charge of the cassette recorder. Both men spoke thoughtfully, in quiet and sometimes urgent voices.

At times their conversations seemed a bit strained to me, as if Dan and Thay never quite managed to get a real dialogue going. It felt a bit like two different conversations or chapters of two books spliced into each other. I think that was partly because Dan's use and style of language and Thay's were so different, and perhaps their modes of expression had a hard time meshing.

I remember one day Dan expressing to me how difficult it was for him to connect with the Buddhist sutras (and he was certainly making an effort to read them during his stay), how different they were from the writings of the New Testament, more philosophical and abstract, not like the flesh-and-blood, real-people feel of the Gospels.

Outside of the evenings spent recording their conversations, there were moments of wonderful connection between Dan and Thay and other community members, simple human moments of celebration and empathy. For example, Dan insisted on cooking a meal for us—it may have been for Easter day. He and I walked to the local open market one morning, and he selected a magnificent fish to bake. I served as his kitchen assistant and delighted in the sheer joy he took in cooking, how he selected and experimented with ingredients and seasonings, how he treated the fish with affectionate and grateful regard. (Though Thay later returned to complete vegetarianism, during the Paris years he did at times eat meat and fish when these were offered to him.) It was clear how much Dan wanted to create something delicious for Thay. It was a celebratory and loving meal, enjoyed at the little low table in the main room.

I remember that on Easter Monday, Dan and I

Jim Forest

took the metro into Paris for a brisk walk and a stop at a cafe for a celebratory coffee and cognac. We were on the steps of a church, and Dan imagined out loud what it must have been like on the first Easter Monday for Jesus's disciples. Dan was so filled with joy.

Dan carried a sense of vibrant celebration about him—that is one of the things I remember most. It was not an easy time physically for him. He was suffering from serious back pain issues and sleeping on a mattress on the floor (Thay had lent him his own room) was difficult, but he never mentioned it to anyone besides myself.

One morning Dan emerged with the long rough draft of a poem and asked me to read it. The title was something like "The Monk Who Never Sleeps," and it was a poem about the Vietnam War and Thay's unrelenting insomnia—how Thay remained constantly awake, present to the devastation in Vietnam. It was a poem of profound empathy and certainly reflected how moved Dan was by his experience spending time with Thay.

I know that part of the reason he had come to Sceaux was for retreat and rest, and to learn from Thay's Buddhist witness. I think of those two extraordinary men, one with unrelenting back pain, one with unrelenting insomnia—as if each quietly carried battle wounds from their dedication to peace work. And it was evident that both men felt a desire to support the other as a real friend, that both felt gratitude for the other.

"I felt as if I were back in Vietnam," Dan told me that summer after his return. "In fact I was even more in Vietnam in Paris than I had been in Hanoi, a Vietnam where no bombs were falling, a Vietnam of poetry and peace even though there was an undercurrent of grief."[212]

*"Healing those months among my Buddhist friends brought, what balm in Gilead!. . . I think of the suffering—exile for the monk, prison for the priest. Perhaps it was the wasting war, homesickness, the death of those we loved that lent our words a transfusion. They flow in our veins, those words, they endure as we endured, through and through; then to now."*

—Afterword,
The Raft Is Not the Shore

# On Pilgrimage to Ireland

Responding to an invitation from the Student Christian Movement, Dan agreed to lead a retreat on inter-Christian dialogue, peacemaking, and reconciliation at the Glencree Center in the Wicklow Mountains near Dublin in an Ireland both emerald green and blood red. For a raucous five or six days in March 1975, an unlikely, unhomogenized crowd gathered from both north and south—Protestant and Catholic, lay and clerical, feminists, Irish Republican Army (IRA) supporters, students, teachers, and several Jesuits.

Pro-IRA mural in Belfast.

It was far from easygoing. "The air was so hot with contention," Dan recalled, "that by the third day, a suggestion seemed imperative: that we retire for a day from the business at hand and make our separate ways into the hills nearby, to take counsel with ourselves and perhaps allow a more peaceable spirit to speak." The quiet day proved medicinal. "That evening we offered the cooks and scullions a dinner prepared by ourselves instead of them. There followed music and dancing and hilarity. By the next morning we were prepared for a different rhythm."[213]

At the close of the retreat, a much larger audience, mainly of Dubliners, gathered to hear Dan speak on the role of churches in a violent world. As usual, Dan centered on the challenge of leading a disarmed life. Was it not the life Jesus and his disciples led? A life without

Members of the Provisional IRA.

*"No humans, not even those armed and at war against my country, can be regarded as legitimate targets. Christians may not kill, period. Christians may not be complicit in killing, period. May not hurl napalm at children. May not bury alive in the desert the nameless soldiers. May not launch the smart bomb against women and children in the shelter."* —Testimony

bloodshed? Should not Christians be noteworthy for their refusal to kill?

After the lecture and discussion, an unexpected invitation was whispered into Dan's ear. "I was approached," said Dan, "by a rather taciturn man inquiring as to my interest in sitting for a while with a few friends of the Irish resistance. His words were sufficiently veiled to convey an impression that something unusual was in the air. I agreed, and a group rather quickly came together in a remote room of the house."

Dan discovered he was meeting with three members of the Provisional wing of the IRA, including the founder of the Provos who had lately been released from prison.[214] There was also a priest, "whose function," Dan commented, "seemed to be to preside at the funerals of IRA warriors summarily removed from this world." The third person refused to name himself; Dan had the impression the man was on the run. As Dan reported, "What ensued was . . . a heated and ragged exchange around topics like violence, nonviolence, piety, denials of complicity, settings-right of the record, denunciations of the British, affirmations of loyalty to the church— a curious Irish stew of every ingredient and savor and surprise, from prime beef to Missus Murphy's overalls. It was ludicrous and tragic, it was music hall and street bloodshed, it summoned the rambunctious ghosts of Parnell and O'Connell and the dead of the Easter uprising, without forgetting the Blessed Virgin Mary and our holy father the Pope. And the rosary. And the bombs. Which may God be our judge, it isn't our people who [plant them] but the British, who as long as they occupy our fair land, every Irish lad will be in arms, so help me God."

The Provos founder, never lost for words, dominated the exchange. "We huddled there, he chain-smoked with his nervous chubby hands, his suit shapeless as a sack, he overweight, foolish, nondescript, yet crowned with the indefensible dignity of the prisoner, the pris-

oner of conscience—the dignity of even the wrong conscience. I was appalled, and I loved him. Our eyes met,
we knew something. We stood in the same leaky boat,
the botched *currach* of the world, opposite numbers, the
transplanted Irish and the rooted. Each with a taste of
jail in his mouth, the look, hangdog and stubborn, of
the ex-prisoner. He calling the shots, and I deflecting
them."

It was the "bloody British," the Provos founder declared, who were responsible for the bombings, doing
so just to implicate the Provisional IRA. He personally
renounced violence. "And yet he hedged curi-
ously about the question of nonviolence. . . . He
was fingering his rosary by now; just as a priest
was part of the paraphernalia of terror, so now
was the Blessed Virgin. And in the presence of
these two *numina*, the Virgin and the celibate
warrior, the one to bury the dead, the other
to raise them to paradise—in light of these
two, the events of this world were small potatoes, indeed. Bombs, bullets, strikes, sabotage,
votes, constituencies, Catholics, Protestants,
gun-running, the corpse in the alley, the long
somber procession to the grave, the volleys skyward,
the black box sinking, the indomitable women—it was
death for portion and tithe and prospect. The British be
damned, on with the wars of the just! . . . Ireland, dead
or alive, was their business, not mine."

Mural of IRA hunger-striker
Bobby Sands.

Dan learned a few things that afternoon. At the top
of the list: "In order to kill and call the killing politics,
you must justify the killing. And the best way to justify
killing is to deny that one kills at all. The hand signs the
death warrant, the mind rips it up, denies it exists. And
someone dies—always, inevitably, the children, the old,
the defenseless."

Such denials and lies, Dan reflected, always lay at
the root of state creation. "The guns have an altogether
uncanny tendency to take over. Eventually they rule the

gunmen. One kills, after a while, with a high and even euphoric detachment. As though when a body thuds to earth, and the smoking gun is lowered once more, one sees with elation a cleared space, an obstacle removed. A mirage, no doubt, a utopia, but how seductive! The gunman breathes easier, salvation is at hand."[215]

Dan was to return to Ireland again and again—or to "ire-land," as he spelled it in one letter.[216]

In 1981 IRA prisoner Bobby Sands and many others went on a hunger strike to protest the conditions at the Long Kesh Prison as well as to claim the right of free association with other prisoners, the right to organize educational and recreational pursuits, and the right to one visit, one letter, and one parcel per week. Ten of the fasters died. Bobby Sands's death—he had been elected to Parliament while in prison—was global news. Asked a few days before his death if he had a last wish, he said, "I would like to meet Father Berrigan." Responding as soon as the news reached him, Dan, together with former US attorney general Ramsey Clark, flew to Belfast, went to the prison, and tried to enter. Within hours they learned that Prime Minister Margaret Thatcher herself had ruled that neither Dan nor Clark were to be allowed entrance. The two of them joined in the vigil outside the prison as Sands slowly died. During those days, Dan met with, consoled, and prayed with the wives of the prisoners as well as others who had gathered. In a letter to me he noted, "I have taken a great measure of heat since our visit [accused by some of being an IRA supporter]; it is hard to keep insisting one is merely trying to defend the right of *all* prisoners everywhere to a minimal human environment and treatment."[217] When he and John Dear went over together in the following years, they often met with widows of the fasters.

From December 1997 through early January 1998 Dan and Bill McNichols spent two weeks with John Dear, then living in Belfast and Derry for his Jesuit tertianship year. By then, McNichols comments, "Dan had become a living icon in Ireland."

"We spent a week in Belfast," John recalls, "visiting Catholic leaders who had been working to end the war. One was Rosemary Nelson, the leading Catholic human rights lawyer in Northern Ireland, a quiet, intelligent, compassionate person who was blown up in her car six months after our visit."

In Belfast with Nobel Peace Prize laureate Mairead Corrigan Maguire.
Courtesy John Dear

On January 1, 1998, Nobel Peace Prize laureate Mairead Maguire held an open meeting at the Peace People House near Queens University at which she officially nominated Dan and Phil for the Nobel Prize "in recognition of a lifetime of dedication to the cause of promoting peace, justice, and human rights around the world. These two brothers are the most prominent faith-based voices for peace and nonviolence in the United States.... The Berrigans have inspired many people through their nonviolent civil disobedience actions against war. They have taken onto themselves much suffering but always refuse to inflict pain or suffering on others, as they act for peace and justice."

# "Everybody should live"

A North Vietnamese tank rolls through the gate of the Presidential Palace in Saigon signifying the fall of South Vietnam. AP.

On April 30, 1975, with the capture of Saigon by Hanoi-backed forces, the Vietnam War came to an abrupt end. It was an event involving the hurried withdrawal of US civilian and military personnel in Saigon, along with thousands of South Vietnamese who were linked with the defeated regime, in the largest helicopter evacuation in history. The war had cost more than a million Vietnamese lives, an estimated eighty-four thousand of them children, plus more than fifty-eight thousand American lives. Millions more had been wounded both in body and soul. Vast areas of Vietnam's countryside had been drenched in blood and polluted with toxic chemicals.

"At the end of the war," Dan recalled, "I was teaching at the University of Detroit. I sat there that night in front of a television and they were doing a recap of the war and the antiwar protests. And I found myself just crying and crying. I felt utterly crushed by the memory of it all. The whole thing was so horrible and so endless."[218]

At the time I was editing *Fellowship*, the monthly magazine of the Fellowship of Reconciliation. Dan was one of seventeen prominent antiwar activists who responded to my invitation to comment in a special issue on this border-crossing event. "The war's end," I wrote in my invitation, "offers a moment for meditation on the lessons to be learned, the amnesia to be avoided, and the ways in which we can better become a peacemaking community."

Dan's contribution was an appeal to peace activists to focus their energies on saving unborn lives from abortion. As the text has never been republished, and as it vividly reveals Dan's readiness to step out onto thin ice even among his peers, here is the full text. It began with a poem:

**For the Vietnamese Children**
Having no tears like
having no money
the squeeze is on
O where shall I replenish
the springs of my eyes?
the children ring me round
tin cups in dead hands
clamoring
"Give us tears you great ones
You gave us blood and named us
I, You, He, She, after
statues, sheiks, saints,
scoundrels, yourselves
then you stole our blood
to make your bread
Don't say 'we don't know where'
It's we who don't know
where where where
You've spun us blindfold
in a game, you great ones
We stop, you great ones
We stop, we topple
no eyes no hands

*"War, abortion, the death penalty. In the judgment of anyone with eyes to see, these have become simply another form of 'daily behavior.' We confront these crimes day by day in the media, in the images of a permanent war against the living—the disposable, the vulnerable, as the Nazis defined these, 'the lives of no value.'"* —Testimony

no cups
no, no tears
It's like death, except
for your death, they weep
but for us
no one knows
no one knows
no one
knows."

The poem gave way to prose:

I'm not sure I can offer much beyond this verse. I am struck recently by the harrowing fact that the chief assault [in war] is against children. The sentence of Bonhoeffer keeps invading me: "How are the unborn to live?" When I go to my theological class here in Detroit, my classroom window faces a sign on a mad main avenue: "Abortions"—and a phone number. As though one were offering groceries, tax advice or used cars. It strikes me that Bonhoeffer's sentence takes on a new horrific resonance. How are the unborn to live?

Have we ever heard of, say, Buddhist abortionists? In the past five years, it is said, some two million nearly born people in our midst have been so disposed of. Perhaps someday soon people who did get born may invade such centers, where doctors relieve women of the unwelcome burden named You or I. And may burn their files or pour blood (all of us are fetuses before we are Jim, Laura, Daniel) and thereby draw another line.

Maybe we have a few new questions about old matters.

1) Is our morality in any sense superior to that of those ancient peoples who commonly exposed the newborn to death, as unwelcome aspirants to the sweet air of life?

*"My life is, as I am often informed, disruptive."*
—Ten Commandments for the
Long Haul

2) Can we help everyone walk into the full spectrum and rainbow of life, from womb to old age, so that no one is expendable?

3) Especially in the religious pacifist community, we who believe no political idolatry can excuse the taking of life, can we help remind and symbolize the splendid range of nonviolence; from before birth to the aged?

4) How do we remind people, our people, of the virulence of short-term solutions, "definitive solutions"? Every unwanted fetus being, equivalently, a Jew or Black? Or a Vietnamese? Or a soul in despair?

5) Are we not all, from conception on, biological and spiritual fetuses, who are destined to grow or to die? What is a human vocation anyway?

6) Was not our first political act just getting born?

7) Can we separate, and suffer for, the crucial distinction between sane family planning, and murder of fellow humans?

8) Does acceptance of abortion not lead to acceptance of euthanasia?

9) Is not every form of imposed death, from abortion to drugs to suicide to war, a call to form communities of life?

I guess what I'm asking is whether pacifists might risk, as we have already risked so much on other unpalatable questions, rethinking the acceptance of abortion? Even as we recognize that its opponents as well as its adherents are sometimes mad?

We have had to raise hard questions in the past about the readiness of so much of the "peace" movement to see death occur, so long as the perpetrator be a "liberator." May we not also helpfully question other current dogmas of our western, war-ridden, itchy, competing and mechanistic selves?

Maybe in mutual nurture of unwanted life, male and female rage can join their lost longing, in an old Christian, Jewish, Buddhist aching, in a reach

Cornell University, Division of Rare and Manuscript Collections (Michael Parkhurst)

of longing and say, "No one should die!" Maybe the most "criminal" (as we were before imprisoned criminals for not assisting in the murder of Vietnamese) and hopeful statement of the seventies is a nonviolent statement, "Everyone should live."[219]

Publishing Dan's anti-abortion article got me into a great deal of hot water with some of my friends and colleagues and put my job at risk, as I told Dan by phone a week or two after the June issue's publication. Dan wasn't astonished. "Sorry to hear it," said Dan, "but not at all surprised. I've been getting some heat, too. I expected it. Beware of irate pacifists! Thank God they don't have guns. Abortion is the one form of killing humans that most pacifists now support—being pro-abortion has become the litmus test for being pro-woman."

Dan noted how words, phrases, and slogans have been enlisted to dehumanize the human being in the womb. "It's an unborn child only if it's wanted; if unwanted it's demoted to embryo or fetus. To dare recognizing that it's an unborn child, and thus deserves protection, is to be against choice, and choice is what the American way of life—of death—is all about."

Dan sitting-in at an abortion clinic in Rochester, 1989.

For many people, "pro-life" simply means opposition to abortion and nothing more. Rare are those who are consistently pro-life—that is. trying in every arena and every stage of life to prevent killing, thus opposing capital punishment, war, euthanasia, abortion, or death caused by social neglect. Dan was one of the few. It made him a minority even within minorities.

The following year, the fall of 1976, I got into renewed trouble among some of my peers for a concern over human rights issues in postwar, reunified Vietnam. Dan and Phil were also involved.

In the spring of 1973, two years before the war's end, Dan and Phil had written to North Vietnam's prime minister "in grief and distress of spirit" because of convincing reports that American prisoners of war had been tortured. Their letter angered many antiwar activists at the time, worried that it lent credibility to US justification for its continuing military intervention. Several months later Hanoi responded, dismissing the charges as lies. Dan and Phil, far from convinced, called on their fellow peace activists not to view Hanoi through rose-colored glasses. No government, they argued, should be romanticized. What was needed was an across-the-board renunciation of all violence against humans for whatever reason, no matter who was responsible.

After the war ended, Thich Nhat Hanh began passing on reliable reports to me of major human rights abuses in a reunited, Hanoi-ruled Vietnam. Many of the prisoners in what the Hanoi government euphemistically called "reeducation camps" were people who had previously been prisoners of the Saigon regime. Many were Buddhist monks.

Following the self-immolation of twelve nuns,[220] I drafted a letter appealing to Hanoi's leaders to allow access to the camps for Red Cross representatives and observers from Amnesty International. Seeking signers, I was pleased but hardly surprised that both Dan and Phil quickly lent their names, as did many prominent opponents of the Vietnam War. But then a mini–civil war erupted among peace activists, with critics of the letter charging either that the allegations were false or that, even if true, it was inappropriate for Americans, no matter how active they had been in resisting the war, to censure or seek to counsel the Hanoi regime. One colleague, a staff member of a Quaker group, the American Friends Service Committee, phoned to advise me to back off— otherwise "this will cost you your career in the peace movement." (It was only that day that it occurred to me that one might make peace work a career; I had thought of it as a vocation.)

One of the letter's unshakeable signers, Joan Baez, called to tell me she had been warned that "Jim Forest is probably a CIA agent." "I told her," Joan continued,

*SOME*

*Some stood up once and sat down.*
  *Some walked a mile and walked away.*

*Some stood up twice and sat down*
  *I've had it, they said. . . .*

*Some walked and walked and walked.*
  *They walked the earth*
  *they walked the waters*
  *they walked the air.*

*Why do you stand?*
  *they were asked, and*
  *why do you walk?*

*Because of the children, they said, and*
  *because of the heart, and*
  *because of the bread*

*Because*
  *the cause*
  *is the heart's beat*
  *and the children born*
  *and risen bread.*
      —Steadfastness of the Saints

Cornell University, Division of Rare and Manuscript Collections

"that Jim Forest is much too nice, and much too disorganized, to work for the CIA!" She then sang me a song she had recently composed.[221]

Remarkably the controversy made Phil Berrigan withdraw his name from the letter. Phil in turn persuaded Dan to do the same. Dan, obviously embarrassed, explained rather lamely that he would never have signed in the first place had he known the letter would become public, though he promised "to question our friends in Vietnam" about the charges. Not long after, aware of how bitterly disappointed Nhat Hanh was by Dan's withdrawal of his name, Dan called to apologize. "Forgive me," he said. "I was a coward." Writing to Thich Nhat Hanh, he said it has been "a serious blunder [made] under intense pressure that I will regret for a long time."[222]

The episode wasn't Dan's finest hour; I never saw him so ashamed of himself. When Joan Baez later published a similar appeal as a full-page ad in *The New York Times*, Dan (but again not Phil) was among the signers. Dan went on to make repeated personal appeals in support of prisoners of conscience to the Hanoi regime. In a letter to Prime Minister Pham Van Dong sent in May 1978, he lamented the death in custody of a prominent Buddhist monk, Thich Thien Minh, and appealed for the release of other monks still in captivity. "The world has come to expect much of the new government of Vietnam, but these expectations are seriously unfulfilled."

# Contaminated Weapons

In 1966, after returning from his first trip to Latin America, Dan had briefly questioned whether nonviolent approaches could provide an effective means of overcoming the military dictatorships that ruled so many countries in that continent. In the years that followed, Dan became increasingly convinced that there was no alternative to nonviolent methods and attitudes for those who sought to model their actions on the example and teaching of Jesus. On this issue he entered into a public debate with his friend and fellow poet and priest Ernesto Cardenal, who took part in Nicaragua's Sandinista revolution and, after its victory, became minister of culture.

In November 1977, in an interview published in the Costa Rican journal *Tiempo*, Cardenal, who had once been a Trappist novice under Thomas Merton, recalled how he had initially favored nonviolent methods of struggle. However, after the destruction of his community, Solentiname, by troops of the Somoza dictatorship, he had been forced to realize that, in the Nicaraguan context, "a nonviolent struggle is not practical, and that Gandhi himself would be in agreement with us."

"Above all," Cardenal argued, "the Gospel teaches us that the Word of God is not simply to be heard, but should be practiced." In the Nicaraguan situation, in which so many peasants were suffering persecution and terror, imprisonment, torture, and murder, "the only

Ernesto Cardenal. Maryknoll/Eric Wheater

Cardenal saying Mass with the
community of Solentiname, Nicaragua.
Maryknoll/Eric Wheater

practical witness that could be given was to take up arms with the [revolutionary movement] Frente Sandinista." Those who did this "did it for one reason only: for their love of the Kingdom of God, for their ardent desire to build a just society, a Kingdom of God, concrete and real, here on earth. When the hour arrived, our young men and women fought valiantly, and as Christians." The young people, said Cardenal, "fought without hatred, in spite of everything, without hating the police, poor peasants like themselves, exploited."

Cardenal saw the choice of violence as tragic but necessary. "We would prefer that there not be fighting in Nicaragua, but this is not the fault of the people, the oppressed, who only defend themselves. One day there will be no more fighting in Nicaragua, no more peasant police killing other peasants. Rather, there will be an abundance of schools, of child care centers, hospitals and clinics for everyone, food and adequate housing for all the people, art and diversions for everyone, and most importantly, love between them all. And it is for this that we struggle."

Dan wrote an open letter in response, addressing Cardenal as "dear brother":

Let me say that the questions you raise are among the most crucial that Christians can spell out today. Indeed, in your own country, your life raises them. . . . They are far more than a matter of domestic importance. . . .

You discuss quite freely and approvingly the violence of a violated people, yourselves. You align yourself with that violence, regretfully but firmly, irrevocably. I am sobered and saddened by this. I think of the consequences of your choice, within Nicaragua and far beyond. I sense how the web of violence spins another thread, draws you in, and so many others for whom your example is primary, who do not think for themselves, judging that a priest and poet will lead them in the true way.

I think how fatally easy it is, in a world demented and enchanted with the myth of shortcuts and definitive solutions, when nonviolence appears increasingly naïve, old hat, freakish—how easy it is to cross over, to seize the gun.

It may be true, as you say, that "Gandhi would agree with us." Or it may not be true. . . . It may be true that Christ would agree with you. I do not believe He would, but I am willing to concede your argument, for the sake of argument.

You may be correct in reporting that "those young Christians fought without hate . . . and especially without hate for the guards" they shortly killed (though this must be cold comfort to the dead). Your vision may one day be verified of a Nicaragua free of "*campesino* guards killing other *campesinos* . . ." The utopia you ache for may one day be realized in Nicaragua: "an abundance of schools, child-care centers, hospitals, and clinics for everyone . . . and most importantly, love between everyone." This may all be true: the guns may bring on the kingdom. But I do not believe it.

So the young men of Solentiname resolved to take up arms. They did it for one reason: "on account of their love for the kingdom of God." Now here we certainly speak within a tradition! In every crusade that ever marched across Christendom, murder—the most secular of undertakings, the most worldly, the one that enlists and rewards us along with the other

Art from the community of Solentiname.

*"Every war in history, in the minds of practically all those who prepare for it or initiate it or respond to it or make money from it or propagandize it or research it or deploy it or go off to kill in it or are wounded in it or survive it—or write encyclicals about it or mount the pulpit to sanctify it—all of these find a way to set down the same thing. Namely, the current war is a good war. It is a virtuous war, a just war, an old war (self-justifying), a war to end all wars. And the above justifications, from the point of view of biblical understanding, are pure scandal."*

—To Dwell in Peace

enlistees of Caesar—this undertaking is invariably baptized in religious ideology: the kingdom of God.

Of course we have choices, of course we must decide. When all is said, we find that the Gospel makes sense, that it strikes against our motives and actions or it does not. Can that word make sense at all today?

"Thou shalt not kill." "Love one another as I have loved you." "If your enemy strikes you on the right cheek, turn to him the other as well." Practically everyone in the world, citizens and believers alike, consign such words to the images on church walls or the embroideries on front parlors.

We really are stuck. Christians are stuck with this Christ, the impossible, unteachable, unreformable loser. Revolutionaries must correct him, set him aright. That absurd form, shivering under the cross winds of power, must be made acceptable, relevant. So a gun is painted into his empty hands. Now he is human! Now he is like us.

Correction! Correction! we cry to those ignorant Gospel scribes, Matthew and the rest. He was not like that, he was not helpless, he was not gentle, he was under no one's heel, no one pushed him around! He would have taken up a gun if one had been at hand, he would have taken up arms, "solely for one reason; on account of his love for the kingdom of God." Did he not have fantasies like ours, in hours out of the public glare, when he too itched for the quick solution, his eyes narrowed like gun sights?

Dear brother Ernesto, when I was underground in 1970 . . . I had long hours to think of these things. At that time I wrote: "The death of a single human is too heavy a price to pay for the vindication of any principle, however sacred." I should add that at the time, many among the antiwar Left were playing around with bombings, in disarray and despair.

I am grateful that I wrote those words. I find no reason eight years later to amend or deny them.

Indeed, in this bloody century, religion has little to offer, little that is not contaminated or broken or in bad faith. But one thing we have: our refusal to take up bombs or guns, aimed at the flesh of brothers and sisters, whom we persist in defining as such, refusing the enmities pushed at us by war-making state or war-blessing church.

This is a long loneliness, and a thankless one. One says "no" when every ache of the heart would say "yes." We, too, long for a community on the land, heartening liturgies, our own turf, the arts, a place where sane ecology can heal us. And the big boot comes down. It destroys everything we have built. And we recoil. Perhaps in shock, perhaps in a change of heart, we begin to savor on our tongues a language that is current all around us: phrases like "legitimate violence," "limited retaliation," "killing for the love of the kingdom." And the phrases make sense—we have crossed over. We are now [like] any army. . . . We have disappeared into this world, into bloody, secular history. We cannot adroitly handle both gospel and gun; so we drop the gospel, an impediment in any case.

And our weapons? They are contaminated in what they do and condemned in what they cannot do. There is blood on them, as on our hands. And like our hands, they cannot heal injustice or succor the homeless.

How can they signal the advent of the kingdom of God? How can we, who hold them? We announce only another bloody victory for the emperor of necessity, whose name in the Bible is Death.

Shall [Death] have dominion?

Brother, I think of you so often. And pray with you. And hope against hope.[223]

In May and June 1984, seven years after his exchange with Cardenal, Dan and fellow Jesuit Dennis Leder spent a month in Central America visiting both El Salvador,

Triumphant Sandinistas enter Managua, July 1979.

governed by a US-backed military junta, and Nicaragua, in its sixth year of US-opposed Sandinista rule.

In Nicaragua, Dan took part in a dialogue with leaders of the revolutionary government, including Cardenal, now minister of culture. The exchange was, for Dan, deeply disappointing. Asking what provisions were made for conscientious objectors, he was told that military service was obligatory for all without exception. Dan listened with "a sinking spirit." Was not respect of conscience essential for a revolution that defined itself as "a revolution of conscience"? A question was raised about concerns Amnesty International had published regarding the treatment of minorities and dissidents, the use of "preventive detention" and forced removals from the land. While everyone present knew that the Sandinista leadership had made a number of serious mistakes, neither Cardenal nor others in the government admitted that any of their policies had gone off track. Dan was saddened that Cardenal presented a wrinkle-free portrait of "the revolution as a kind of absolute platonic form, beyond question or critique—essentially a romantic view."[224] (A decade later, in 1994, Cardenal left the Sandinista party, protesting its authoritarianism, and joined an opposition group. Cardenal stated, "I think an authentic capitalism would be more desirable than a false revolution.")

While in El Salvador Dan and Leder listened to testimonies of torture, murder, and war, but also of peacemaking and community building. While in the capital city of San Salvador, they visited staff and faculty of the Universidad Centroamericana, including theologian and rector Ignacio Ellacuría and the five other Jesuits who, five years later, would be assassinated by government soldiers. There were also discussions with Jon Sobrino, one of the leading voices of liberation theology. "These learned Christians, theorists, weavers of the volatile biblical words and themes," Dan noted, were "first of all listeners, and not merely to one another, to [fellow] academics . . . but listeners to the unlikely poor."[225]

Jesuit Fr. Ignacio Ellacuría, assassinated with his community in November 1989.

# Swords into Plowshares

In 1969 Phil had fallen in love with Elizabeth McAlister. The feeling was mutual. The following year, sitting together in an empty office of a church in the Bronx, they exchanged vows, declaring themselves husband and wife.[226] It was an event without witnesses and unknown at the time even to Dan. Neither Phil nor Liz withdrew from their respective religious communities, nor was there any honeymoon. Phil was soon back in prison.

In June 1973, six months after Phil's release,[227] the two obtained a marriage license and legalized their union at a ceremony in the living room of Liz's mother's home in Upper Montclair, New Jersey. Paul Mayer and Dan were witnesses along with Jerry and Carol Berrigan and others close to the couple.

In a homily for the event, Dan recalled a Vietnamese proverb: "When something difficult is attempted, it is like breaking a rock with an egg." Dan saw in this image a metaphor for marriage: "Truly, our dear friends, this morning Phil and Liz have decided to break a rock with an egg, and so all sorts of rhythms have been set in motion by this most unexpected act, an act which seems so in accord with nature as to be almost against nature. That is to say against the rock, which has no future, they have set the unborn egg, teeming with future, teeming with hope, containing all their tomorrows."

*"In the day of the toad and the night of the long swords, Philip wears his humanity like a Buddha, a jewel in the forehead. He and others like him light up the national darkness. And the darkness, to borrow a phrase, does not comprehend."* —Testimony

217

Liz and Phil at Jonah House. Cornell University, Division of Rare and Manuscript Collections

*"The community of Jonah House has gone its way, against all odds, unrepentantly opposed to nuclear violence and its lethal spin-offs— the decrepitude of political life, domestic violence on a spiraling scale, sexism, racism, executions, and the vile social triage being worked against the poor."*
—Testimony

Later in the day, dozens of friends gathered for a celebration of their bond at the diocesan house adjacent to the Cathedral of St. John the Divine in upper Manhattan, a manorlike building made available for the occasion by a supportive Episcopal bishop, Paul Moore.

Phil and Liz moved into a run-down building in a battered neighborhood in west Baltimore and christened it Jonah House.[228] The name was apt. It had been Jonah's prophetic task to go to the city of Nineveh, roughly equivalent in the ancient world to today's Washington, DC, and prevent its destruction. Jonah wasn't an eager recruit to the city-saving ministry; his initial response was to flee from God's attention by sailing to distant Tarshish. It took a wild storm and a three-day detour as indigestible cargo in a whale's belly to get Jonah back on course and to accept his prophetic mission. "If God could use Jonah for the works of justice," Liz remarked, "there is hope for each of us."

From the start, Jonah House was both a community and a base for organizing. The first actions, launched in the summer of 1973, were a series of "White House Pray-Ins" protesting the US bombing of Cambodia, which was a significant expansion of the Vietnam War. In the months and years that followed, the Jonah House community held a vigil in front of Henry Kissinger's home, attempted to dig graves on the White House lawn, did the same on Secretary of Defense Donald Rumsfeld's front lawn, and planted trees as a life symbol at a Connecticut naval base housing nuclear-missile-armed Trident submarines. In 1976 they attempted a meeting with newly elected president Jimmy Carter in Plains, Georgia; denied the opportunity, they raised banners protesting nuclear weapons. Year after year they joined with other peace groups in disrupting arms bazaars in Washington, lavish events that Phil described as "the obscenity to eclipse all obscenities—big hoopla, blacks and Hispanics offering cocktails, scantily clad hostesses beckoning on the military jocks and dignitaries to buy their deadly wares."

Organizing protests that led to arrest and jail time became Phil's default setting. When not locked up, Phil joined with others in the community in defraying household expenses as house painters.

"While my father had the most experience in that trade," Phil's son Jerry told me, "having paid for college by painting houses during the summer with my uncle Jerry, and while he would often be on the highest ladder on the job site, there was an element in this aspect of communal life—as there was in many aspects—of relinquishment of authority to the communal process. The community would agree together what jobs to take on and when. There was a communal evaluation of the status of the bank account—a common purse—and at a weekly scheduling meeting members would sign up for certain days on the current paint job as well as meal preparation and child care and leadership of the weekly Sunday liturgy. It wasn't easy. Participation in community involves denial of self, sharing authority, encouraging others to come forward and take more responsibility. In the long run, many people found my father quite impossible to take and I understand why. On the other hand, few appreciate how difficult community life was for my parents, as stable, deep, and conservative as they were in so many ways, inviting people in to a living experiment in Gospel nonviolence, dealing with people's brokenness and neuroses. It's all done in the hope that something will stick and that we all might become a little more Christ-like than we have been so far. As we see in the Gospel, Jesus's first public act was building a community of disciples."

Dan visited often and, to "thicken the soup," passed along checks he had received for leading retreats and giving lectures.

In the midst of all the hard work and organizing, Phil and Liz became parents of three new Berrigans: Frida (April 1, 1974), Jerry (April 17, 1975), and Kate (November 5, 1981). On the occasions when both Phil and Liz were in jail simultaneously, other members of the

Liz and Phil with Jerry and Frida
Courtesy Frida Berrigan

Phil and Frida at a protest. Cornell University, Division of Rare and Manuscript Collections (Bob Strawn)

*"We do not go to the Pentagon and White House to offer an 'alternative policy,' an 'alternative politic,' whatever that might mean. Our task is simply to proclaim the sin of mass destruction, the blasphemy against the God of life implied in weapons of mass killing."*

—Portraits

community cared for the children. All three were home-schooled.

On December 22, 1976, the beloved Berrigan matriarch, Frida, age ninety-one, died. "Toward the end," Dan wrote, "the only sentence her wasted body could form was a simple 'I love you.' We who love her will never hear those words spoken in such a way again." Her three younger sons, Phil, Dan, and Jerry, along with Liz, decided to commemorate Frida's life with an act of civil disobedience on the steps of the Pentagon on December 28, on the church calendar the day commemorating Herod's slaughter of the innocent. "Some seventy-five people from east and west gathered there," Dan reported. "We were denying Herod his historical prey—here and now, the children of the world. Twenty-nine of us were arrested for pouring our blood on the pillars and chaining ourselves to the portals. Many of the Pentagon resisters were given heavy sentences, among them Elizabeth McAlister." Liz was sentenced to sixty days.

In 1978 Dan wrote a confessional letter to Phil in which he aired the question of whether he should engage, as Phil was urging, in another act of Catonsville-like civil disobedience that might result in a year or more in prison. His poor health, Dan explained, was a restraining factor, "There's the question of my back and eyes, which are stable . . . diet, and lotsa vitamin supplements. There's no question without these [my health] would worsen. . . . On the other hand—[there is the primary matter of] the call. Which is a mystery and respected as such; and [ought at least to] mitigate the above and put it in place. No question that all through your months [in prison], I've felt the deep divine logic of your stance, being there. Right as crystal or the timing of the sun. Right for me too. This remains unshaken, a matter of [the] gospel rightly grasped. I feel also . . . no great stake in this world whether in the Jesuits, apart from a few friends, or the writing or caroming about the country. My real stake is in you and Liz and Jerry and Carol and the [children]. . . . I would like to consider myself spiritually prepared to gulp hard and leap in; what else can one do? This is about the closest I can get to a confession these days. . . . Bless me."[229]

Phil responded, "If I had your back and eyes, I'd be doing less jail than you're doing. Most of my courage comes from a strong back."

Yet Dan was not at all hesitant in taking part in acts of protest and civil disobedience that involved arrest and the risk of short stays in jail.

On Ash Wednesday 1980, while teaching on the Book of Revelation and religious nonviolence at the Jesuit School of Theology in Berkeley, Dan took part in a sit-in in the outer office of the president of the University of California–Berkeley. The university was and remains responsible for Livermore Laboratories, an institution that describes itself as "a premier research and development institution for science and technology applied to national security." Under this cosmetic wrapping, the work of Livermore Labs centers on the development and design of new nuclear weapons.

"They let us cool our posteriors for some nine hours," Dan recalled, "giving us time to reflect, pray, spread ashes, affix pictures of bombs to their walls, fast and sing and be silent by turn. . . . Then, about midnight, they decided to 'clear the property.'" What might have been a night in jail turned out to be, Dan noted, "an experience of trash removal."

In the roulette of civil disobedience, on this occasion there were no arrests. "In the course of our sit-in," Dan recalled, "one of the office subalterns screamed, 'And you

Top and Above: Dan at Pentagon protest. Cornell University, Division of Rare and Manuscript Collections

221

call yourselves religious people, coming in here under the shroud of God.' This immediately after we had poured ashes on the floor. Meantime, up the hill [where Livermore Labs are located] . . . I am told that the bomb concocters are also preparing to 'carbon test' the Shroud of Turin.[230] Is the shroud of God for real? Will we know at last? We may know yet, in a far different way than anticipated, and the shroud of God may be vast enough to stretch across the corpse of all humanity."[231]

The year 1980 marked a turning point. One of the war-related sites that had drawn the attention of the Jonah House community was General Electric's Nuclear Re-Entry Division Assembly Facility in King of Prussia, Pennsylvania, not far from Philadelphia. The local Brandywine Peace Community had been conducting vigils and minor acts of civil disobedience there since 1977. The founder of the Brandywine community, Bob Smith, met Jonah House member John Schuchardt, a former Marine officer who earlier on had worked as an attorney and public defender. Smith explained that the General Electric plant provided a key element in the development of first-strike nuclear weaponry.[232] A significant action at King of Prussia, Smith and Schuchardt agreed, would publicize both what General Electric was producing and its role in US preparations for initiating nuclear war.

Molly Rush, of the Merton Center in Pittsburgh, recalled Isaiah's prophecy: "They shall beat their swords into plowshares and their spears into pruning hooks."[233] "What if we were to do what Isaiah envisioned?" asked Rush. "We could just walk in there and get at one of those things." A plan began to take shape of entering the GE facility and using hammers to damage a partially assembled warhead—the shield for a Mark 12-A reentry vehicle. The shield prevents the H-bomb contained within it from melting as the missile comes back into the atmosphere en route to its target. The shields were made by General Electric and then shipped to Pantax in Amarillo, Texas, to be joined to nuclear warheads.

Phil at Pentagon protest. Cornell University, Division of Rare and Manuscript Collections

The Jonah House community hosted a meeting to explore various questions. If they entered the plant, how would people working there react? Would such an action make a contribution to the cause of nuclear disarmament? They also evaluated the risks. If charged with sabotage, the penalty could be grim. "I had the feeling," said Schuchardt, "that I could spend the rest of my life in prison." Still, he asked himself, might that not be a small price to pay in order to make nuclear war less likely? It was a question that resonated with others at Jonah House, not least Phil.

One aspect of the challenge was that only specialists really understood much about first-strike weaponry and reentry vehicles. Phil contacted Robert Aldridge, a former nuclear engineer turned peace advocate, who educated him and the others about the weapon system's intricacies and purpose.

Mark 12-A warhead.

It wasn't easy finding people prepared to join such a high-risk action. Ultimately there were seven volunteers: Carl Kabat, a Catholic priest; Anne Montgomery, a nun as well as daughter of a retired admiral; Dean Hammer, a Yale Divinity School graduate; Molly Rush, a wife and mother of six; Elmer Maas, a former college teacher; plus John Schuchardt and Phil. As he had done just before Catonsville, at the last minute Phil managed to persuade Dan to join the first "Plowshares" action as the group's eighth and final recruit.

A few days before the action Dan sent a brief note to Robert Ellsberg: "The next weeks will bring some changes here too. We're going to [pour] some blood at a nuclear shroud factory (shroud is the way they describe what they do there!) in Pennsylvania. I'm fairly sure the penalties will be fairly severe. So I'm rounding off things here, leaving [my] apartment in the hands of Bob Keck to be sublet after a month or so if the sentence goes long. Please send a prayer. . . ."[234]

On September 9 the raiders, armed with clawless hammers, moved unhindered into the GE plant. While

*"In a biblical sense, the Bomb has already detonated in our midst. In a classical sense, the form precedes the fact; we must have imagined, internalized, been possessed by the bomb, before we could consent to concoct it. . . . The moral fallout is anomie, compulsive violence, glorification of blood and border, distraction from the truth of life. After years of this we can scarcely call ourselves literate in the gospel. We read with dead eyes."*

—Portraits

The Plowshares 8:
Fr. Carl Kabat, Elmer Maas,
Phil Berrigan, Molly Rush,
Dan Berrigan, Sr. Anne Montgomery,
John Schuchardt, Dean Hammer.

Father Kabat and Sister Anne distracted two guards, the rest of the group entered the target building and proceeded to shatter part of two Mark 12-A missile shields, then poured blood onto blueprints and equipment before kneeling in a circle, holding hands, and singing hymns. Police arrived forty-five minutes later to arrest them. The eight were charged with ten felony and misdemeanor counts.

"GE's Mark 12-A," Dan wrote to friends, "is designed to enclose three H-bombs each with its own target. . . . Our act hurt no one, unlike what this weapon is designed for. GE claims we caused thousands of dollars of property damage. We claim we saved lives."[235]

The judge assigned to the initial hearing met lawyers for both sides, telling them he didn't want another Harrisburg trial with huge crowds of supporters and opponents. If the district attorney agreed, he would drop charges and allow the eight to make explanatory speeches. Otherwise, if the defendants insisted on a trial, they faced up to ten years in prison. Both Schuchardt and Phil were adamant about having a trial. They wanted the world to know what General Electric was manufacturing and the nature of such doomsday weapons. Not least, they were defending international law established at the Nuremberg trials, which they insisted allowed people to interfere with preparations for war.

The trial, held in March 1981 in Norristown, Pennsylvania, involved a day-by-day struggle by the accused to address the issues that lay behind their action: the prevention of nuclear war, the development of first-strike nuclear weapons, and the gross immorality and illegality of a war involving a city's destruction and the deaths of millions.

The judge assigned to preside, Samuel Salus II, was both unsympathetic and rigid; in a letter to me at the time, Dan referred to "his innate blindness & rancor."[236] For Salus, the only question for the court and jury to decide was whether the defendants had committed the specific actions with which they were charged. Why they did so and what legal justification their actions might claim was not the court's concern. Attempts to present exculpatory evidence would not be tolerated.

During the trial, Dan was permitted to sum up the inspirations and motivations that led him to join in the Plowshares action:

> The question of why we did our action takes me back to those years when my conscience was being formed, back to a family that was poor, and to a father and mother who taught, quite simply, by living what they taught. And if I could put their message very shortly, it would go something like this: In a thousand ways they showed that you do what is right because it is right, that your conscience is a matter between you and God, that nobody owns you. If I have a precious memory of my mother and father that lasts to this day, it is simply that they lived as

*"In confronting G.E., we choose to obey God's law of life, rather than corporate summons of death. Our beating of swords into plowshares is a way to finalize this biblical call. In our action, we draw on a deep-rooted faith in Christ, who changed the course of history through his willingness to suffer rather than to kill. We are filled with hope for our world and for our children, as we join this act of resistance."*
—From the "Statement of the Plowshares 8," Portraits

though nobody owned them. They cheated no one. They worked hard for a living. They were poor, and perhaps most precious of all, they shared what they had. And that was enough, because in the life of a young child, the first steps of conscience are as important as the first steps of one's feet. They set the direction where life will go. And I feel that direction was set for my brothers and myself. There is a direct line between the way my parents turned our steps and this action. That is no crooked line.[237]

As for the damage that he and the other seven had done to weapons of mass destruction, the reasoning behind it was not difficult to express or understand, said Dan:

*Both Isaiah and Micah drew on the hammer, as an implied symbol of spiritual rebirth, of conversion to compassion and justice, of a new face put not just on things, but on the soul. A new face turned toward God and one another. . . . Thus the hammer becomes a symbol of the outlawing of war. If war were outlawed, we asked ourselves, what would the world look like? What would that other, improbable, even unimaginable shape be? Isaiah is a visionary, and a practical one. . . . He sees a world in the form of— a plowshare."* —Testimony

The only message I have to the world is: we are not allowed to kill innocent people. We are not allowed to be complicit in murder. We are not allowed to be silent while preparations for mass murder proceed in our name, with our money, secretly. . . . It's terrible for me to live in a time where I have nothing to say to human beings except, "Stop killing." There are other beautiful things that I would love to be saying to people. There are other projects I could be very helpful at. And I can't do them. I cannot. Because everything is endangered. Everything is up for grabs. Ours is a kind of primitive situation, even though we would call ourselves sophisticated. Our plight is very primitive from a Christian point of view. We are back where we started. Thou shalt not kill. We are not allowed to kill. Everything today comes down to that—everything.[238]

Addressing Judge Salus, Dan added these memorable words:

We could not *not* do this. We were pushed to this by all our lives. When I say we could not *not* do this, I

CONTEMPT

MOLLY
DEAN
ANNE
DAN

CARL
ELMER
PHIL
JOHN

mean, among other things, that with every cowardly bone in my body, I wished that I hadn't had to enter that GE plant. I wish I hadn't had to do it. And that has been true every time I was arrested all these years. My stomach turns over. I feel sick. I feel afraid. I don't want to go through this again. I hate jail. I don't do well there physically. But I cannot not go on because I have learned that we must not kill if we are Christians. And I am supposed to be a disciple. So at some point your cowardly bones get moving, and you say, "Here it goes again," and you do it. And you have a certain peace because you did it, as I do here this morning in speaking with you.[239]

At the end of the trial, in response to Judge Salus's rage at the defendants' persistent attempts to enter into dialogue with the court and to present legal justifications for what they had done, the eight stood up and turned their backs on him. "One by one," Dan wrote me days later, "the audience rose and did likewise."

All eight were found guilty. Dan, Phil, Kabat, and Schuchardt received three- to ten-year sentences, the others eighteen months to five years. They were quickly bailed out and, despite Salus, ended up serving remarkably little time—in Phil's case, the longest, just five

Plowshares defendants turn their back on the judge.

*"It was a kind of Stonehenge moment in the mind . . . a solid wall of wills, a stupendous silent no to the absurd puppetry."*
—Portraits

*"We await sentencing. A pallid phrase indeed in face of our passionate intent to continue resisting the machinery of mega-death. . . . May Easter summon us forth with a trumpet blast from tombs of dread and inertia. Tombs blocked at mouth with—missiles. Come, mighty angel, roll them back!"*

—Portraits

Dan with actor Martin Sheen.
Ed Hedemann

months. But for nearly a decade, while the appeal process dragged on, the eight lived month-to-month under the shadow of impending imprisonment.

The trial was re-created in Emile de Antonio's 1982 film *In the King of Prussia*, which starred Martin Sheen, playing Judge Salus, and featured the Plowshares Eight playing themselves.[240] During filming Sheen developed bonds of friendship with both Dan and Phil. Sheen often visited Dan in the years that followed and several times was arrested with him. "Mother Teresa," Sheen has said, "brought me back into the Church and Dan Berrigan kept me there."

Another consequence of the King of Prussia action was a short film made by television journalist Mike Wallace for the CBS weekly news program *60 Minutes*. Called "The Brothers Berrigan," Wallace filmed a Plowshares action in Missouri and interviewed Dan and Phil. At one point, Wallace asked Dan, "Do you think you will live to see the end of nuclear weapons, which you are so desperately trying to bring about?" Without hesitation, Dan responded, "I'm not desperate about anything. I'm just peacefully pointing out that we don't need nuclear weapons. We don't have to have a nuclear world."

The King of Prussia action gave Phil and Jonah House a new organizing focus—the Plowshares movement. In the years that followed, a small core of committed men and women hammered and poured blood on MX missiles, Trident submarines, B-52 bombers, and various components of nuclear weapons. Though journalists often treated such protests as nonevents, "those involved," as Murray Polner and Jim O'Grady wrote in *Disarmed and Dangerous*, "tenaciously insisted that the government's nuclear weapons first-strike strategy was a crime, that indiscriminate sales of extraordinarily devastating weapons abroad was obscene, and that politicians and generals alike are bound by precepts of international law."[241] The actions were a wake-up call even if few were listening. When a television reporter noted in 1981 that Dan was not getting as much attention as he once had, he replied, "I don't think we ever felt our conscience was tied to the other end of a TV cord."[242]

Liz took part in one such action on Thanksgiving Day in 1983 when she and six others hammered on the bomb-bay doors of a B-52 that was being outfitted to carry nuclear-armed cruise missiles. The judge who presided at the trial described her as a "professional protester."

Frida Berrigan recalls what it was like when both her parents were locked up simultaneously:

Liz, Phil, and Frida. Courtesy Frida Berrigan

This was not an easy time. Mom and Dad had not planned on being in jail at the same time. I turned three and my brother turned two while they were away. We all struggled with being apart. Jerry and I were taken care of by two community members—Ladon Sheets and Joan Burd. They were not strangers; both had been core members of the community for years, but they went from being occasional babysitters and playmates to being our primary caregivers without a lot of notice or preparation. . . . We were too young to have very distinct memories of that time, but I do remember that it was tough for us and our parents. Jerry had nightmares and often woke up crying. He also fell against the coffee table and broke his two front teeth while they were away. In *The Time's Discipline*, Mom wrote: "It isn't hard to be in jail; it is a different way of being. But being away from one's little ones, unable to respond to Jerry's crying at night, is terrible."[243]

Phil and Liz afterward resolved never to risk leaving the children without at least one parent at home.

Though Dan took part only in the first Plowshares

Supporters of the Plowshares 8.

action, he backed them all. "Plowshares actions," comments John Dear, "became a major focus for Dan for the rest of his life. They were Dan's way of speaking against war and nuclear weapons, talking about the God of peace and God's will for nuclear disarmament, and how to follow Jesus today."[244]

On April 10, 1990, a decade after the first Plowshares action and nine years after the trial, thanks mainly to the efforts of lawyers Ramsey Clark, Peter Goldberger, and Joseph Cosgrove, the appeal process finally ended with a vindication.

A new judge, James Buckingham, had been assigned to review the earlier trial and alter the sentences if he saw fit.

An impassioned oral statement by Dan was the high point of the hearing:

> The charges [brought against us in the 1981 trial] were a juridical effort to name not so much our crimes as ourselves. One is tempted to say in light of the biblical events commemorated this Holy Week, the charges were attempts not only to name, but to nail us. I urge you to view with alarm, therefore, the felonious faces you see before you this day. The defendants, according to this court, are breakers and enterers, conspirators, destroyers, worse and worse and so on and so on. . . .
>
> When one thinks of it, this naming and nailing of people has been going on at a great rate in our lifetime. One thinks of the naming of Nelson Mandela by the South African state some twenty-six years ago. He was called dangerous, violent, a conspirator plotting the overthrow of law and order. One thinks of the repeated naming and nailing of Vaclav Havel by the Czechoslovakian state over the years. He was called disruptive, an enemy of the state, a hooligan. One thinks of noble Sakharov and his long ordeal [in Soviet Russia], condemned and vilified as traitor to the state.

One thinks inevitably this week of another naming and nailing. It occurred in a court very like this, in the first century of our era. The Accused was hauled in, successive judges had at Him, as did the tempestuous crowd. He was named repeatedly, scornfully by the Roman state and its satellite religionists and thugs: would-be destroyer of temple property, withholder of tribute money, blasphemer, pretender to a lost throne. The charges were sharp as nails. The names attached to Him quite literally held firm. He was convicted and capitally disposed of.

And yet, and yet. Even though the law has claimed so often to speak the last word concerning the accused, to name the final name, to drive the nails deep—yet some event down the road of time, an intervention, a change of heart, a change of climate, these keep intruding. A far different word is heard. It slowly attaches itself to such as Mandela, Havel, Sakharov, Jesus, and countless other noble criminals. This seems to be a constant of history, whether in our lifetime or long before.

Dan with Plowshares co-defendant Sr. Anne Montgomery, and Paul Mayer.
Ed Hedemann

No court in fact seems able to speak a last word or to drive a final nail, even in a coffin. The names fade and fall to rot in the rude weathers of time. The nails rust and spring apart. Which is to say, justice, in contrast to the law, tends to get heard eventually, to forge new names on behalf of the vilified, to raise the very dead.

Next Dan reflected on the iconic image of Justice found in courthouses around the world:

The eyes of this woman are blindfolded. She bears a scale in hand, as though, prevented from seeing the world, she still could weigh, estimate rightly, set wrongs right. She also bears a sword, for she is vowed to truth and consequence. Blind justice. The image, I think, conveys a great irony. She is blind, one thinks, in order that justice may not be swamped by the passing show, by the passions and storms that shake the earth we walk. Justice is blind in order that justice may see, longer and deeper and within and beyond the passion and prejudice of the hour. She is blind for another reason as well: in order that justice may hear more acutely, as the blind often do; may hearken to the voices of the ancestors and the unborn, the inarticulate and victimized and scorned. She must hear what others are deaf to, as she must see what others are blind to. And Justice holds in hand a scale; in order that she may touch and sift and weigh . . . the law of the land . . . that she may judge the tyrannical burden of that law, as it weighs heavy on our conscience, on our courts, on our churches, on our poor; as under that burden the world itself falls to kneel in fear of nuclear Armageddon.

That blindfolded Justice! How deeply the vision penetrates, how nicely she sorts out and balances innocence and guilt, crime and consequence. How, contrary to expectation, special interest, greed and fear and folly, Justice cries aloud—for Justice. And in consequence, justice at last! Vile verdicts are reversed, vilifying names are renounced, murderous nails are loosened!

Given patience and steadfastness in the accused, this comes to pass. Justice is attained. Sometimes in one's own lifetime, sometimes after. Thus Mandela becomes an only hope of a tormented and degraded society. Havel is elected president of his country. Sakharov is rehabilitated in death. And the nails spring from the hands of the mysterious victim of Good Friday.

On a larger stage, our own lifetime, the murdered Jesuits, the murdered women of El Salvador are invoked and honored, the children dead in a bloody swath from Bethlehem to Soweto, rise and sing. Our cloud of witnesses, witnesses for the defense! . . . Such are the momentous reversals suffered by lawless law and disordered order. Such reversals we note and rejoice in. How the vile names come unstuck and the murderous nails fall to rust, how the law is struck blind, how blind Justice penetrates the heart of truth and, in God's good time, rights the wrong!

The courtroom was as still as a monastery at midnight as Dan finished his appeal, addressing a heavenly court even more than the court in Norristown:

Let this be said. The judgments rendered out today . . . are in better hands than ours, better hands than our judges. In the hands, let us pray, of a holy Defendant once reviled and misnamed in an earthly court, named and finally nailed in infamy. His wounds, we believe, are healed, and glorious. And His name is above every name, every earthly power and dominion—including the power and dominion of this court, or of any earthly court. It is to Him, finally, we proffer our argument. The argument goes this way. If the children of the world will be accounted safer for our imprisonment, so be it. We go in a good spirit. If the earth will be accounted free of nuclear illness and insult for our imprisonment, so be it. We go in a good spirit. If first-strike weaponry is to be judged within the law, and we outside the law, so be it. We go to prison in a good spirit.[245]

Dan under arrest at the White House.

Judge Buckingham listened throughout with receptive attentiveness. "As I look over their records," he declared, "the crimes are for the most part fairly minor. It is crystal clear that it was a nonviolent affair. The de-

*"When you are hauled into court, prepare no defense. Despite the admonition, we always prepare, and deliver where allowed, statements to the court; though it must be added that we do so without great enthusiasm and with care that legal punctilio be subject to our conscience. The point of the command seems to be not so much a prohibition against stating one's case as an urging to keep one's intent clear. In defending oneself, one's aim is not self-justification, but service of the truth."*

—Ten Commandments for the Long Haul

Phil under arrest at the Pentagon.
Cornell University, Division of Rare and Manuscript Collections

fendants were attempting to make a statement of their deeply felt convictions. I agree with many of those convictions. We are all concerned about nuclear war." He then sentenced the eight to time served plus twenty-three months of probation.

Buckingham was nearly as surprised with his ruling as were the defendants. He said in court that, driving to Norristown that morning, he had intended to send the eight back to prison. "When I came down here today," he said, "my ideas were a little different. Counsel and the defendants were very persuasive."

When Phil walked out of the courtroom, he told reporters he had "mixed feelings" about Buckingham's decision. "We got a warm, decent judge who was lenient and then slapped probation on us," Phil said, "but [by being freed instead of jailed] our action will be forgotten and so too will GE's war-making. Being on probation will not hinder me—I am ready to go back to jail."

In contrast, a grateful, relieved, and cheerful Dan displayed a toothbrush he had brought "just in case I was locked up tonight, but it seems I won't be needing this after all."

After spending all of the 1980s making plans that always had to be tentative, with a three- to ten-year prison sentence hanging over him, Dan had been freed once again from the lions' den.

As the nineties began, Dan had decided that he would not participate in more Plowshares actions and questioned whether seeking prolonged prison sentences was the best choice for Phil, Liz, and others close to Jonah House. Phil did not agree; he was to be in and out of prison until the last year of his life while Dan would focus on acts of civil disobedience with symbolic impact but not likely to result in heavy penalties.

Now in its fourth decade, the Plowshares movement continues through its actions—more than a hundred to date. Those engaged enter military bases and weapons factories, often with astonishing ease, damaging or disabling weapons of war when possible, pouring blood, painting biblical passages on walls, and calmly awaiting arrest and whatever follows.

One of the most dramatic Plowshares actions, and the one that has achieved by far the most public attention, happened in 2012 when Sister Megan Rice (age eighty-two), Michael Walli, and Greg Boertje-Obed managed to cut their way though several fences in Oak Ridge, Tennessee, entering a zone in which deadly force against intruders was authorized, and gained access to the Y-12 National Security Complex. Y-12 is the storage site for eight hundred thousand pounds of weapons-grade uranium, the material that undergoes fusion when a nuclear bomb is detonated. While not entering the building, they streaked its white exterior walls with their own

Cornell University, Division of Rare and Manuscript Collections

blood, squirted from baby bottles, and spray-painted the building with such phrases as "The fruit of justice is peace." The scandal of lax security at Oak Ridge, known as "the Fort Knox of uranium," led to urgent congressional hearings.[246]

The usual result of Plowshares actions was imprisonment for the raiders, with the length of the sentences varying dramatically depending on the mood and outlook of the judge. Remarkably, in November 1984, one of the judges, Miles Lord of the Federal District Court

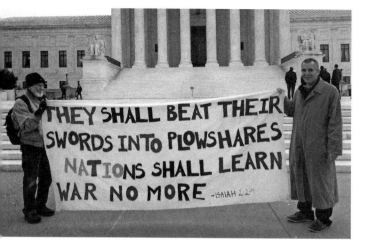

Top: Steve Kelly, S.J., and Joe Morton protesting before the Supreme Court.
Courtesy Frida Berrigan

Above: Blood on the Pentagon.
Cornell University, Division of Rare and Manuscript Collections

in Minneapolis, decided that damaging a component intended for a nuclear-armed Trident submarine deserved respect. He used the occasion of sentencing the two defendants who stood before him to deliver a searing condemnation of nuclear weapons and the political inertia that keeps churning them out. Those who inflicted damage to weapons of mass destruction were making, he remarked, "a desperate plea to the American people and its government to stop the military madness which [those being tried] sincerely believe will destroy all of us, friend and enemy alike."

He saw no public good that would be served in putting the defendants behind bars:

As I ponder over the punishment to be meted out to these two people who were attempting to unbuild weapons of mass destruction, we must ask ourselves: Can it be that those of us who build weapons to kill are engaged in a more sanctified endeavor than those who would by their acts attempt to counsel moderation and mediation as an alternative method of settling international disputes? Why are we so fascinated by a power so great that we cannot comprehend its magnitude? What is so sacred about a bomb, so romantic about a missile? Why do we condemn and hang individual killers while extolling the virtues of warmongers? What is that fatal fascination which attracts us to the thought of mass destruction of our brethren in another country?

Announcing that his conscience was clear, Judge Lord sentenced the defendants to six months imprisonment, suspended.[247]

# Room for Disagreement

O n occasion Dan could be painfully thin-skinned, impatient, and sarcastic. It was rare, but there were disagreements that tested friendship to what might have been the breaking point. In one letter I reminded him that friends often hesitated in expressing criticisms or raising hard questions with him: "Your gifts do not include making it easy for friends to say what you are not likely to appreciate hearing."[248] In another: "There is a tendency to think: 'How dare I to raise such questions—I am not finding better ways to tackle this—and I'm not going in and out of prison—so I have no right to object.'"[249]

My hardest encounter with this side of Dan followed a 1985 interview with the *National Catholic Reporter* in which I expressed some reservations about Plowshares actions as a means of promoting disarmament. "I wonder," I had said, "if the damage caused by Plowshare actions makes it any more likely that the people who make the weapons or want them are brought closer to disarmament? If I had a gun and someone damaged or stole it from me, I would be inclined to get another gun and maybe even two. I might be more fear-driven than ever."[250]

Dan took my comments personally and was deeply offended, responding with a letter that went off in my hands like a hand grenade. "If the quotes from you . . .

Dan Berrigan during a visit in Holland.
Jim Forest

Dan and Phil, 1975. Cornell University, Division of Rare and Manuscript Collections

*"Most people are carnivorous. This is more than a casual observation. They don't want you on the program, they want you on the menu. . . . Practically no one has the stomach to love you if you don't love yourself. They just endure you. So do you. . . . You have to be a little insane to avoid going totally bananas today."*
—Ten Commandments for the Long Haul

are substantially accurate," he said, "I think you have seriously hurt our friendship and have been unjust to sister and brother Christians, many of whom are in prison—the cruelest cut of all."[251] In my response I said, "It disturbs me that you are quick to assume the worst and find me 'as austere and harsh as any judge or prosecutor we've ever met with.' I would have hoped for something more tentative." Of course Dan apologized, as I did to him, but repairing our bond took several letters in both directions.

By 1987 Dan also was privately raising questions about the direction of the Plowshares movement. "I sense a loss of the modesty of the first [King of Prussia] enterprise," Dan said in a letter to Phil regarding a recent action, "where the hammers were small, as was the damage in [dollar] terms, the whole thing quite manageable in the explaining, and public understanding easier come by. I felt more peaceableness and equanimity of spirit in discussing those early acts than I do now. I wish we could get things back to base, so to speak. To announce a quarter million in damage is to set the head spinning, and (I think) obscures the intent, which I take it was first of all to induce public awakening through the symbols themselves, rather than to attempt a direct impeding of the [war-making] machine (impossible in any case)."[252]

Though reassured by Phil's response, Dan's letter was one of the rare ones in their correspondence when the brothers were at odds with each other, but not the only one.

Another problem that tested their relationship was Phil's long-running resentment that the spotlight of public attention and admiration fell mainly on Dan. After the two returned from a two-week lecture trip in Germany in May 1989, Phil fired off a letter to Dan in which he complained that he had felt like "an appendage to you, your acolyte or something on that order. The simplest request [to you] for a sweater in that nasty Berlin weather was met with inaction; or [my request for] an English speaking newspaper . . . inaction, too. . . ."[253]

Phil accused Dan of being an inattentive listener. "We [at Jonah House] listen to you with attention, relish, gratitude. You don't listen that well to us, creating a frequent impression [of being] condescending and patronizing. You weren't listening too well in Berlin. And that had me in a quandary, much more so than our [German] friends. Perhaps I'm off the wall in this, perhaps I'm stumbling over my own ego, allowing feelings to create false issues, even unjust ones. If that is so, tell me. Moreover, if certain purple patches of mine are offensive, crude, domineering, tell me. And I'll do my best with them. Coming home on the plane, it seemed sane to conclude that we shouldn't work together again without a better understanding."

In his response a week later, Dan said he had sensed "something was amiss" and was glad Phil had begun the process of clearing the air.

> I've been through some hard times lately, since Germany, as evidently you have too. It's kept me kneeling in prayer as hasn't happened in a long time. Such questions kept troubling, festering: What went wrong on that trek? In what had I offended my brother? I did a long review of conscience, and prayed with all my heart for you, for your family, for myself even, so deep I was in darkness since that evening in Berlin, when the thing broke open. Then your letter.
>
> How could it be, I tormented myself, that two

*"Above all, I would like to be found faithful. . . . In so mad a time, I asked myself, was I to aid and abet my country? Was this the proper function of a Christian, a Jesuit? Or was I to resist my country? And if the latter, to whom could I go with my anger and torment? Who would say to me, 'You must resist'? Who would say, 'Break the iniquitous law; it is a chain on all our limbs'? Who would say, 'Your direction is just; walk it; and I will walk with you'?"*
—Portraits

*"I hope that our no, the no of my brothers, my family, my friends, to the Vietnam war, and our continuing no to the nuclear arms race—that this no is uttered within a larger yes. . . . A yes to all creation and community, to all decency and candor, to all gentleness and courage, to the vast range of human charisms."*

—Portraits

brothers, who so love and respect one another, could have such different views of the same events—almost as though they were receiving and sending signals from two planets? I am still dumbfounded. . . .

Your words about you being my "acolyte" are particularly unfair and leave me bewildered. . . . When a question arose as to who would speak in public I constantly deferred to you. In my mind and conduct, in Berlin you were my equal at every point (as you are in my heart) and my teacher as well.

Why this talk of competition—as though you must declare that your contribution to peace work is equal to mine? For my part, I have no least doubt that your courage and steadfastness are unique. . . . I have no interest in comparing your work with mine, as though we were in a game of winners and losers.

Over the years, I've seen myself perforce as a listener and learner in your regard. This has not always been easy for me, but I've taken that stance, since your opinions on people, politics, peacemaking, etc., are usually offered not as occasions for discussion but as incontrovertible. I seldom if ever feel invited to offer something about my work, my community, my troubles—nor do I often gain the impression I have some something to offer. So I clam up. . . .

When I was trying to get to the question "why me?" it occurred to me that for a long time, I've been a kind of lightning rod for your wrath, never understanding why, yet taking it, letting you shake my bones. But no more, not in Berlin or anywhere.

Dear brother, there's a certain violence that afflicts you. It reminds me of our father, and his way of "taking it out" on his own. In the old days, I used to cringe from him; and later from you; but no more.

Maybe we're also talking about two ways of doing the job we've long ago set our lives to. I learn from your way, or try to, and swallow the differences.

You have much greater trouble accepting mine. And there we are, in [our] mid and late sixties.

You conclude that we can't work together without a better understanding. I agree with all my heart. . . . My own conclusion, after days of prayer and trying to gain some light, is that your treatment of me, and your letter, does you small honor. There are difficulties in your life much deeper than myself. I am small potatoes; a symptom—and at times a victim.[254]

In the collected letters there is no response, but nine months later, shortly before the long-awaited King of Prussia resentencing, Dan again wrote about matters in which their views didn't mesh:

Cornell University, Division of Rare and Manuscript Collections

I've come to think that certain events in our own past . . . are more important than we've allowed. . . . I recall that my worst times . . . (few thank God), are connected with [the issue of] jail time.

Let me start way back, far back as Danbury and your verbal assault on me there, for, as I remember, something to do with my excesses in the visitors' room. As I came through a fog of anguish to understand things, [your] fury had less to do with my peccadillos at the time, than with [your] trying to tell me something very difficult; [your] love for Liz; that in fact you had already married in spirit. I had of course in no way been prepared for this. How could I be? And yet I stood with you both, and the vow you made. . . .

Dan recalled Phil talking about his "demons" and "a particularly hellish jail time" that spring and summer, but added that "it doesn't help me much as to what causes periodic outrage, as far as I can understand it, connected to my life and goings on. To be told, to come to understand, would at least clear the air, which up to this point, is smogged with uncertainty. . . . Right now I think we're

*"My fitful and nightmarish life had finally exposed the betrayal, a false supposition about Jesus, a supposition as powerful as it was universal. Namely, that true knowledge of Jesus could be separated from experience of the cross."* —Portraits

Dan and Phil, 1985. NCR

drifting. I don't understand why or in what I seem to keep offending. Or why such events are always connected with jail. If this is not resolved, I guess we all have to hang out in limbo—a place where I lose you and you me. I wonder why, I wonder what my sins are. Why do you on occasion grow so furious at me? What can we do to come to a better love, a better friendship? Why am I periodically in the way of this?"

In contrast with Phil, Dan favored an approach in the pending King of Prussia Plowshares appeal that would aim at shorter rather than longer sentences:

There are the deepest reasons I know of, in the lives of [our codefendants] Dean [Hammer] and John [Schuchardt] and myself to fight this latest legal lynching. I've nearly died in jail; whether it is a good thing for me to return there, and almost inevitably have to be plucked from there, is another question that gives pause. Whether jail time is good for Phil, and for Jonah House, is something I question as well, for reasons above. For my part, I'll fight being jailed. To the last ditch.

If the Plowshares prisoners and the peace movement don't understand, so much the worse. But I believe our friends in jail will, if we speak honestly about our situations. What the future holds as to better or worse times to be locked up, I leave to God. Meantime I have good work to do, in or out. As do all of us. Innumerable ways, as your letter says, of giving life and liberty. This is the clumsy best I can do, for now. . . .[255]

*"In a sense that makes sense to me, my friends are already delivered. They are delivered from fear and trembling before the power of the state; also from inertia and moral amnesia. They are fit subjects for the miracle we call resurrection."*
—Essential Writings

Dan's last letter must have helped; Phil gave way to Dan's counsel. In the twelve years of letters that followed, there are many expressions of love, gratitude, and mutual respect, but I have the impression that some of the deeper issues that troubled them remained unresolved.

# Listener of Last Resort

In 1978 Dan learned of St. Rose's Home, a hospice for destitute patients dying of cancer, from a young Catholic Worker friend who was serving there as an orderly. St. Rose's founder was Rose Hawthorne Lathrop, daughter of Nathaniel Hawthorne, the novelist best known for *The Scarlet Letter*. In 1896, following the death of her husband and her conversion to Catholicism, Rose Hawthorne moved into a slum tenement in New York's Lower East Side and began providing nursing care for penniless neighbors afflicted with cancer. A community of similarly minded women gradually took shape. St. Rose's, now operated by the Hawthorne Dominican Sisters, is today one of three such homes in the United States.

St. Rose's Home.

"I was in the usual spinning orbit of teaching, writing, and pilgrimaging to the Pentagon to throw ashes and blood at the idols," Dan wrote. "Something was lacking; whether true icons, physical work, or still testing. I phoned the sister in charge. Could I hire out as a part-time volunteer?"[256]

For four years Dan was a familiar presence at St. Rose's, helping patients—referred to as guests by the nuns and staff—in whatever way was needful. He listened, talked, shared silences, made beds, cleaned, prayed, and met relatives and friends of those being cared for. Being at St. Rose's "keeps me sane," he told me in a letter. "I am a bit exhausted by it all but immensely grateful for the un-utterably beautiful presence and glances of the dying."[257]

In an interview, Dan described his usual activities: "I appear at bedside, hold their hands, ready for what-ever service seems required or helpful. They can take me or leave me, as can the nuns, orderlies, families. I do not bring the holy oils, or administer the sacrament of the sick, or give communion, except on special occasions. . . . I come and go, a kind of marginal figure in that shell-shocked lunar, no-person land which is laid claim to by both life and death."[258]

"I don't know whether you have ever smelled can-cer," Dan once remarked to a reporter, "cancer of the nose, cancer of the face, which is the most terrible to look upon and to smell; cancer of the brain; cancer of the lungs. We see it all, smell it all, hold it all in our arms."[259]

I visited St. Rose's one night and was stunned by the spectral nighttime noise. The guests were asleep or trying to sleep. The dominant sound came from scarecrow bod-ics struggling to breathe, every breath a Herculean labor. Each breath ended with a question mark: was that the last one?

In *We Die before We Live: Talking with the Very Ill*, a book about his work at St. Rose's and some of those whom he came to know as a volunteer orderly, Dan stressed that what the nuns and their helpers did for their guests was done gratis: "In payment for such care, such friendship, no money crossed the palm. No guest paid, no one could pay. It was a rule of the order, strictly ad-hered to. It struck me: here we had a stunning instance of the ethical cemented into natural law. The rule was all but metaphysical: no money." It went even further—not a penny was received from insurance companies or from city, state, or federal sources.

"Who could have believed it?" Dan asked. What a contrast with the surrounding world, where "things which should be available to all inevitably cost a great deal. The few things which are still free of price tags are pol-

*"You don't have to be poor in America to die badly. You just have to be dying; the rest is sup-plied. And by 'dying badly,' I don't refer to immediate physical care, on which, bad or good, the rich have the usual monopoly Let me speak of the obverse, 'dying well,' as St. Rose's has helped me understand the term. 'Dying well' implies a sense of one's self, a hand on the rudder, a mind that despite rip tides and near swamping is reasonably able to give and take, to read signals and send them out. . . .'"*

—We Die Before We Live

luted: air, parks, vistas. But in any sane scheme of things, that almost unimaginable world that shone on our retinas like a mirage, like the kingdom of God, would not good medical care be free to all?"[260]

sojo.net

The nuns' guests were the very people, Dan reflected, "whom I see on the subway and bus en route to the hospital: the working poor. Now and again, we greet a different guest of the days of the tolling bell—a kind of sub-subway person, a prisoner, an addict, alcoholic, a classic outsider, outside the economy, outside the social contract. In either case, poor or outcast, the people we serve have only the most tenuous handhold on America. They have lived and are about to die at the edge of almost everything that constitutes the Dream: money, profession, opportunity, the upward escalator. . . . The moorings that bind these lives to the mainland have never been that firm; now they are slipped with ease. There is detachment in the air, good humor, even a sense of celebration at times. . . . Up to the final letting go, the prelude is not depression or damp; it is sunny, warm of will."[261]

For Dan, care of the dying was another form of peacemaking—a reconnecting of near and far, us and them, friend and enemy, the loved and unloved, the well and the ill, the seen and the unseen.

Dan regarded what he saw dry-eyed. "We corrupt our sense of reality by sentimentalizing it," he said. "The abstractions poison the soul, reduce our lives and deaths to market commodities, subject death itself to the technicians of death, whether psychological or technological. It is all, in fact, one: the brutalizing of ourselves, the degradation of language. I am trying to suggest that we are inevitably sentimental until we become political, especially in matters of life and death. Our understanding, our car-

*"A bitter truth. We, our children, our fair land . . . are all endangered. . . . Only an act of God can snatch us from the folly of death, universal, self-inflicted. . . . The act of God is simply a covenant in which, hand in hand, we bespeak our trust in God, our stake in the world and its creatures, in truthful living and good outcome. Come what may. The act of God is enacted by us, here and now, each day; or it is not."*

—We Die Before We Live

ing, are summoned to embrace the fate of all, the common weal and woe. And when, at length, our sense of death has reached outward to embrace the enemy, the stranger, the outcast, dissolving petty differences and distance, and declared its peace with all creation—at that point we may claim a human sense that is something more than a threat or a bared weapon. And in the instance of cancer, such a sense allows us to travel gracefully from fact to metaphor. Better still, to oscillate between the two, touching each pole, the cancer close at hand, the dying across the world; the cancer at St. Rose's, the dying, the perennial dying of [cancer of] the survivors of Hiroshima."

The sentence, "I am trying to suggest that we are inevitably sentimental until we become political, especially in matters of life and death," calls for comment. I once asked Dan what he meant by the word "political." I couldn't recall him ever voting. He pursed his lips and widened his eyes, then said, "I don't mean party politics. I have a hard time telling Republican from Democrat. They are in unity when it comes to killing the current enemy and compete to outspend each other on methods of killing. I mean politics in the Greek sense, 'affairs of the city,' that is, matters that concern everyone. For example, war—war and killing, widows and orphans."

In 1981 an unknown illness, a year later named AIDS, was first clinically observed in the United States. The beginning of what would become a pandemic, it was to shift Dan from St. Rose's Home to St. Vincent's Hospital, ground zero for New York's AIDS crisis.

In its first thirty-five years, AIDS has taken the lives of 35 million people and still kills by the thousands every month, especially in regions where medication is unavailable or unaffordable. Gay men have been the hardest hit, but are far from alone in their suffering.

In 1984 Dan met a young Jesuit, William Hart McNichols, today a well-known iconographer, who was then one of the rare Catholic priests working with AIDS patients.

*"In those early ventures of mine among the sick, almost everything was in the nature of a first, clumsy try: would one be welcome, would one be shown the door? How would one be received? How would a greeting, even an innocuous statement, be taken? It was all quite chancy. So much had to be a matter of faith, on both sides."*
—To Dwell in Peace

"I was waiting for a subway train at the 59th Street station," McNichols recalls. "The train arrived, the doors opened, and there was Dan Berrigan looking like a homeless leprechaun rather than the fierce prophet I had imagined when reading his books. . . . Swaying on the center pole, I introduced myself, then sat down next to him, and there our friendship began. I quickly discovered that Dan was fascinated by what I was doing and interested in working with the St. Vincent's Hospice. I put him in contact with Sister Patrice Murphy, who headed the project. She was delighted to have him lend a helping hand. Dan was at home with everyone and brought his great gifts of companionship and joyful affection to so many men and women with AIDS."[262]

Fr. William Hart McNichols. Courtesy W.H. McNichols

Dan started volunteering a day each week at St. Vincent's in July 1984. For twelve years he walked the wards talking with AIDS patients and getting to know them, available to all but keeping an eye out for those who had no family or friends coming to visit. Many of the patients were children or kids in their teens. "The work at the [St. Vincent's] hospice is emotionally tough," he said in a letter to Phil, "more so than it was at St. Rose's, where older people dying seemed more in the course of nature and easier to take."[263]

It was an undertaking that had ever-expanding borders in Dan's life. The poet Denise Levertov told this story of Dan:

A friend of mine in New York City, a young man who had been my student, then my secretary, and then my continuing dear friend, had AIDS, and I felt

NEW YORK CITY **REMEMBERS**

## AIDS CANDLELIGHT VIGIL
### CENTRAL PARK BANDSHELL
### AT 72nd STREET
Sponsored by AIDS RESOURCE CENTER

DEDICATED TO THE MEMORY OF MICHAEL HIRSCH, EDWARD MURPHY, AND ALL WHO HAVE DIED OF AIDS

## JUNE 17, 1989 at 7:30 PM

Flyer for an AIDS vigil: Art by William Hart McNichols

that—so many friends of his, including his partners having died—he was much too isolated. I decided to ask Dan to put him in touch with some AIDS assistance service. . . . Steve was not a Catholic, but I felt he would be responsive to any practical suggestions Dan might offer. . . . The very day he received my letter Dan called him, much to Steve's astonishment and gratification, and not long afterward, when Steve was hospitalized, visited him. Steve died almost the next day.[264]

Maureen McCafferty made contact with Dan in 1985 when her former husband was dying of AIDS. "There weren't too many clergy ministering to these men in those days but Dan was," Maureen recalled. "He came to visit Paul on several occasions, brought him communion, said Mass, and made Paul feel safe enough that he died peacefully." Maureen and Dan became good friends. In the years that followed, they often had meals together, some cooked by Dan, some by Maureen. Maureen was one of the four people with Dan when he died.

Via a parent or sister or nun or friend, a spouse or former spouse, names and addresses of the AIDS afflicted had a way of making their way to Dan. One visit tended to lead to another until death intervened. A typical first sentence: "I heard from so-and-so that you were ill and thought I would drop by and see how it's going." He never identified himself as "Father Daniel," just Dan. "I wanted to make it as clear as possible that I was seeking no conversions or last-minute confessions," he told me. Dan often presided at funerals of people whom he had met only months or weeks before. He described himself as "a listener of last resort."

Catholic Worker Carl Siciliano recalls Dan "brought gifts, arriving with flowers or cookies, books, a milkshake, a container of clam chowder . . . He invites [his newfound friends] to meals at his apartment when they are healthy enough for the journey uptown. He takes them to restaurants. He invites one man living as a guest in someone's tiny spare room to stay in his apartment while he spends some weeks teaching at a distant university. He invites another man to stay at a cottage he has use of on Block Island to escape a brutal heat wave, but alas when the time came the man had become too ill for the journey. . . . As the men grew sicker he fed and bathed them. He washed their soiled clothes. He panicked when they did not answer their phones. He sat with them for hours in the hospital as they declined. Talking with them while they still have the ability to communicate, offering silent companionship when they are rendered unable to speak. Often merely holding their hands . . . The suffering that comes upon his friends is horrific. Some became covered in lesions. Some went blind. Some are rendered unable to eat or suffered from endless diarrhea."[265]

These were the years when to have AIDS was, to many whose idea of God centered more on hell than heaven, proof positive that the victims were leading notorious lives and fully deserved their suffering. Especially in the early years, it was a disease many preferred not to call by name, an illness that, in Dan's words, "carries a baleful light of the supernatural . . . mated with deviant conduct, conjuring up dark corners where the unspeakable festers away."[266]

Often the people Dan met had been raised Catholic but had become estranged, feeling the Church had judged them great sinners and abandoned them. "The pilot who drops bombs on homes and hospitals is lauded as a patriot and model citizen and is welcome to receive communion in any church," Dan told me, "but the man who has loved the wrong person in the wrong way is seen as deserving of every agony."

One of the patients Dan befriended was Luke—a master chef, trained in France, owner of a restaurant in Brooklyn—who one day, three years before Dan entered his life, discovered he was bearing the AIDS virus. When

*"The gods of death. Their tactic is the breaking down of the promise of immunity from death, the immunity that we name faith, or grace, or love of God, or one another. Let no one be immune! Let hearts be hardened. Let compassion be obliterated. Let all be persuaded, by hook and crook, by bomb and brutality, that death is, in effect, a good way of life."*
—To Dwell in Peace

Dan met him, Luke's immune system was in ruins. He had both cancer and pneumonia. "Luke's hospital room was altogether familiar," Dan wrote. "I could have entered it blindfolded."

Luke was one of the fortunate ones; he hadn't been abandoned. His parents were almost daily visitors, and his parish priest frequently dropped in. All were bewildered. What could anyone say, the priest or Dan or the parents or Luke? Silence and small talk were far more merciful than pious slogans and deathbed clichés.

"In Luke's best moments he was accepting," Dan wrote, "taking what came with a laconic, understanding nobility." On the way to the elevator, Luke's mother asked if her son would die "a good Catholic"—could Dan see to that? "Know it or not," Dan later wrote, "the son was already seeing to that. On his own, with their goodness at his side."

To everyone's surprise, Luke survived that particular hospital stay, returning home to his apartment in Manhattan's Chelsea neighborhood. "There he held court, gray-faced, his hair a mere scrap of coarse straw, but on his face a smile that turned the heart over. . . . No giving up." Violating the dietitian's orders, Dan had brought along a wedge of Luke's favorite cheese, brie. "I'm not supposed to have it," said Luke, "but what the hell."

A few days later Luke was back in the hospital— Dan the first to get the news. "Within days," Dan wrote, "Luke was in better hands than ours. Faith, though blind with tears, assures us it is so."

"In the evening we shall be judged by love," Dan wrote in *Sorrow Built a Bridge*. The words were borrowed from St. John of the Cross. It was a sentence also dear to Dorothy Day, who used an even more compact translation: "Love is the measure." After Luke's death the words came back to Dan. "I think of Luke and of what a mild and gentle judgment his will be. My friend will be judged by love. Which is to say he will not be judged but embraced."[267]

*"I need to be saved. I must be saved, lest I be pounded into a shape of moral bafflement, the misshape of normalized abnormality. A shape that resembles no true history and tradition; but only violence and its offspring, its purveyors, its yea-sayers. I cannot do this on my own, save myself. . . . No, I must be salvaged by others. By grace, by Christ. Saved, from 'the times, which are evil.' So it is said in Scripture, a news simply put, in terms one can take or leave. And despite all, as I believe, good news."* —To Dwell in Peace

# Life at West 98th Street

After leaving Danbury Prison in 1972, Dan developed ties with the West Side Jesuit Community living at 220 West 98th Street, a World War II–era twelve-story building just off Broadway. About seventy-five Jesuits were then in residence. Later on the neighborhood was gentrified, but in the seventies it was a down-at-the-heels area in which muggings were not uncommon and drug dealers easy to find. In 1973 Dan moved in and remained there until 2009, when rent increases forced the community, then shrunk to about twenty, to move. For the many years it lasted, the community at West 98th Street provided Dan with his first long-term home since joining the Society of Jesus.

In 1973, when Dan first brought me there to visit, he was clearly delighted to be part of a Jesuit household in which he felt genuinely welcome. No more cold shoulder, no more changed locks, no more possessions in boxes outside the front door. Showing me around, he brought me to a spacious area that had been converted into a common room with many couches arranged to facilitate conversations. Off to one side was a dining area. I was welcome to have a meal there any evening, Dan told me. "Be here by 6:15. The cook leaves the food on steam heaters and we take turns washing the dishes." In the back was a television room, isolated so that it wouldn't disturb anyone. It was all quite homey, even if institutional.

220 West 98th St. in New York City.
Robert Ellsberg

Walls in Dan's apartment, adorned with art and photographs.
John Dear

Yet it was evident that Dan also felt a trace of guilt in the relative comfort in which the Jesuits were living. The common room included a nautically themed, well-stocked bar such as one might find in a small Manhattan hotel, except this one lacked a cash register. "If this is the holy poverty," Dan remarked, "bring on the holy chastity!"

"Dan first lived in apartment 7J," John Dear tells me, "sharing it with Bob Keck, Bob Springer, Jack McSherry, and Fred O'Connor, an older Jesuit who was a spiritual director. Dan's room there was twelve-by-twelve feet with a window looking out on a brick wall. I lived in it in 1987 and couldn't believe that, at the height of his fame, Dan lived in that tiny room. Then in 1982 he moved into apartment 11L. It gradually filled with art. There was a table for dinner, chairs for guests, and a wall of books. In the bedroom he had his desk and a computer. Next to the low, narrow bed was a wall of photos of friends and saints that he called his "nonwailing wall." There was a small kitchen decorated with serigraphs made by his friend Corita Kent. Last but not least, his bathroom was papered with photos and magazine covers plus pages of the Oval Office transcripts in which he and Phil were mentioned—Nixon and White House chief of staff Bob Haldeman discussing the Berrigans, Haldeman wondering where the Berrigans got their money for legal defense and Nixon responding, 'They're loaded, they've got millions.'"

Fellow Jesuit Luke Hansen recalls the environment as he encountered it during his first meeting with Dan: "It was easy to recognize his apartment door—it was covered with slogans [one of which declared], 'When Jesus said love your enemies he probably meant don't kill them.' . . . Inside his door rested a beautiful wood sculpture of Franz Jägerstätter crushing the Nazi swastika. On the wall, there were photos of Dan sitting with Thomas Merton; Dan being arrested with Martin Sheen; the last photo taken of Phil; a photo of Phil, Liz, and their oldest child, Frida; and a courtroom drawing of the King of Prussia Eight turning their backs on the judge."

John Dear provides a brief account of Dan's daily rhythm at the time: "Dan spent about thirty minutes in silence and prayer every morning, sitting in the presence of Jesus, of God, with his own soul, as he would say. Then by 9 a.m. he would start writing and write till noon. After a light lunch, he always took a walk, either to Central Park or along the Hudson River, sometimes with a friend. If he had a visitor who wanted to speak with him, he might meet the visitor at 3 or 4. Then he would join the Jesuit community for evening Eucharist and dinner in the common room. At every Mass Dan always prayed the same intention: 'For the prisoners of conscience, we pray: Hear us, O Lord.' In the late evening, Bob Keck or myself would visit him, have a drink, and talk about life and the world."[268]

A vivid account of living under the same roof with Dan comes from Don Moore, priest, professor of theology at Fordham, and head of the 98th Street Jesuit Community. Dan was, said Moore, "disturbing, demanding, and delightful . . . a constant disturber of community living whether at community celebrations of the Eucharist, monthly community meetings, semi-annual weekends away, or our occasional week-long retreats together."[269]

One of Dan's "disturbing" traits was his habit of "re-

*PSALM 119*

*A double heart be far from me,*
 *Lord*
*I love your commands*
*my hope is your promise*

*A lying tongue be far from me*
*I love your promise*
*my hope is your law*

*Far from me a violent will*
*your will is my hope*
*I love your commands*

*To witness your law*
*to love your commands*
*be my first love.*

*—Uncommon Prayer*

phrasing simple questions, pointing out something we had overlooked, or suggesting other aspects of a problem that tend to shatter our accustomed and comfortable way of viewing our community life or of dealing with outside issues. We suddenly find ourselves treating the given agenda in a much different way. Who are we as Jesuits? What is our purpose as community? Why are we living together? . . . Where are we in our prayer together? What more can we be doing for one another, for our Jesuit province, for the Society, for the church, and, most important, for our world, our city, and our sisters and brothers who live in this neighborhood, a neighborhood where half the funerals are for victims of AIDS?"

Dan was, Moore continued, "constantly bringing us back to the fundamentals of our Jesuit and religious life."

Though connected to many communities, the community Dan most relied on for support and encouragement was the household of Jesuits with whom he lived. Moore recalled how much it meant to Dan if even one member of the community managed to be present for a hearing, trial, demonstration, or poetry reading. Dan compelled those living with him to ask themselves how they could be of greater support to him "in his various endeavors, in the risks he undertakes for us all. How can we be more involved with him and for him? And the obvious corollary of such questioning: How can we manifest greater support and love and concern for one another? Dan is indeed a disturber of community life; he is a reminder of the enormous responsibility that comes with community living."

Dan didn't allow his housemates "the luxury of viewing community simply as something we slide into as a matter of convenience; it is, after all, something we choose for our own sake, for the world's sake, for the sake of the greater glory of God." To live in community with Dan was "to recognize the basic driving force of his life, as well as the basic driving force in that community's life. To be with him in any kind of faith sharing, speaking of

*"The only Jesuits who look me up or want to talk seriously are by and large third world types, beats, people in personal turmoil at the misdirection, misfirings, injustices, concrete impasse of things. I can't offer them much except a certain wry skill in surviving the Sillys on Stilts. I'm still around; not much more."*
—Ten Commandments for the
Long Haul

The 98th St. Jesuit community.
Courtesy Benincasa

our own experiences of prayer, or simply relating where we are in our own Jesuit lives, is to recognize how much he strives to discern and to respond to the promptings of the Spirit in his own life."

Through all such "disturbances," Moore reflected, Dan "helped us to confront the demands that community life should be making upon each one of us." In Dan's mind, it was everyone's responsibility if someone was "shouldering a burden alone, whether overwork; change of ministry; difficulties with superiors; problems of loneliness, self-doubt, or discouragement; or, perhaps of greatest importance, being confronted with a terminal illness. These are problems that also concern community."

Moore recalled the way Dan had restructured his life in the period when one member of the community, Lew Cox, was suffering from cancer, of which he died in December 1986. "Because of the understanding of community that Dan had so strongly helped to engender, it was clear from the first diagnosis of Lew's inoperable cancer that this was a community problem, a community concern, a community commitment. The community to a man, led in many ways by Dan, rallied around Lew; we would be with him to the very end." Cox's diagnosis had resulted from an exploratory operation performed on Ash Wednesday, 1986. During Cox's eight remaining months, "Dan was continually a model of care, concern and compassion. It almost seemed that the months and years he had spent in volunteer assistance to those dying of cancer and of AIDS were in reality a preparation for leading us in our care for Lew. These were days and weeks of intense and profound community living. In his homily at Lew's funeral, Dan talked about his last Eucharist with Lew less than forty-eight hours before his death. They had talked and prayed together over Mark's rendition of the storm at sea and the obvious parallels with the cancer that was slowly sapping Lew's many vital energies, providing a unique opportunity for faith and hope in God's saving power."

John Dear and Dan on the ferry to Block Island. Courtesy John Dear

Within the 98th Street community, each member's problems were, to the extent that he wished, the community's problems. "This is as it should be; we are not alone, and we are all, in St. Paul's terms, ministers of reconciliation. This community attitude is due in no small way to Dan's persistence in urging us to meet the demands of our living together. I am convinced that every member [of the community] is today a better Jesuit because of Dan's presence in our midst."

Last but far from least, Moore found living with Dan in community was "in so many ways sheer delight. Just as he can be disturbing and demanding, he can also abruptly relieve our tension. Many a long evening session has ended with one of his favorite interventions: 'Enough of serious talk—we all deserve a drink!' And the ensuing hour or so of relaxation helps us all to grasp a bit more clearly and personally whatever the topics of our discussion had been."

One of the blessings Dan brought to community life was his transformation, on weekends when he wasn't away, into Daniel the gourmet chef. "I'm sure each Jesuit in the community has more than once received the message from Dan: 'I'm having a few friends in for supper Sunday evening. Why not join us?' The 'friends' may turn out to be other Jesuits or anyone from Ramsey Clark to Martin Sheen to members of Pax Christi or the Catholic Worker to a neighbor dying of AIDS." On such evenings, one could "count not only on gourmet cooking but gourmet conversations." This was, Moore noted, "Dan's way of saying to each one of us: 'Hey, you are really significant in my life.'"

William Hart McNichols remembers how greatly he admired Dan as a writer and poet and yet avoided meeting him for fear of "Dan Berrigan, the fire-breathing prophet." "Later, when I moved into the same Jesuit community on 98th Street," McNichols recalls, "I discovered how much fun Dan could be. All my projected fears and categories just dissolved. Here was a real prophet and a man who could also be a great and loyal friend."

But even at 98th Street, there had been a few who would have been relieved to see Dan move elsewhere or even be expelled from the Society of Jesus. McNichols comments on the antipathy Dan awoke in some of his fellow Jesuits:

I also saw, at times, some hostile people around him hurling their projections, sins of omission, and competition at this gentle man. The main reason, it seemed to me, was that he had been given the "Joseph coat." This ambiguous favor of father-to-son from the book of Genesis brought the original Joseph nothing but jealousy and separation. It wasn't enough that Dan-

*APARTMENT 11-L*

*These are the rooms I go from.*
*An angel commands it; Go from here.*
*I go*
*to break the bones of death, to crack*
*the code of havocking dreams. I go*
*    from here*
*to judgment, to judges*
*by Rouault, Daumier, Goya,*
*their hammer crack of doom.*
*I go. Then I'm told*
*by a guardian angel of the rooms*
*    I'm told—*
*When you go from here*
*faces of those you love*
*turn to the wall, and weep.*
*I have an angel's word.*

*And when I return*
*older, sad at times, so little of death*
*    undone*
*despite all sacrifice and rage*
*Lo, something savory, exotic*
*steams in a pot, the table fitly laid.*

*And the typewriter's iron mask*
*melts in a smile, and the keys*
*like a lover's hands*
*compose a love letter;*
*Welcome. Believe. Endure.*

                        *—A Sunday in Hell*

iel Berrigan was lauded as a great writer, poet, and theologian, but now he was a symbol, an archetype, a sometimes maligned and unwilling prophet. All this, to say the least, was a heavy coat for him to bear. It still seems to me that this obvious gift (even to his enemies) of the coat of many talents, a sign of the Father's love and promise, is what stirs up people the most. But Dan's life struggling with the scriptures, and then feeding others with what he finds, is food to him. This living prayer nurtures him, soothes the despair, and calls him to continue his many creative ways of peacemaking under the benediction of the Savior: "How blessed are the peacemakers; they shall be recognized as the children of God."[270]

But the great majority of those living at 98th Street felt blessed to have Dan's presence, and it was mutual. A healthy community life revives and refreshes its members, Dan wrote to Phil in August 1991: "Someone said last night at Ignatius Day liturgy that he felt he was growing younger rather than older. He put the reversal down to the fine community we have here. As Poppa would say, I subscribe to that. Or, put me down for fifty."[271]

At the time, Dan was seventy. He had been a Jesuit for fifty-two years.

Though Dan's life on West 98th Street was comfortable, there were many nights when he chose discomfort. "Throughout the 1980s," John Dear bears witness, "once a month Dan spent a night in the local homeless shelter run by the Holy Family Franciscan Church. Two people would manage everything—set up the cots, put out the blankets, get the coffee and food ready, open the doors at six, get everyone to bed at eight, get everyone up at six, prepare coffee and breakfast, manage the showers and finally at half past eight, when the parish school would begin, close the shelter down for the day. The shelter had beds for fifty. Dan never talked about this—few knew about it. Its one expression was a book he entitled *Stations*,[272] a set of poems

*"The tormented, lost wanderers of our city are all about us; they huddle, sleep, awaken, stagger about, hold out their beggar hands. We wear their presence like a great societal shroud—our own. In them that other city, a city of shame, stirs to life. Day and night. . . . The homeless live out, in dreadful, literal detail, the poverty we would rather conceal—from God, from ourselves. They are icons of the 'other side' of ourselves; they are icons of modern life turned inside out. That shroud again, its seams and rents shamefully exposed."*
—Stations: The Way of the Cross

about the homeless walking the stations of the cross."

Dan had a place of retreat—Block Island, a comma of land just ten miles square anchored between the coast of Rhode Island and the eastern tip of Long Island. For many years its permanent population, not quite a thousand people, included lawyer and theologian William Stringfellow and poet Tony Towne. The two described themselves as lay monastics. Their house achieved status as a footnote

John Dear and Dan at Block Island.
Courtesy John Dear

in history for having been Dan Berrigan's hideout at the very end of his season of avoiding the FBI. Following his release from Danbury in 1972, Dan returned to the Stringfellow-Towne home once or twice every year until 2010; in the years that followed, he was too frail for the journey.

In the early 1980s, his hosts built Dan his own small house on a field overlooking the ocean, a cabin of gray wood in the New England tradition, with a deck around it. It had a high ceiling with dark wooden beams, dark wood for the floor, a handmade wooden desk, bookshelves, a wood-burning stove, a kitchen area in one corner, as well as a bathroom and a cell-like bedroom, the walls of which served as a photo album of family and friends. On a white wall of the main room Dan wrote a prayer:

Where the house
dares
stand
at Land's End
and the sea

Block Island house, where Dan often stayed. Jim Keane

turns in sleep
ponderous menacing
and our spirit fails and runs
—landward seaward askelter—
we pray You
protect
from the law's
clawed
outreach
from the Second Death
from Envy's Tooth
from Doom's Great Knell
all
who dwell here.

Written beneath was a steadily expanding list of names of those who had made use of the house—friends, family, fellow Jesuits, pilgrims, exhausted activists, guests suffering from AIDS, honeymooners. . . .

As a Jesuit, Dan could own no substantial property, so Stringfellow offered the cabin to his order. As the Society didn't want it, a trust, the Eschaton Foundation, was set up by Stringfellow. Meanwhile, so long as he was able, use and care of the house was in Dan's hands.

"Dan went there every year, sometimes twice a year, staying normally for about ten days," John Dear recalls. "In the early years he went on his own, in the last decade or so, with me or Bob Keck or both of us. We would get rooms in town. Dan spent many hours sitting on the deck, doing nothing but read, write, and be silent. Or he would walk down the cliff to the beach. It was here that Dan wrote much of his poetry."

Dan loved his retreat on Block Island—it was his micro-hermitage. But 220 West 98th Street was home. "If I could live anywhere in the world," he told Robert Ellsberg when they were walking nearby, "it would be in this city, in this neighborhood, on this block."

# The Mission

I n 1985, not long after returning from travels in El Salvador and Nicaragua, filmmaker Roland Joffé came to Dan's apartment with a proposal: would he take part in a forthcoming movie about the Jesuit missions in Latin America in the eighteenth century? After consulting with his provincial, Dan agreed. Through much of the spring and summer of 1985—April through August—Dan was in Colombia, Argentina, Brazil, and Paraguay for the filming of *The Mission*, directed by Joffé, written by Robert Bolt and starring Robert De Niro and Jeremy Irons, with Liam Neeson in a supporting role. Dan served as an adviser and also played the part of a Jesuit priest, Father Sebastian.

Inspired by historical events in which Jesuits had participated, the drama and Dan were well matched. Though appearing in many scenes, Dan's only spoken line, appropriately, was the word "no." But his most important contributions to the production were off-camera. He worked closely with both principal actors, in Irons's case even doing a weekend retreat with him (a very compact version of St. Ignatius Loyola's Spiritual Exercises) and, on another occasion, fasting with him for a day. Dan celebrated Mass for those actors and crew members who wished to take part. He also helped in the development of several key scenes.

The film, set in the mid-eighteenth century, involves

*"As to the thing with DeNiro and Joffe, they came here one night with the project which I liked. They put me through my traces here, and I like them, and I think's coming through. I'd like to show the world what a Jesuit like the one Bolt portrays might look like—since at least in this rare land, there doesn't seem to be a plethora of same."*
—Dan to Phil, February 5, 1985

*"Let us not hesitate to invoke the martyrs. They preferred living acts to dead symbols. For this we honor them.*

*They risked death at the hands of the violent, rather than compromising and pussyfooting. For this we honor them. . . .*

*They named the idols, for our sake also. For this we honor them.*

*They endured in a tranquil spirit obloquy and contempt, from Christians and others, oligarchs, bishops, politicians. For this we honor them."*

—Testimony

a Spanish Jesuit priest, Father Gabriel (played by Jeremy Irons), who enters the western Paraguayan jungle to establish a mission station and convert a native Guarani community to Christianity. Risking martyrdom, Gabriel travels to the towering Iguazu Falls, makes the perilous climb to the top, and—aware he is being watched by unseen faces—plays his oboe as if he were in Eden. Captivated by the music, the Guarani warriors spare his life and take him to their village. The seed of a mission is planted.

The film jumps forward several years. The mission is now established, in every sense a success but also an object of envy to the colonists. We meet slaver Rodrigo Mendoza (played by Robert De Niro), a man who abducts native people and sells them to plantation owners. After returning from a kidnapping raid, he discovers his fiancée making love to his brother and kills him in a duel. Though acquitted of murder, Mendoza sinks into severe depression for what he regards as his commission of an unforgivable sin. In the movie's pivotal scene, Gabriel visits Mendoza and challenges him to embrace a healing penance: coming to the aid of the very people he had been enslaving. With Mendoza's assent, a resurrection begins. Mendoza accompanies Gabriel and several other Jesuits on their return to the Guarani village while dragging behind him a self-imposed burden—the heavy armor and sword that represent his former life. There are tense moments when the Guarani recognize Mendoza, but after seeing him in his humbled state and in the company of Father Gabriel, one of them cuts away his penitential load in a gesture of forgiveness. Astounded by the Guaranis' absolution and acceptance, Mendoza decides not only to help the Guarani but to become a Jesuit.

Such Jesuit missions actually existed. Under Spanish rule, these had been enclaves of relative security in which slavery was banned, but the Treaty of Madrid of 1750 reapportioned Latin America. The missions would now be on land ruled by Portugal, under which slavery was legal.

Cardinal Altamirano is sent to survey the missions, but even if he attempts to protect them, the Guarani are certain to be enslaved anyway. If the Jesuits resist, the entire order faces suppression.[273]

At Gabriel's invitation, the cardinal visits the mission and is amazed at the Guarani's industry, artistry, musical talent, and spiritual vitality. Even so, he sees no alternative but to close the mission and instructs the Guarani that they must leave, describing this as "God's will." The Guarani leader challenges his claim, arguing, "It was God's will to develop the mission. Does God change his mind?" Despite the threat of excommunication, Gabriel and Mendoza choose to remain with the Guarani even in the face of attack, but they are divided on how to respond. Gabriel rejects violence as a violation of the Gospel while Mendoza decides, along with many of the Guarani men, to defend the mission with weapons.

When a colonist army attacks, the Guarani warriors prove no match for the rifle- and cannon-armed soldiers. After Mendoza is fatally wounded, the soldiers enter the village, but upon seeing the unarmed women and children within the church, the soldiers are reluctant to fire. Carrying a monstrance containing the consecrated bread of the Blessed Sacrament, Gabriel leads the unarmed people toward the attackers. Undeterred, the colonial commander orders a renewed assault. Gabriel, together with many of

Dan on the set of *The Mission*.
Cornell University, Division of Rare and Manuscript Collections

Dan and Jeremy Irons.
Cornell University, Division of Rare and Manuscript
Collections

the Guarani, is gunned down. After his death, a child picks up the Blessed Sacrament and leads the procession, only also to be shot. A handful of Guarani escape into the jungle. Days later, several young survivors return to the scene of the massacre and salvage a few belongings, including a violin, then set off up the river, going deeper into the jungle. A final title declares that many priests continue to struggle for the rights of indigenous people. The text of John 1:5 is displayed: "The light shineth in the darkness, and the darkness hath not overcome it."

Throughout the filming, Dan kept a journal, later published as *The Mission*,[274] that combined observations about local culture; the Guarani tribe who play themselves; the cast and crew; the history of the Church in Latin America; the Jesuits in that early, more radical period of their history; and his own part in helping prepare the actors, especially Irons and De Niro, for key scenes. Martin Sheen thought Dan's diary "one of the best books on filmmaking" he had ever read.

Dan helped Joffé rethink the film's ending. Scriptwriter Robert Bolt had imagined Gabriel and those with him simply being murdered as they prayed on their knees in the mission church. The idea of Gabriel leading a eucharistic procession toward the soldiers was Dan's—an active nonviolent response instead of passivity. Dan described it as "a gesture of faith"[275] that "confronts the worst and evokes the best in the massed adversaries."[276] The choice for both Mendoza and Gabriel, Dan noted, "is quite simple—how one is to die, with gun in hand . . . or sacrament in hand."[277]

One of the film's central issues is nonviolence versus violence, a topic rarely addressed by Hollywood. The film, Dan notes, "refuses to take sides. No one is condemned or vindicated; the angel of death hangs over criminal and virtuous alike. . . . In the matter of death there are no exemptions, only differences, but the differences are of moment, the film dares to hint."[278]

Dan also respected the film's attempt to highlight an

extraordinary effort undertaken by Jesuits to defy colonial ambitions: "The actors are attempting something audacious, miming the incandescent spirits of Jesuits who blazed a path through the eighteenth-century jungle of ignorance, lust and avarice and create so splendid a utopia on behalf of others. . . . One still gasps in wonderment." But colonial Europe would not permit such an endeavor to survive: "The Jesuits, along with all their works, the culture they had built for one hundred and fifty laborious years out of Indian despair and burgeoning hope, their neophytes and ample farms and flourishing trade, the liturgy and music . . . all were crushed."[279]

It's not a movie with a happy ending: "So the mission perished," Dan reflected, "as the best-laid plans and hopes of the Jesuits have always perished, whether in China, India, or Paraguay. One mourns, but one also knows that this genius that invites destruction has no acceptable alternatives, anymore than the Gospel has, whose divine Protagonist, we are told, also spoke the unpalatable truth, and so invited destruction."[280]

*The Mission* won the 1986 Cannes Film Festival Best Film Award and was nominated for seven Oscars, including Best Picture.[281]

One of the surprises in Dan's film journal is his response to a question put to him by Robert De Niro, "What is it in Jesuit life that you clung to?" "It was the life itself," Dan responded. "It was friendship, community, the promise of support for one another, a vision of great work to be done, which those before you had done so well."[282]

In a postcard sent to Nancy and me while he was still filming, Dan wrote, "Hope against hope so splendid a story can be worthily told. It has confirmed my vocation even this late in the game as I read about heroes and risk takers who make me both proud + ashamed."[283] In a letter sent to us after his return home, he commented, "I'm glad I went. . . . It's my best way of saying thank you to the Order for almost 50 years of undullness."[284]

*"Something is undoubtedly awry. I have no sense of 'growing old,' no conception of what the phrase might mean, except as weird incantation, or a declaration by the gimlet-eyed cultures that one is no longer a unit of production. Granted a minatory creak or two, I am left only with a sense that something foolish is being pushed at me, something known as 'aging.' . . . This when all the while the clock of the soul, mysterious and infallible as the clock of all living things, whispers only of deeper depths and another season."*

—The Steadfastness of the Saints

# Kairos

Credit: John Toolan

att Daloisio of the New York Catholic Worker tells the story of meeting Dan at a retreat in 1999 at Kirkridge in Pennsylvania. When it ended they shared an hourlong ride to the nearest train station. "I jumped at the opportunity," Daloisio remembers, "to spend an hour in the car with this person who had become a hero in my life. . . . I spoke at breakneck speed for the first forty-five minutes going through my list of questions and Dan patiently listening. Finally Dan mercifully stopped me. With that mischievous smile and twinkle in his eye that I would be fortunate to see so many times over the coming years, Dan said that he had one answer to every question I had asked: 'The answer to all of your questions is one word: *community*.' He explained that it was both ridiculous and futile to try and answer any of these questions alone—that only in community could we not only discern better the question, but then live the answers."[285]

Throughout his life Dan lived in community, beginning with the Berrigan tribe and proceeding through a succession of Jesuit communities. From the early 1960s onward he was also part of various auxiliary communities, from the Catholic Peace Fellowship to the Kairos Community. (*Kairos* is a Greek word meaning the propitious moment for the performance of an action, an event occurring in the fullness of time.)

Luke Hansen, then a Jesuit novice, first met Dan in 2007 in the dining room of the West Side Jesuit Community. "Following the community's dinner," he recalled, "we walked over to the Holy Name parish rectory where the Kairos Community meets every other week to pray with the scriptures and discuss peacemaking."

The Kairos Community, a core element during the last third of Dan's life, was founded by Dan, along with Elmer Maas, Anne Montgomery, and several other peace activists, and continues to this day. Kairos has organized countless acts of peace witness, usually with a component of civil disobedience, at many military-connected sites in and around New York City. Timing was usually connected to a Kairos calendar that begins on Martin Luther King's birthday in January, includes both Ash Wednesday and Good Friday, moves on to Hiroshima Day on August 6 or Nagasaki Day August 9, and ends December 28 with the Feast of the Holy Innocents. In a given year Dan might be arrested as many as five times.

"How many times have you been arrested?" Dan was often asked. "Apparently not enough," was one of his responses. (John Dear estimates that Dan was arrested at least 250 times. "No priest in American history," says John, "was handcuffed more often than Dan.")

During the last decades of his active life, Dan's approach to demonstrations involving civil disobedience took on a different sheen. "He continued to be arrested time after time throughout the nineties and into the second decade of the twenty-first century," his friend and lawyer Joe Cosgrove commented, "but his witness came across differently. Dan was less and less interested in using the courtroom as a vehicle for witness. I represented Dan in all but a few of his arrests in protest actions. Normally his court appearances were brief. This allowed me to argue for summary dismissal, usually granted, with Dan neither seeking nor being asked to speak. One time, when the judge was reluctant to outright dismiss the charges but was willing not to impose sentence if the

*"They also ask frequently: 'Where does your hope come from, how do you keep going?' Which seems to me a serious question, but composed out of insufficient evidence, a question having about it a certain immodest aura, which I'm being invited to stand under. . . . I like Philip's typically laconic answer: 'Your hope is where your ass is.'"*

—Ten Commandments for the Long Haul

Top: At a Nagasaki Day protest, 2002.
Felton Davis

Above: With actor Martin Sheen.

defendants pleaded guilty, I expected Dan to reject the offer—pleading guilty was never part of the strictures of passive resistance adopted by the peace movement. But, as I explained to Dan what this meant, he just shrugged his shoulders as if to say he didn't care."[286]

One of the places often singled out by Kairos was the USS *Intrepid*, a retired aircraft carrier that became a military museum in 1974. Since 1986 the ship has been moored on the Hudson River side of Manhattan at West 46th Street.

Another frequent target of Kairos prayer and protest actions was the Riverside Research Institute, a strategic think tank and weapons development center that was for many years housed in a building near Times Square. The institute's roots go back to the Manhattan Project, the ultra-secret project that developed the nuclear bombs dropped on Hiroshima and Nagasaki. Friends in Kairos estimate that Dan was arrested at the Riverside Research Institute at least a hundred times.

In 1986 Dan and actor Martin Sheen were arrested together at a Kairos-arranged antinuclear protest. "I was in New York doing a film," Sheen recalls, "and had a day off. I heard about a demonstration over at 42nd Street trying to block the entrance to [the Riverside Research Institute]. . . . I went to that demonstration and Dan was there. It was my first arrest for a noble cause, and it was the happiest day of my life. I'll never forget it. It was so disarming. Dan was, you know, kind of leading the group in prayer and singing. And the police finally arrived and said, 'Now, come on, you guys. You've got two minutes to disperse.' And Dan said to the presiding officer, 'Come on, officer, you believe in this cause. Get in here and join us.' And he backed away and said, 'Oh, no, no, Father, please, please don't.' Dan made it so human, so down to earth."[287]

Often the police made their arrests gently, but not always. John Dear recalls an especially harsh arrest on Good Friday, 2001:

Dan, myself and others from Kairos were arrested for kneeling at the entrance of the USS *Intrepid*. Normally we would be put in a van, taken to the nearest precinct, booked and released by 4 p.m. Not that day. We only learned later that Mayor [Rudy] Giuliani had secretly signed an ordinance requiring that all protest groups involving more than ten people had to be booked, go through the system, be locked up for the night, then appear the next day

With John Dear at a protest at the *Intrepid*. Courtesy John Dear

in court. We were chained together, feet, waists and wrists, all connected to each other, and taken to the nearest precinct, but that turned out to be too full for the men in our group. The women were taken and the rest of us driven on. We went from precinct to precinct till one in the morning. All the precinct cells were full. Finally, they took us to the Lower Manhattan jail called 'The Tombs' but for some reason they couldn't park the van nearby. The eight of us, chained together, surrounded by men with machine guns, had to walk five long blocks in Arctic weather. I was directly behind Dan. We were freezing and exhausted and could only walk a few inches each per step. It's amazing we didn't fall over. It was one of the worst nights of our lives—horrible and humiliating. By three in the morning Dan was released. The rest of us were put in a cell that was so crowded we could only stand shoulder to shoulder. We were at the point of nausea, we had not slept, couldn't lie down, had eaten nothing since our arrest, and were chilled to the bone. At 10 a.m., we were finally brought before a judge and released. Later, we sued the city. A judge found in our favor, against Giuliani. The notori-

*"Every time I face arrest, my heart turns over. The fear is so strong at times as to be a matter of physical illness, nausea. . . . My cowardly heart longs in every fiber to have done with this charade. . . . You walk with your fear as you would walk with an illness, determined that it will not down you. . . . This I think is a clue; to disallow fear the last word, the word that wins."*

—Ten Commandments for the Long Haul

With attorney Ramsey Clark and his wife Georgia. Courtesy Carla Berrigan

ous ordinance was dropped. We even received some money, about $500 each as I recall.[288]

Dan's lawyer Joe Cosgrove adds, "Ramsey Clark and I filed a federal civil rights case against Giuliani—it had the delicious title *Daniel Berrigan vs. Rudolph Giuliani*. After much pretrial proceedings, the City of New York settled with those who were arrested. In fact, a number of other cases arose out of this. We were helped by the New York Civil Liberties Union, which started their own action first. By the end of litigation, the City ended up paying many other people for the way they were treated, at last count in the neighborhood of $500,000."[289]

The ordeal gave birth to one of Dan's last poems, "Payment":

It was something akin
To paying your way
(No saving metaphor
To be sure)
Paying
For the next mile
The next heartbeat
The next sunset
Something owed life,
The sheer beauty,
Yes, the heartbreak—
Small price, all said
Handcuffed,
Driven in a chain gang
Across Manhattan
At cold midnight,
Something paid
To strike
The manacles Christ bore
And bears in the world.
Does the metaphor befit?
I'm unsure.
That way it might.[290]

Yet another flashpoint for Kairos were the city's military induction centers. Luke Nephew, a cofounder of the Peace Poets, recalls taking part in a class Dan was teaching at Fordham that unexpectedly led him to one such center:

The class was called "Revelation: The Nightmare of God." Father Dan explained [what John the Evangelist had meant by] "the mark of the beast." The Roman Empire used to tattoo DC on people, which stood for Divine Caesar. It meant that you were recognizing Caesar as holy and you were declaring that you would worship the empire. At the end of class, he said, "Alright, for our next class, don't show up here." The class murmurs a general "Huh?" "We'll meet at Bryant Park and 42nd Street. From there we will walk to the US Military Recruiting Station because that is where they put the mark of Caesar on people today." My classmates and I looked at each other with eyebrows raised. Two days later, our class marched through the busy chaos of 42nd Street. We walked slowly and in silence, carrying cardboard coffins. The pictures some of the people carried showed people shredded by bombs and women wailing at the sky. When we arrived, our teacher and about twelve others locked arms and stood in front of the door of the recruiting station. Inside, the military men looked confused and tried to open the door, but the group refused to move. Class had turned into a march, and it was now turning into direct action. Our teacher was teaching by example. Within ten minutes the little triangle in the middle of Times Square was covered with police who were ordering the protesters to leave. Instead of obeying the police orders, they were singing. . . . Minutes later, our teacher and his fellow peacemakers were being tossed in the back of the paddy wagon. The salty water of profound sadness in his eyes, our teacher gave us a solemn nod as if to say, "This is the bare minimum of what is necessary." . . .

*"To say, 'I am the way' is to say, 'I am the way out. Come, imagine a way out. Then put foot on it.'*

*To say, 'I am the truth' is to say, 'I am not the untruth. Come speak the truth.'*

*To say, 'I am the life' is to say, 'I have risen from death. Come, don't get used to death, don't inflict death, get up, resist death, rise from death.'"* —Testimony

The paddy wagon shut its doors. The police ordered the crowd to disperse. The blue and red lights flashed across the scene and our teacher [with other Kairos members] was driven deeper into the belly of the beast. Class dismissed. Education commenced.[291]

John Dear remembers a Kairos gathering one night in the winter of 1986. One of the group reported that staff at the famous Morgan Library, housing one of the world's principal collections of rare books, had been annoyed with the presence of homeless people near the library entrance on East 36th Street. Embedded in the pavement adjacent to the library were large grates through which heat poured upward from a subway tunnel below. Because it was freezing outside, the grates were being slept on by homeless people who had nowhere else to go. The Morgan Library administration found this unsightly and responded by covering the grates with barbed wire. "The question was raised, 'What can we do?' There was a long moment of silence, then Dan said, 'Cut it!' It was as simple as that. I was young and shocked and a little scared, but everyone in the circle said okay, great, let's go tomorrow—we'll have a prayer service and then cut the barbed wire. Someone in the group agreed to obtain wire cutters. I was assigned to contact the press. The following morning we cut the barbed wire! Perhaps because the press was present, the police didn't interfere. There were no arrests. Best of all, the Morgan Library never reinstalled the barbed wire."

Participating in a Kairos community action, Dan's last arrest took place aboard the USS *Intrepid* on Good Friday, April 2, 2011, five weeks short of his ninetieth birthday.

Dan's last participation in a protest demonstration occurred late the following year, October 2012, at Zuccotti Park in Manhattan's financial district to support the Occupy movement.[292] Joe Cosgrove recalls the day:

Protesting at the *Intrepid.*
Ed Hedemann

Dan's mobility by this time was such that getting him to and from such a demonstration was a task unto itself. Catholic Worker Carmen Trotta and I collaborated—Carmen got Dan into a taxi and escorted him to Lower Manhattan. I met the cab and walked arm in arm with Dan to the nearby demonstration. There was an earnestness in Dan's walk that seemed to say he had one more point to make. When we got to the crowded plaza, he was immediately recognized—people parted like the Red Sea. Dan and I moved toward the center where someone had set a chair at the bottom of stairs leading to the plaza. As he sat, the crowd gathered around him with a reverence befitting his spiritual elder status. When the demonstration ended, I drove Dan back to the Jesuit retirement facility—Murray-Weigel Hall at Fordham University. I don't know if Dan realized that this was his last demonstration—he said very little along the way home. But throughout the time there, he was the epitome of what he always encouraged in others: to know where one stands—or in this case, sits—and stand there. In his quiet, utter silence in this last demonstration, Dan's witness could not have been louder.[293]

Last arrest at the *Intrepid*, April 2, 2011.

In the many actions in which Dan took part during the last third of his life, most of them Kairos-generated, Dan was the person most likely to be photographed, a fact of life for Dan but one in which he never felt comfortable. One of the core traits fellow Jesuit Luke Hansen discovered in Dan was that he wasn't looking for adulation or disciples: "Dan didn't want people to follow him. He wanted people to follow the Gospel. He repeatedly encouraged me, 'Stay focused on the Gospel and let the rest take care of itself.'"

What disturbed Dan to his roots was how often the Gospel and other biblical texts are read, honored, and even memorized, but ignored in day-to-day life. "In early November 2001," John Dear recalls, "I came home [to the West Side Jesuit Community] and heard on NPR that the US Catholic bishops had met that day in Washington and voted 190 to 4 in support of the US bombing of Afghanistan. After the vote a special Mass was held at the Shrine of the Immaculate Conception, with the secretary of defense and the Pentagon's Joint Chiefs of Staff sitting in the first row. One of the Joint Chiefs did the first reading—the Ten Commandments, including 'Thou shalt not kill'! I went up to Dan's apartment to have a glass of wine and told him this. He paused and said, 'You know, we should just throw out the Gospels. From now on we should process into Mass carrying the Air Force rule book and in the middle of Mass, incense it, and open it to read the new commandment, 'Kill your enemies.'"[294]

Side by side with Dan's highly visible persistence in acts of protest was his less known devotion to the visual arts, the more public activity in part sustained by the latter. How many knew Dan Berrigan had a long-running fascination with the paintings of the sixteenth-century Italian artist Caravaggio?

"From the late 1990s onward," Joe Cosgrove recalls, "one of our regular topics of conversation was the work and life of Caravaggio. The brilliance of his work seemed to hypnotize Dan. For years Dan and I engaged in a detailed study of Caravaggio, sharing scholarly works written about him and undertaking a review of prints of his paintings or, when possible, seeing them in person at the Metropolitan Museum of Art and elsewhere. Dan was particularly captured by descriptions of a particular lost work of Caravaggio, *The Fenaroli Resurrection*, which disappeared sometime after the late eighteenth century. We only had written accounts to go by. These testify that the risen Christ was shown as shockingly human—no shafts of light, no cherubs, no immaculate white flowing

*"Love your enemies? The Word of God in our midst? But we were at war! The moment war was launched, we all became realists. The Word of God might apply elsewhere (or elsewhen) or to simpler times or to one-to-one conflict or to pacifists and religious (whoever these latter might be; for the most part they are mum as the others.) . . . The time is short. Reject the errant history, the pseudo-tradition. There can be no just war. There never was one."* —Testimony

linen robe but an emaciated, lately dead man blinking into the daylight like a prisoner in rags who has been unexpectedly released. The descriptions we found hit Dan like nothing else I'd ever seen. Shortly before Philip's death, Dan sent him a letter—and copied me—with one scholar's description of the lost painting. 'Imagine,' Dan wrote, 'if this were our image of the risen Christ . . . a Christ reluctant and broken.' Dan and I spoke often of this image, and how different our Church would be if we viewed the risen Christ as a stunned survivor of death. Certainly Dan could identify with such a Jesus. Dan was reminded of the many AIDS patients he'd tended to who, as he often told me, looked like concentration camp prisoners. Dan held fast to this concept of the resurrection for the last decade and a half of his life. It seemed to give him hope."[295]

The resurrection was at the core of Dan's life, not merely as a theological doctrine to which one might assent intellectually but as a lived experience and a way of life. As he wrote,

> Since 1980 and all the Plowshares actions, some of us continue to labor to break the demonic clutch on our souls of the ethic of Mars, of wars and rumor of wars, inevitable wars, just wars, necessary wars, victorious wars, and say our no in acts of hope. For us, all these repeated arrests, the interminable jailings, the life of our small communities, the discipline of nonviolence, these have embodied an ethic of resurrection. Simply put, we long to taste that event, its thunders and quakes, its great Yes. We want to test the resurrection in our bones. To see if we might live in hope, instead of the thicket of cultural despair, nuclear despair, a world of perpetual war. We want to taste the resurrection. May I say we have not been disappointed.[296]

With attorney Joe Cosgrove.
Robert Ellsberg

# Phil's Death

Rick Reinhard

I n December 2001 Phil returned to Jonah House after completing what proved to be his final incarceration. At age seventy-eight, he had now spent eleven years of his life in prison for efforts to outlaw nuclear weapons and prevent wars or speed their end. He felt exhausted and needed a cane. Hip surgery proved necessary.

In September 2002 Phil wrote to Dan reporting his first indication of having cancer. "I went to [my physician] yesterday to get an opinion on month-old general lassitude and weakness. . . . She started testing me and the bottom dropped out. A possible blood clot near my lungs etc etc etc. She held me overnight—no sleep, always another test, and meanwhile her fear was proven illusory. So Liz brought me home—no sleep, no food for nearly 24 hrs. and both arms looking like pin cushions. It's terrible to fall into the hands of doctors with technology at their call! Now it's my liver. I informed her that my liver has been the best—no pain. And I've never been an excessive drinker. No matter, I must return for a 'scan' test. Whereas, the only thing clarified is that I'm losing weight—maybe 20 pounds."[297]

In a brief note a few weeks later, Phil told Dan he was "awaiting a report of the liver biopsy. Soon."[298]

The biopsy's findings were grim: inoperable stage IV cancer of the liver. Phil's decline was rapid. He reconciled himself to the probability of death with the simple declaration, "I pray for healing daily, but if not that, may God's will be done!"

Frida, Phil and Liz's oldest child, describes the last phase of her father's life:

The doctors said they could treat [the cancer] with chemotherapy, but the chances of a full recovery were slight. Dad was up for trying chemo . . . but after one round of chemo, he said, "No more." Mom gathered us all in—not just my brother and sister and me, but the whole community. Hundreds of people came to take care of him, of us, of one another. They came to help him die and to help us grieve. And through all of this, [my mother] made it happen—laughter, tears, raucous memory sharing, meatballs, roses, and torches. . . .

[Dad] asked us to pray for healing and for our faith to be strong in the months to come. He asked us to start preparing for a life without him. He was not afraid, he told us. He loved us and he was sad, but he would be ready. And then, with clear eyes and a lot of compassion, he got down to the hard work of dying with dignity.

The hallmark of the next few months was gratitude. I would sit and read with him. "Thanks, Freeds," he'd say. My sister would bring him a drink. "Thanks, love," he'd say. My brother [Jerry] would spend time with him. "Thanks for giving an old man a lift," he'd say. My mom, the Jonah House community, the continuous stream of friends and relatives who came to say hello, spend some time, and say good-bye all experienced the same thing—thanksgiving. Dad allowed no gesture, however small, to go unappreciated.

When some of the day-to-day care became too much for us, we brought in hospice care. They were amazing. They respected what we were doing—loving our dad on his journey to death. Letting him die

Phil and Liz. Courtesy Frida Berrigan

the way he lived: surrounded by people, surrounded by love, resisting the medical-industrial complex. Dad stopped eating and did not want to drink. His breath grew labored. Magnified by the baby monitor in his room, his breathing became the off-kilter metronome of our days, as we planned the funeral, shared stories and memories, prayed, cried and laughed. On December 6, 2002, sometime after dinner, he died. He died at Jonah House, and more than thirty of his friends, family, and community members were there. We had walked the last weeks with him.[299]

Frida's brother Jerry recalls "sitting with Dad in the days before he died. It was cold and snowing outside. His breathing was labored. I had the distinct impression that his spirit was flying around somewhere, moving freely, connected only very tenuously by an ever-fraying thread to his body, which, for now, anchored him down. I knew that when his spirit left his body, he would be truly free."[300]

Phil wrote a final statement in the days before his death: "I die with the conviction, held since 1968 and Catonsville, that nuclear weapons are the scourge of the earth; to mine for them, manufacture them, deploy them, use them, is a curse against God, the human family, and the earth itself."

Hundreds gathered for the wake and funeral. Frida writes,

Dan and Liz visit Phil in jail, along with Kate and Frida Berrigan. Courtesy Frida Berrigan

The pine box that my brother and friends made was ready, beautifully painted by the iconographer Bill McNichols. We prepared the body and laid him in the coffin in dry ice. The wake and funeral were at Saint Peter Claver, where Dad had served as a priest decades earlier. The night after the wake, we gathered around him one last time and then nailed the coffin closed. I remember my Uncle Jim, my dad's oldest living brother at the time, driving nails deep with just two whacks of the hammer.... The next morning was cold, clear, and so beautiful. Dad was loaded onto the back of a pickup truck and my sister Kate, our sister-in-law Molly, and I rode in the truck with him. Other people carried signs and banners as we processed the mile or so to the church for the funeral Mass.... It was a strangely happy occasion. Dad was gone, but he was still so present in the room full of people who loved him.[301]

Top and Above: Phil Berrigan's funeral procession. Steve Dear

"I am convinced," wrote his brother Jerry, "that Phil's death resulted from his prison diet. Eleven years of meals permeated with drugs and chemicals intended to pacify prisoners, to forestall inmate rebelliousness, took a life's toll."

John Dear presided at the funeral Mass, and Dan preached the homily. One of Dan's themes was Phil's balance/imbalance of patience and impatience:

> The two seem complementary, a kind of high-wire balancing act of the spirit. From 1967 [the year of the Baltimore Four] to the day of his death, Philip must learn patience.... He learned patience through

bolts and bars, through stop clocks and time served, at the icy hands of judges and guards and wardens; he must learn it through the war-making state and a complicit church, through long sacrifice and small return, through thirty-five years of American wars and scarcely a week of genuine peace. So he learned patience from many unpromising teachers. It was like an iron yoke placed on his shoulder. And oh, he was impatient.... If Philip's patience was marmoreal, his impatience was a lifted hammer. The blow struck marble, repeatedly. What we had at the end was a masterwork of grace, of human sweetness. We gazed on him with a kind of awe.[302]

Frida and Kate read aloud the eulogy they had coauthored:

We have visited our Dad in many prisons—Danbury, Allentown, Elkton, Lorton, Peterson, Hagerstown, Cumberland County, Baltimore County. We have spent time with him in all these dead spaces: spaces meant to intimidate and cow and beat down; spaces that repel and resist children, laughter, loving and family; spaces meant to communicate a clear message of who is in charge; spaces with stupid rules about how and when and for how long to touch and hold; spaces where you talk into a phone and look through smudged plastic....

But our Dad never seemed touched by that

Courtesy Carla Berrigan

weight. Even in prison, even in those awful spaces, he was free. In prison, as in the outside world, his work and life were to resist violence and oppression, to understand and try to live by God's word, to build community and help people learn to love one another.

When we visited our Dad in prison we paid no heed to the rules. . . . We filled those places with love, with family, with stories and laughter and strategizing. He was free in prison and he showed us that freedom has nothing to do with where your body is and who holds the keys and who makes the rules. It has everything to do with where your heart is, and being fearless and full of hope.[303]

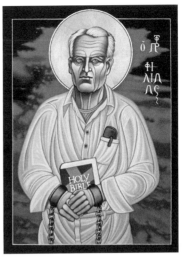

Icon of Phil Berrigan by William Hart McNichols.

Jerry recently wrote to me about aspects of Phil's prayer life:

My father prayed for a deeper appreciation of all friends and colleagues in the work, and he prayed for courage for all who would dare resist war, and he prayed even for our enemies, the men with guns, the men at the Pentagon and the State Department and at 1600 Pennsylvania Avenue. . . . These are our enemies, the "Masters of War" that Dylan scourged. All of them, all of us, when all else is stripped away, he would pray, are human beings, reachable, changeable, somehow, we hope. In his better moments, he prayed for all.[304]

Phil is buried in St. Peter's Cemetery, adjacent to Jonah House. The gravestone is a Celtic standing cross.

"I would like to be remembered," Phil wrote in his autobiography, *Fighting the Lamb's War*, "as a Catholic who tried to be a Christian."

John Dear, who directs Dan's literary trust, tells me that Dan-as-poet was buried with Phil: "After the funeral Dan just stopped writing poetry."

*"Toward Sunday noon, we assembled in Bryant Park and began a solemn procession, bearing placards with Phil's photo and quotes from his writings. Our goal was the* SS Intrepid, *a hideous, overbearing war museum anchored in the Hudson river. There 29 of us crossed a police line and were arrested. All honor to a noble spirit. Philip lives!"*
—Dan, October 2003, The Berrigan Letters

# A Visitation of Prophets

Portrait of Dan by Robert McGovern.

Dan was a prolific writer, averaging a book every year beginning with *Time without Number* in 1957. The collector of the complete works of Daniel Berrigan needs a bookcase with room for nearly sixty volumes.

During the last two decades of his life, Dan's published work centered on biblical studies and meditations. He produced books on Genesis, Exodus, Deuteronomy, Job, Lamentations, the Psalms, the Acts of the Apostles, and Revelation. The prophets—among them Isaiah, Ezekiel, Jeremiah, and Daniel—became a major focus of his writings. Dan's literary method was to weave together a prophet's text with his own free-flowing commentary, the latter coming like a parade of boxers jabbing fiercely at a punching bag.

In each prophet Dan found himself being addressed and challenged by a biblical ancestor. There was a ready-made affinity. The prophets of Israel and Dan Berrigan of New York City were God-afflicted men inclined to gestures that spoke louder than words; were outraged with injustice; uncompromising and outspoken; often irritating; often overcome by sorrow and anger for the ways their countrymen ignored divine commandments, abused creation, hated their neighbor, and worshiped almost anything but God.

Dan saw each of the prophets "as God's compassionate

and clairvoyant and inclusive image . . . Each prophet strives for a divine (which is to say, truly human) breakthrough in the human tribe. Lacerating, intemperate, relentless, the prophets raise the question again and again, in images furious and glorious, poetic and demanding: What is a human being?"[305]

It was through the prophets that the God of mercy, the God of compassion, the God of self-giving love, is most vividly revealed, in contrast to the nightmare god of pitiless condemnations and executions, the great punisher, the everlasting warden of the inferno. As Dan noted in a letter to Robert Ellsberg, "My sense is that God isn't in any recognizable way self-revealed until 800–500 BCE and the prophets."[306]

A golden thread running through the books of the prophets, Dan noted, is "a very strong bias in favor of the victim and a very strong sense of judgment of evil structures and those who run them. The prophets and Christ talk about the God who stands at the bottom with the victims and with the 'widows and orphans' and witnesses with them in the world, from that terrifying vantage point which is like the bottom of the dry well that Jeremiah was thrown into. That vantage point defines the crime and sin; that point of view of the victim indicts the unjust, the oppressor, the killer, the warmaker. And the message is very clear. It's a very clear indictment of every superpower from Babylon to Washington."[307]

In a magazine interview he took another stab at describing the prophetic vocation: "[The prophets are] speaking to every segment of any culture. They're giving hope to those who are under the heel." At the same time the prophets are "making those, like ourselves—who are somewhat in possession [of power]—uneasy. And then, to authority, they're absolutely ruthless about the kind of power that crushes people and wages wars."[308]

It's not a vocation with a safety net—the biblical prophets didn't fare well or win much applause. As Dan pointed out, "Jeremiah was martyred in Egypt by

Book covers of *Isaiah* and *Jeremiah*, with art by Robert McGovern.

Dan protesting at the *Intrepid.*
Courtesy Carla Berrigan

his own people when he sought refuge there, and then the tradition about Isaiah says he was also murdered. It goes that way for the minor prophets, too, although with less certainty. But we can be fairly sure that they were kicked out if they weren't killed. . . . The only [prophet we might describe as] effective was the [nonhistorical] clown Jonah. He did a big thing in Nineveh—converting everybody. . . . Everybody, even the beasts, went into mourning and fasting, and this whole enormous city, which never really existed on the scale described in the Book of Jonah, is converted just because this guy opens his mouth. . . . It's a send-up of the whole prophetic mission, because in actuality every one of the prophets was worked over and buried. Every one of them was involved in a horrendous kind of irony: they were ordered by God to speak up but were told at the outset that nobody would listen to them."

"What makes the books of the prophets unique," Dan noted, "is that there's no comparable document of that era— from the eighth to the fifth century before Christ. There's nothing like it in any other literature."

There are, Dan pointed out, not only prophets but antiprophets, the latter who, alleging that they speak for God, heap blessings on kings, presidents, and prime ministers as the bombs rain down and the wretched die of hunger.

"Antiprophets were just lackeys of the king, blessing his decisions. Whereas the Hebrew prophets were offering a very stern and forbidding judgment upon what was going on in the corridors of power," Dan commented. "One way of testing the prophet is the presence of the antiprophet. . . . We can exercise some judgment about the people who hang around the powers that be and bless what they're doing."

Dan offered the example of Jeremiah, "who says unequivocally to his people, 'You're going to be driven into exile and you're going to be there for seventy years and every one of you who goes into exile is going to die there, and some of your children will die there.' The antiprophets, on the other hand, are saying, 'We have the Word of God, too, and we say the city will not fall. Some people will go into exile, but they'll be back here in four or five years.' Because Jeremiah's word comes true, we recognize him as the prophet, but he had to go through exile and death without any proof. Very tough. Identifying the true prophets is not a matter of personality, it's a matter of truthfulness."

Asked if prophets have to suffer, Dan pointed to Isaiah: "Isaiah is the clearest example of someone who had a good time for a while because he had influence and respect in the corridors of power, but then the war clouds gathered and God's Word became more austere about what was going to come. That is when Isaiah finds out who he really is, and then we get Isaiah's songs of the suffering servant. The power play, for Isaiah, is finished. He is no longer a servant of the king but of God."

Asked if he had a favorite prophet, Dan singled out Isaiah: "When Jesus announces who he is in the synagogue, he opens the scroll to Isaiah.[309] . . . Even apart from that, I would love Isaiah, but knowing Jesus loved him really adds something, too."

It also impressed Dan that Isaiah was part of a community: "We tend to think of the prophets as loners, but that is not true of any of them. All of what went on got in the scroll somehow—somebody listened and somebody took notes. So there was community all over the place, as far as I can judge, and these writings went through many minds and hearts and pens before they arrived in our hands. It's very good that we at the other end of this tradition are meant to absorb it in community because that's the way it got started and transmitted."

Ezekiel, who envisioned the resurrection of a multitude of slain warriors whose bones filled a desolate valley,[310] was another prophet especially dear to Dan:

Such a mad hope! It took the form of a supreme vi-

*"My thesis is simple and, I trust, audacious: each of the prophets, in the present instance Jeremiah, is an 'other' of Yahweh. As God's compassionate and clairvoyant and inclusive image, each prophet strives for a divine (which is to say, truly human) breakthrough in the human tribe. Lacerating, intemperate, relentless, the prophets raise the question again and again, in images furious and glorious, poetic and demanding: What is a human being?"*

—Jeremiah

Dan at UC Berkeley. Mev Puleo

sion, of the "dry bones" scattered in the wasteland. From exile, shame, defeat, a dead end—came the revelation. We must understand that for Ezekiel's people, all evidence, rumor, the false promises of yea-sayers, everything that shored up a kind of cultural optimism had been swept away, dissolved. Despair rode the saddle of the world; life had become its own "worst case." Ah, then it was that the heart of Ezekiel saw and his tongue was loosened. Hope stood free, sang its song of prevailing. In a place of pure desolation, an entire ecology speaks of the prevailing of death. A sere landscape of dry bones. No sign of life. And then—a sign. One after another, the bones stand upright, connect one to another, grow animate. Skulls speak aloud. And death lodged in cadavers like a parasite, in institutions like a colony of termites—death shall have no dominion![311]

Dan also devoted a book to his biblical namesake, Daniel,[312] a Jew-in-exile who served the Babylonian king honestly but not unconditionally. When he refused to worship idols as the king commanded, Daniel was thrown into the lions' den to be eaten alive. Instead he was given divine protection and the next day walked away from the lions unharmed. In the text's Christian reading, Daniel provides a prophetic sign of Christ's death and resurrection. The Book of Daniel also includes the story of the three young men thrown into a furnace where they sing a rhapsodic canticle that sees all creation as joyfully engaged in blessing the Lord. They too are spared the doom ordered by the king.

Dan saw the Babylonian furnace as a metaphor for war:

The episode lies too close for comfort. Close indeed, and torrid. Scorching, a near memory of furnaces of our lifetime, stoked against the innocent. So we incline to put the image of the furnace at a distance, as we do other horrors of the age: cluster bombs, land mines, smart missiles, napalm, rubber bullets; successive incursions, whether in Vietnam, Iraq, Grenada, or Central America. The plain fact is that our nation, along with its nuclear cronies, is quite prepared to thrust enormous numbers of humans into furnaces fiercely stoked. Of the preparation and commission of such crimes, of their technique and strategic advantage, we have learned a great deal. But of repentance we have learned precisely nothing. As a nation, nothing. As a church, perhaps something. It seems impossible to keep one's own story from dovetailing with the story of Daniel and his friends. Always some peaceable action brusquely summons those I love into the hot belly of the legal juggernaut![313]

Dan stressed that attention to the prophets gives additional evidence, if more were needed, that one need not achieve a state of inner tranquility before engaging in peace work. "The notion that one has to achieve peace of mind before stretching out one's hand to one's neighbor," Dan wrote in an essay for the Jewish journal *Tikkun* in 1998, "is a distortion of our human experience, and ultimately a dodge of our responsibility. Life is a rollercoaster, and one had better buckle one's belt and take the trip. This focus on equanimity is actually a narrow-minded, selfish approach to reality dressed up within the language of spirituality. . . . Open up the book of Jeremiah and you do not find a person looking for inner peace. Jeremiah goes through mountains and valleys. That kind of richness I find very appealing, whereas the kind of spirituality that looks for a flat emotional landscape brought on by the endless search for inner peace and equanimity I find disturbing, a quest that goes nowhere."[314]

Mev Puleo

# Thompson Street and Murray-Weigel Hall

Franciscan friary on 147 Thompson St., where Dan was relocated.

In 2009 the twenty members of the West Side Jesuit Community were forced to give up their apartments at 220 West 98th Street, having lost a prolonged legal battle that sought to keep the rents down. A law had been passed in 1987 whereby corporate bodies such as the New York Province of the Society of Jesus could not lease an entire apartment complex; rather each individual apartment had to be in the name of a single party. As a result, when a given Jesuit was reassigned or died, his apartment reverted to the landlord. By then the community had been greatly whittled down; ten of them—Dan was one—desired to continue living together. The New York Province, honoring the request of this remnant, managed to find new quarters, an unused Franciscan friary at 147 Thompson Street in Manhattan's Soho district, three blocks south of Washington Square in Greenwich Village.

"The friary needed a lot of work," one member of the community, Joe Towle, wrote, "but it had ten bedrooms and an ample kitchen. The kitchen thrilled Merrick Dean, our cook. The kitchen at 98th Street had been slightly bigger than a phone booth. It didn't hurt that she found Raffetto's fresh pasta store just around the corner. So Merrick came with us, concluding more than twenty-five years of caring for our comestible needs and wants. The new digs had a large dining room, two large basement spaces that were converted into a house library and a waterhole for welcoming lay friends and colleagues and to enable us to continue the long tradition of the feast days that had so nourished our community life. We also had a glass-enclosed back addition that came to serve as a solarium and a greenhouse—it enabled us to seat our normal number of friends for the monthly gathering."

"Dan was very weak by this time," John Dear recalls. "The large front room just to the left of the entrance was assigned to him, but it wasn't ready. They also had to remodel the bathroom and put in handrails for Dan. This took several months, and since he didn't have a place to live, for several months he lived at Murray-Weigel Hall, the Jesuit infirmary at Fordham University, until his room was ready." Meanwhile John unpacked Dan's belongings, set up his room, and hung his pictures.

"Dan loved the community," notes John, "but missed the Upper West Side. Also his strength was fading. He became very frail, so much so that he began to spend afternoons in bed. Often he skipped breakfast or lunch or both. He began to lose weight. As he was lean to begin with, this became a concern. We bought him a refrigerator and set it up in his room, and the community cook, Merrick, made special veggie sandwiches for him and put them in his little fridge. This helped, but even so still he became increasingly frail."

It was while Dan was part of the Thompson Street community that, in late October 2011, I had my next-to-last visit with him. I had given a talk earlier that evening at the Catholic Worker's Maryhouse on East 3rd Street. Afterward Carmen Trotta, Mike Baxter, Tom Cornell, and I walked across town via Houston Street. It was past eleven when we rang the doorbell. I was worried that

Dan with Jim Forest.

*SHOW ME YOUR FACE, O GOD / PSALM 61*

*At land's end,*
  *Where the sea turns in sleep*
*ponderous, menacing*
  *and my spirit fails and runs*
*landward, seaward, askelter*

*I pray you*
  *make new*
*this hireling heart*
    *O*
*turn your face to me*
*—winged, majestic, angelic—*

  *tireless,*
   *a tide*
  *my prayer goes up—*
  *show me your face, O God!*

Jim Forest

Dan would be long asleep. "Dan is still a night person," Carmen assured me. And awake he was, delighted to welcome us, eager to talk, full of questions about health, family, children, grandchildren. His recollections of the early days of the Catholic Peace Fellowship were vivid. Though physically something of a scarecrow, his memory was laser-sharp, his sense of humor undiminished. I gave him a copy of my latest children's book, *Saint George and the Dragon*,[315] explaining that the dragon represents anything evil and whatever makes us panic. Dan looked through the illustrations with the attentiveness of a ten-year-old. "It's never too late to battle dragons," Dan remarked.[316]

In 2012 it was decided that Dan—now ninety years old—should return for a time to Murray-Weigel Hall just to regain his strength. "This was a common practice," John Dear explains. "Often, elderly Jesuits went there to recuperate and then returned to their communities. Dan began eating three meals a day—the nurses more or less forced him to eat!—but he still slept most of the time. He stopped writing, eventually stopped reading, never watched television, and became very quiet and passive. Bob Keck, another member of the Thompson Street community, moved there too, and though Dan had regained his strength and was going to move back, he decided to stay and keep Bob company. Eventually, the provincial announced that Dan would always stay there, that he was now too weak to move back. While Dan was upset over this, the rest of us were quietly grateful. The fact was he could no longer be on his own. He wasn't sick, never took a pill, had no complaints, but he just wouldn't eat and spent hours each day sleeping. He accepted the arrangement but it was never his desire to remain. He was forced to stay and he was miserable about it. He had a private room and excellent care—the nurses loved him!—but not the living space and freedom he was used to. It was painful."

My last visit with Dan was in mid-December 2012.

Robert Ellsberg and I drove together from the Orbis office at Maryknoll. It was mid-afternoon when we walked into his room, a gray space without any of the paintings, wood cuts, serigraphs, photos, pins, bumper stickers, and posters that ordinarily made his rooms extraordinary.[317] Dan lay in a hospital bed. My first impression was that he had died and we happened to be the first to know it. He lay under a light blanket as still as a corpse and seemed not to be breathing. Only by looking closely could we discover a slow pulse in his neck. Robert and I sat in chairs on opposite sides of the bed, said nothing, and waited. I noticed several books on a stool near the bed.

After a while Dan's eyes blinked open. It was a Lazarus moment. Instantly awake, he glanced at us and said, "Visitors! How good to see you!" He pried himself up and we had a lively conversation. Then John Dear arrived, just off the plane from a trip to Afghanistan, with much to report about his travels. Dan was fascinated. Several of John's

Dan at Murray-Weigel Hall, with John Dear and Robert Ellsberg.
Jim Forest

stories stirred Dan to laughter. A bell rang and Dan announced it was "time for a martini—perfect timing!" Using a walker, Dan led the way to the infirmary's common room and dining area where the bar was open and the community of elderly Jesuits was slowly gathering. What did we talk about? Afghanistan, of course, but also family. Age ninety, Dan still remembered that Robert's son Nicholas had gone to Fordham Prep, that one of my sons was named after him, and that my wife, Nancy, was a translator. "Do you still live in that little house in Alkmaar? Is the windmill still there?" He recalled that our guestroom, which he had once occupied, had been slightly larger than a bathtub. (It was during that stay with us that I discovered Dan was addicted to mystery novels. He raided our library in search of mysteries he hadn't read.) He was pleased to know, now that our kids were grown up, that we had a larger guestroom. Suddenly, after a second martini, it was clear Dan was exhausted. We walked with him to his room. He lay down and was immediately asleep. We tiptoed out.

In 2013, when it was clear Dan would complete his life at Murray-Weigel Hall, Al Briceland, superior of the Thompson Street community, asked John Dear to take responsibility for Dan's property. By then Dan had already assigned John as his literary trustee. "So one day I got a car," John recounts, "drove to Thompson Street, filled boxes with everything that had to do with Phil and Liz, drove to Jonah House, and gave it to Liz. Then I filled up the car with any pictures and possessions for Jerry and Carol, and—this time with Dan accompanying me—drove to Syracuse. What was left—tons of pictures, books, and papers—I took charge of. Over time I sorted through all his unpublished and personal papers and shipped them to DePaul University, his final archives, where they are now. I also gave away some pictures and possessions to various friends of Dan's. The rest of his books were given away when the Jesuits finally left Thompson Street."

John also recalls, "Slowly, over his last few years at Fordham, Dan's orbit grew smaller. He could walk only very short distances, could barely hear, would barely eat, and lost many of his friends by outliving them. Yet he never complained. Dan mainly stayed in his room but received a steady stream of visitors, probably a dozen every week. Then around Holy Week 2014 his dear friend Bob Keck died suddenly. All who were close to Bob and Dan came for the wake, a party of about fifty people. By then Dan was silent most of the time but periodically he had good days. At every meal he sat with his old friend Don Moore, who was also frail and could barely walk. After

Dan at Mass at Murray-Weigel.

Bob Keck's death, Don was Dan's closest friend at Murray-Weigel Hall."

There was a brief period when Dan refused to eat as an act of protest after learning that John Dear had been forced to choose between giving up peace work or leaving the Society of Jesus. John reluctantly chose to leave. "While I was in South Africa in 2014," John wrote me, "one day I received urgent e-mails reporting that Dan had gone on a fast to the death to protest the way I had been treated and that Dan would only start eating again if he heard directly from me. This was extraordinary because in his frail health, he could die in a matter of days. I sent a long letter via e-mail to Dan, which was read to him when he woke up the next morning, and he started again to eat."[318]

Jerry Berrigan with Dan at his 80th birthday celebration. Eileen Miller

Dan's niece Carla, Jerry and Carol Berrigan's daughter, shared with me the story of what came to be known as "The Miracle on Maywood Drive":

Dan insisted on being with my father on his 95th birthday, December 20, as he had for every birthday of the last decade. I talked this over with Margaret Monahan, the director at Murray-Weigel. She reminded me that Dan was incredibly frail, not able to walk or stand, not eating, saying very few words, and that there was a possibility he could die on the trip. Even so she would support our decision. Our position was that, if Dan were going to die, where better than with us? Liz and Carmen Trotta made him as comfortable as possible for the five-hour car trip to Syracuse. He arrived with a beaming smile and ready for a celebratory martini! The following morning, as they were packing the car for the return trip, we proposed to Dan that he stay with us a little longer. He stayed on for ten days, which included my father's very large birthday open house through Christmas. He came alive before our eyes, his appetite returning

*"A better argument could not be devised for the eternity of our substance than the ache which is unhealable in this life, for lost friends. . . . Against death the omnipresent, the omnivorous, the would-be omnipotent; whether death's misbegotten misnomer be neutron bomb, or betrayal of Christian by Christian, or acedia of spirit, or the refusals and reprisals that jar our soul off course—against fealty to these, or complicity in these, my friends place a hand over my mouth, an exorcising hand on my brow. Fear not. You shall see our face."*
—Portraits

Top: Dan, John Dear, and Sharon and Joe Cosgrove, April 2016.
Courtesy Joe Cosgrove

Above: Cover of *The Berrigan Letters*, published in April 2016.

with a vengeance, his voice clearly audible, his sense of humor intact! The brothers watched many movies, one of them being "The Mission," which Dan watched with a broad smile, tapping his hand on the chair for emphasis during the more cinematic scenes. Those were magical days! On our return, the staff at Murray-Weigel was incredulous that this was the same Dan who had left ten days earlier! It was Dan's next-to-last visit with my father—he died the following July. Dan was being driven up to be with him, but my father died just before Dan arrived. Dan was able to attend my father's funeral Mass, which was a blessing for us all.[319]

Among Dan's frequent visitors were Joe and Sharon Cosgrove. "One time," Joe recalls, "Dan invited us to lunch on a Saturday and suggested we join him in the chapel for liturgy beforehand. On this occasion it turned out to be a funeral Mass for one of the priests at Murray-Weigel who had died two days before. All the Jesuits, including Dan, concelebrated. I'll never forget the image of these mostly old men, some too weak to stand, extending their feeble hands in conjunction with the principal celebrant at the raising of the cup and bread. Another time, on Ash Wednesday 2015, Martin Sheen and I visited. We had our own little ceremony with Dan applying our ashes—in Martin's case on his forehead, but with an impish smile he placed mine on my nose!"

Joe also described a visit that he and Sharon had with Dan on Christmas Day 2015: "We shared our time with Dan with several Jesuits, two of whom argued as to whether Isaiah was speaking just to the Israelites of ancient times or to us today. You could imagine Dan rolling his eyes as he listened in bemused silence!"

Robert Ellsberg describes his two last visits with Dan: "Jim Douglass was with me for one of them. We went with Dan into the dining room for a drink, and a young guy came over and introduced himself as a Jesuit scholastic. He asked us who we were, and Dan said, 'I'm Dan Berrigan.' The young guy winced with embarrassment. My last visit was very shortly before Dan died. I had brought along the galleys of *The Berrigan Letters*. He was very still and seemingly beyond words, until asked if he would like a drink of water: 'That would be very nice,' he said. I was surprised to find out that in subsequent visits he was well enough to listen as people read from the *Letters*. Right to the end he had his ups and downs."[320]

"Two weeks to the day before he died," wrote Joe Cosgrove, "Sharon and I were with Dan. It was a beautiful spring day. We asked Dan if he'd like to go for a walk around the campus, and he gave a forceful nod. After the nurse bundled him up and put his Ben and Jerry's stocking cap on, we headed out. We asked Dan which way he wanted to go and he pointed his bony finger down a path clearly marked 'Do Not Enter.' It was, we surmised, just another act of civil disobedience! Although it was getting more and more difficult for Dan to speak, he was clearly audible as he pointed out different buildings on the campus where he'd taught. Pointing down another path, he directed us toward the university church. Its doors were open. I asked if he

A last walk at Fordham, April 2016.
Courtesy Joe Cosgrove.

wanted to spend a minute there. He nodded, paused, then pointed inside. I don't know what he was trying to tell us, but something seemed to grasp him at that moment. We stayed in the church awhile, then he nodded and waved us back toward Murray-Weigel Hall. It was the last time Dan ventured outside. We stayed for dinner. Dan seemed invigorated and spoke more than we'd been used to. Although hard to hear him, it was clear that he

Dan at Murray-Weigel with great-niece Madeline and great-nephew Seamus. Courtesy Frida Berrigan

wanted to talk about John Dear and his venture to Rome working on an effort to get the Vatican onboard with a statement on nonviolence. He was so excited—it was as if Dan himself had been on the trip. And then John himself appeared! It was completely unexpected. We all thought he was still in Europe, but there he was, and Dan just shined! As John told the story of his trip in detail, Dan hung on his every word. It was a special night and one that seemed to give Dan a burst of life. As we took him back to his room to say goodnight, we asked the nurse to take a picture of the four of us—so far as I know the last one ever taken of Dan."[321]

"I was fortunate enough to have made a visit to Dan on April 22," says niece Mary Berrigan, "only a couple days before he became gravely ill. I arrived just as Dan was coming from chapel and midday Mass. I joined him in the dining room for lunch. He was especially expressive that day, asking questions and commenting on various things. He pointed out the beauty of the planters in the solarium and made sure I saw them. When I offered him his coffee cup, he raised it to me and so we toasted. After a bit more back-and-forth, Margaret [Monahan, who headed the infirmary staff] wheeled him to his room where he admired the bright, pink daisy I had put in his room. We chatted a bit longer and then I began to sense he was running out of steam. I asked if I could do anything for him before I left. He asked that I lower his blinds. I did that, then kissed him good-bye. I took his hand and he gave me a little reassuring squeeze. I said, 'Peace,' to him, and he replied, 'Peace.'"

# Last Rites

In 2002 Robert Ellsberg had asked Dan if he had any celebrations coming up in the foreseeable future. "Just my funeral," Dan replied. But for that event he had to wait fourteen years.

Having been on death's border for the better part of a week, Dan died just before noon on April 30, 2016, a Saturday, nine days before his ninety-fifth birthday.

Of the many people who had kept a bedside vigil during Dan's last days, four were present at the end: two fellow Jesuits, Joe Towle and Don Moore, and two friends, Patrick Walsh and Maureen McCafferty. Liz McAlister and her three children, Frida, Jerry, and Katie, were three miles away, stuck in traffic on the George Washington Bridge, while niece Carla and her husband Marc were crossing the Hudson on the Tappan Zee Bridge.

Maureen, one of the frequent visitors at Dan's bedside, describes his arrival at the finish line:

> When I walked into his room about noon, the minute I saw Dan lying in bed, eyes looking upward, breath coming with difficulty, I knew, "This was it." I texted Joe Cosgrove that if he wanted to be with Dan, now was the time to hop in his car. Joe Towle called the family—Liz, Frida, Jerry, and Kate who all "just happened" to be doing a retreat together. They hopped in their car. The fact that these four family

Dan in his famous blue shirt.
Robert Ellsberg

Procession from the Catholic Worker to Church of St. Francis Xavier. Felton Davis

members were together was a miracle—Liz was usually in Baltimore, Jerry in Michigan, Kate in California, and Frida in Connecticut. Carla and Marc came down from Syracuse.

As Patrick, Joe, and I were sitting vigil, I decided to talk to Dan—I understood that hearing is the last sense to go in a dying person. I told him his family was on the way, he would soon be meeting his mother, Frida, his brother Phil, and all his other brothers, that he had led a very good life, that we all loved him and would miss him a lot. Joe left the room. Patrick and I were sitting there and I said to Patrick, "I think he has stopped breathing." An aide came in, took his blood pressure, and shook her head. Dan had died.[322]

Dan lived and died in used clothing. On his last day he was wearing pajama bottoms that had belonged to his brother Jerry, who had died the year before.

Dan was bookish to the end. On a low table near his bed was a pile of books. Though no longer able to read on his own, when Dan was conscious, visitors sometimes read to him.

In his closet at Murray-Weigel Hall was a thin navy-blue backpack, "light as a feather," his niece Frida told Jim Dwyer, a reporter for the *New York Times*. "He brought it everywhere. Dan owned nothing. He carried nothing. Whenever I traveled with him—to conferences, speaking engagements, retreats, family occasions—he'd bring that little backpack of nothing. I'd pick him up and ask, 'Is that all you have?' He'd say, 'Yes, that's it. Let's go.'"[323]

"My cousin Carla and I got married fifteen years apart," Frida recalled. "Dan wore the same shirt to both weddings." It was still hanging in the closet. It was among the gifts brought to the altar at the funeral Mass.

"He had two kinds of clothes," Frida added, "threadbare, translucent from wear, and things that he had never worn. He had a shiny old black raincoat that he wore to every demonstration. Just Google the images of him." Another possession was a much-used red stocking cap with a laughing cow on the side that had been sent to him by the ice cream makers Ben & Jerry for whom he had once done an ad. "He wore it all the time."

A private wake was held at Murray-Weigel Hall Wednesday evening, May 4, for the Jesuits and a few close friends. John Dear noticed that the priestly robe Dan's body had been vested in was on backward. Over Dan's chest was a huge white dove surrounded by bright red flames. "It was a robe that otherwise would be used for Mass on Pentecost," John realized, "except, if worn at Mass, the dove and flames would be on the back. But this was perfect! A dove and flames! It reminded me of the fire that burned at Catonsville in 1968."

A public wake that filled the Jesuit church of St. Francis Xavier on West 16th Street was held the next day. The doors were opened at two in the afternoon. Dan's waxy, pale body lay in an open coffin close to the altar. His friend of many years, David Eberhardt, was struck by "Dan's cheap black shoes." At seven o'clock a two-hour program began that featured friends and relatives, each speaking for two minutes. This ended with Dar Williams performing a song about Dan she had written, "I Had No Right."

The funeral took place at ten the next morning, May 6. The Mass of the Resurrection was preceded with a peace march that set off two hours earlier from the Catholic Worker's Maryhouse across town on East

Rain falls on memorial procession.
Felton Davis

3rd Street. Despite pouring rain, hundreds took part. "Somehow it was fitting to walk through the rain to sing Dan home," said Matt Daloisio. The Rude Mechanical Orchestra, a marching band, enlivened the procession as it made its wet way to the West Village church. An array of banners was raised above the boisterous throng—"Our humanity is destroyed by endless war," "Peace is a Way of Life," "Love Your Enemies—Jesus; Kill Your Enemies—Uncle Sam," and more. Many carried quotations from Dan's writings and photos of Dan. On arriving at the church entrance, the marchers sang the black spiritual that anticipates disarmament: "We're gonna lay down our swords and shields down by the riverside. Ain't gonna study war no more!"

The church was packed to standing room with a thousand people or more. Large photos of Dan had been placed around the church.[324]

There was a choir of twenty-eight voices, with mandolin and clarinet. Jesuit provincial John Cecero presided at the liturgy. The cantor was Anne Holland. The altar area was crowded with concelebrating priests, John Dear, Bill McNichols, and Bishop Thomas Gumbleton among them.

The Call to Worship was a poem of Dan's, "We Love," that had been set to music:

> about trees: past is never tall enough,
> future too tall. Another spring will tell.
> Tell another spring

I will be there, and fairer.
I become myself, standing upon
that throat of swan
that striding giant I decree myself.

We love: in trees or men, how many die
forward on the blade.
                  I see men like forests
striding, like swans, royally, always
royally: though lowly afoot, striding unto death.

What we love: there are not blades enough

Dan's friend and fellow Jesuit Stephen Kelly, who has spent eight years in prison for antiwar and antitorture protests, gave the homily. He elicited a roar of laughter and applause at the start with a greeting to the FBI. "We may let members of the FBI assigned here today validate that it is Daniel Berrigan's Funeral Mass of the Resurrection, so they can complete and perhaps close their files."

Kelly concentrated on the implications of the day's Gospel reading, the story of Jesus raising his friend Lazarus from the dead.[325] It's a narrative, said Kelly, "that reveals the condition of humanity and anatomy of freedom to love . . . Seemingly, Jesus arrives too late." [Lazarus had died several days before and was now entombed.] Kelly asked if we, too, like Lazarus, are not "sealed under two tons of stone?" Isn't Lazarus's tomb "an inspired image of our own situation and how God sees us, sealed up in death despite our freedom?"

"We're presented," said Kelly, "with a *kairos* moment of faith: a sliver of light breaks the obscure camouflage, beaming into an otherwise dark hour. Is it really possible that God knows what it's like to have death immanent, bearing down, deluding, threatening annihilation? . . . The immediacy of death threatens to cleave the relationship between Jesus and the one who sent him. How can one obey the guidance and be dependent on the one who

*"One newsman asked, undoubtedly seeking a new twist on a stale pretzel: 'What words would you want inscribed on your tombstone?' I said, gnawing my pretzel: 'May he never rest in peace.'*

*I meant something beyond a joke. In such times as ours, the ego takes its proper measure, not from something so vulgar as crowd appeal, but from the struggle inherent in life itself. If, indeed, the ego is not to stagnate, or lord it over, or utterly give up before the brutal and gargantuan and sinister shape of life."*

—Ten Commandments for the
Long Haul

sent him if afraid? But "greater love has no one than to lay down one's life for a friend. So God does know what it's like to encounter death's whiplash. . . . Always, everywhere, each time, each encounter, risks are included. . . . So what's God going to do? In John's Gospel, in which we're asked for faith—not its opposite, fear—will Jesus practice what he preaches? Will he put confidence in the Father's guidance? Will his love risk facing death as the Father unmasks death?"

Jesus assures Lazarus's sisters that Lazarus will live, Kelly said, but was this just a pie-in-the-sky promise of a resurrection at the end of history? "Jesus went the distance in this anguishing scene. To see him at work is to see life itself overcoming death because he, as a human being, cooperated, obeyed the guidance of the one who sent him. He loved. He lays down his life. He says, 'I will take your place, Lazarus. Come forth, I am not of the power that put you there.' Now there is a different moral power in town. God is going to crack Death's veneer. . . . Through Jesus's obedience the crumbling begins and the hidden hold of death is broken."

Kelly noted another key element in the story: "An assent is awaited. Jesus is asking for the nod from friends, our willingness to remove obstacles to faith, a hurdle to overtake. Will the friends of Lazarus allow this? Will they roll away the stone? The first impediment holds up the scene. The friends object—'But you're going to embarrass us all with a stench!' Jesus insists: 'Believe; do not be ruled by fear, but faith.' . . . But the principalities dictate that resurrection is strictly illegal. It's forbidden to bring us back to life and unbind death's prisoners. Jesus asks others, conspiratorially, to do likewise. But what of the faith of our Daniel? Did he hear in his inner recesses the summons to come forth? Did Philip, his brother, another one who awakened to Christ's voice, help unbind [Dan] from the trappings, the ensnarling bonds, the lure of prestige and credibility?"

In their respective ways, said Kelly, the lives of Dan

*"What now? What is our expectation of Christ? . . . For my own part, I cannot separate His activity in the world from my own. I see Him in the gospel and the Eucharist, but also in the faithful—in the mirror of my own mind and the work of my hands. . . . That is why I am arrested again and again, and will never give up. . . . So believing, I deny to the politicians, the researchers, the generals, their way in the world. They will not prevail. My faith in Christ and my faith in my friends allows me to say this. The word of the death dealers is not the last word about our fate; other hands than theirs are in command of life and death."*

—Ten Commandments for the Long Haul

and Phil Berrigan raise the same urgent question, a question of whether we will choose the resurrection or not: "Are we to remain in a catatonic stupor, asleep, drunk, unconscious or in flat-lined existence . . . with our freedom never used? What good is it if paralyzed in fear? Liberated, but not loving?"

Daniel and Philip Berrigan, Kelly continued, "exposed the historical alliance of the religious leaders . . . colluding with structures of domination. Bomb-blessing has no place in Jesus's self-giving ministry. The imperial power of *Pax Romana* ran aground on the shoals of Christian steadfastness. But through the centuries what was an intimate circle of outcasts and martyrs dissembled and gained in ascendancy the power it was meant to resist, the power that had to be faced. Daniel and Phil untied, illegally, those called forth from out of power's captivity, power's confines. They risked the retaliation of those beholden to death's sway. They touched the idol of the state. Inspired, they, and other draft board raiders, retrieved the place and pre-eminence of the conscientious objector as imitating the love of Christ."

Kelly made a proposal. From time to time the Catholic Church not only formally identifies certain people as saints, having lived Christ-like lives in extraordinary and exemplary ways, but recognizes a few saints as Doctors of the Church, that is, theologians regarded as especially authoritative. "I leave it to your own assessment as to Dan's holiness," Kelly said, adding that in his opinion Dan belonged among the Doctors of the Church. Dan was one of those Christians "who retrieved for the people of God a move from preoccupation with orthodoxy [right belief] to orthopraxis [right practice]."

Kelly concluded with a passage from Dan's book *No*

Funeral Mass for Daniel Berrigan.
Robert Ellsberg

Hearse departs with Dan's coffin.
Robert Ellsberg

*Bars to Manhood*: "These many beautiful days cannot be lived again. But they are compounded in my own flesh and spirit. And I take them in full measure with me toward whatever lies ahead."[326]

The congregation responded to Kelly's reflections with prolonged applause. It was a sermon, remarked David Eberhardt, "to convert even a nonbeliever such as myself."

In preparation for communion, gifts were brought to the altar area by a procession of family members. In addition to bread and wine, the gifts included books Dan had written, articles of clothing he had worn, protest banners, and a hammer that had played a role in a Plowshares action.

Following communion, Liz McAlister read aloud the words Dan had written in preparation for the burning of draft files at Catonsville: "Our apologies, good friends, for the fracture of good order, the burning of paper instead of children, the angering of the orderlies in the front parlor of the charnel house. We could not, so help us God, do otherwise. . . . We have chosen to say with the gift of liberty, if necessary our lives: the violence stops here, the death stops here, the suppression of the truth stops here, this war stops here." A tidal wave of applause followed.

Liz stressed the inseparability of the sacred and political for both Phil and Dan Berrigan. Together they followed a dark path in which failure was a frequent experience—"It never seems to get better, and we walk in that reality," as Liz put it. Dan brought his solidarity with the marginalized and down-and-out, she remarked, into his many university appointments: "While other professors would rail against apathy and indifference, Dan would offer the insights of being out in the streets." Dan shared ways "to dig into resources and live deeply even with so much wrong in the world . . . The gift I walk with most is his practice of talking deeply but briefly at the end of an evening about something in the world and then posing the question: 'What gives you hope these days? What are you doing that gives you hope?'" Dan "remembered the reasons for hope and returned to faith, hope, and love." She implored those who revered Dan not to simply hold him up as an icon "in ways that exempt us from our own responsibility" but rather to follow his example. "How much better would it be if we asked for a double portion of Dan's spirit, and better yet, if we acted on it?"

Other members of the Berrigan clan surrounded Liz as she spoke: Frida, Jerry, and Kate Berrigan, and Carla Berrigan Pittarelli. "It's almost like [my uncle] lived right in the heart of God and reported back to us," said his nephew Jerry. Frida spoke of how much it meant having an uncle who listened so attentively both to her questions and her answers, who took her for long walks, who enjoyed her company at meals, who only ate when others ate, an uncle of such amazing vitality, and then an uncle who abruptly grew weak, began to falter, and who was forced

Family and friends gather after the funeral to reflect on a question from Liz McAlister: "What gives you hope?"
Matt Daloisio

Dan's gravesite. Matt Daloisio

to depend on the strength of others. Now her Uncle Dan was gone—"all that was left was us and our love for him and the things he loved. But that's enough. It's enough, because it has to be."

"Everyone applauded as the hearse drove away with Dan's body," Joe Cosgrove wrote me afterward, "but at the time we knew nothing about his actual interment. Jesuit burials are not only private, they're purely functional. Normally no one is present except a paid gravedigger. Matt Daloisio of the Catholic Worker would have none of that. Matt went on an intelligence mission and found out that the burial was set for May 11 at the Shrine of the Jesuit Martyrs in Auriesville, near Albany, the final resting place of hundreds of deceased Jesuits. Word went out to a few of us—Carla Berrigan Pittarelli, her husband Marc and her brother, Philip; Frida Berrigan and her two small children, Seamus and Madeline; Catholic Workers Carmen Trotta, Bud Courtney, Matt and Amanda Daloisio; and me. We convened at the cemetery where Matt and Amanda handed out programs they'd created for a ceremony. We took turns reading from scripture and from Dan's own works, then prayed for those most in need, and wept as Amanda's sweet voice sang Dan's coffin into the earth. Then the adults took turns shoveling earth over the coffin while the kids played among the gravestones."

While the Jesuits had prepared a headstone similar to all the others that stood vigil in the cemetery, Carla and Marc put their artistry to work and created a supplementary grave marker that included the few words Dan had once proposed as an epitaph:

"It was never dull, alleluia!"

# Afterword:
# Bearing Witness

Dan was the target of sharp criticism through much of his adult life, but lived long enough to witness some remarkable validations. Not least he saw a fellow Jesuit with a similar conscience elected pope and take the name Francis, thus linking his pontificate to the poor man of Assisi who became a missionary of mercy and an enemy of war. He lived to hear the same pope stand before both houses of the US Congress and single out for praise two of Dan's principal mentors, Dorothy Day and Thomas Merton. Just months before Dan's heart stopped beating, the Vatican hosted a global meeting of peacemakers who proposed that it was time to bury the just war doctrine and focus instead on nonviolent methods of conflict resolution and what makes for a just peace. In all the sixteen centuries of the just war theory, it was pointed out at the conference, no national hierarchy had ever condemned as unjust any war in which its nation's military was engaged. Dan was one of those who has helped speed the day when Christians, whether Catholic or otherwise, could no longer attach the adjectives "just" or "holy" to the word "war."

While writing this book I received a letter from David Eberhardt describing Dan's funeral in detail, an event I had missed because the Atlantic Ocean stood in

Obituary for Dan Berrigan in *The Catholic Worker.*

Drawing by Ben Forest.

*"Sometime in your life, hope that you might see one starved man, the look on his face when the bread finally arrives. Hope that you might have baked it or bought or even kneaded it yourself. For that look on his face, for your meeting his eyes across a piece of bread, you might be willing to lose a lot, or suffer a lot, or die a little, even."*

—Daniel Berrigan

the way. David is a poet who has never ceased wrestling with life's larger questions. His often off-the-rails life includes the commission of what was judged a felony in 1967: along with Phil Berrigan, David was one of the four who stained draft files with blood in Baltimore.

"People like to quote," David reminded me, "Dan's self-effacing and self-deprecating view that we do good for its own sake and forget about results. But Americans always want results, and in fact there were results. For starters we ended the draft, for Chrissake. People question the results of the witness actions, but you never know how your action may influence another. Dan Berrigan changed a lot of lives. I call that a result."

Dan Berrigan changed a lot of lives, mine among them. I expect what Dan did and what he said and the example he gave will continue to change people's lives for the foreseeable future.

Dan was easy to love but even late in life he could be a challenging person to be with. While he wasn't a recruiting sergeant, he made clear to all who encountered him that the possibility exists to reshape one's life around the beatitude of peacemaking: "Blessed are the peacemakers for they shall be called children of God." Saying no to any death-centered activity is an integral part of such a commitment. Dan's life raised the question: As a step in the right direction, how about shaking the dust out of your life with a little civil disobedience now and then? Would a sabbatical in jail, even a brief one, be such a bad idea? In any event, get out of the tomb and make some gestures, however modest, that favor life.

In my own case Dan helped me imagine taking a step—burning draft records in Milwaukee in 1968—that I might otherwise not have taken. While I still have troubled feelings about the year my seven-year-old son, Benedict, and I lived apart from each other, it nonetheless gives me pride to have been one of those who put war resistance above personal freedom. (While in prison I had the consolation of attaching on my cell wall a crayon drawing Ben had made for his Sunday school class of me behind bars. It showed me smiling broadly while holding my arms up as if I had won an election.)

Thank you, Dan, for nudging me over the cliff of my own fears.

Dan had powerful convictions but was not self-righteous. One of the things Dan showed me was that you don't have to wag a scolding finger at others in the effort to live and advocate a peaceful life. Accusations seldom change anyone's mind. Glares don't convert. You can be as absolute as Dan about not killing anyone and at the same time enjoy the company of people who don't agree with you and perhaps never will. In his writing and lectures, Dan could be as unyielding on life-and-death issues as Moses with the tablets of the Ten Commandments in hand, but in face-to-face encounters he had an amazing gift to make space for and welcome the other, to tell stories and jokes, to create bridges of affinity and laughter. In Ireland, arguing the virtues of nonviolence with a leader of the far-from-nonviolent IRA, Dan realized how much he liked the man despite their radically different views. It didn't make their differences less significant or their verbal jousting more restrained, but their mutual affection put a dimension of love into their exchange.

As David Eberhardt pointed out, part of the scandal of Dan's acts of witness was his emphasis on doing the true thing even if many judged it as ineffective or merely symbolic. "The good is to be done because it is good," Dan said in an interview, "not because it goes somewhere. I believe if it is done in that spirit it will go somewhere, but I don't know where. I don't think the Bible grants us to know where goodness goes, what direction, what force. I have never been seriously interested in the outcome. I was interested in trying to do it humanly and carefully and nonviolently and let it go. We have not lost everything because we lost today."[327]

Once asked by an Irish journalist if he thought he was on the right track, Dan replied, "Well, I'm embar-

CNS

rassed when I compare what I am with what I should be." It was a modest response.

Dan loved the word "modesty" and used it often. Be modest about what you are doing, be modest in your expectations of what your acts of witness will accomplish, be modest about who you are. Do your best but get used to failure. It's God who made the world and God who saves it, not you. But be confident that whatever you do to safeguard life is not wasted.

Dan, like many others involved in antiwar protest, was often described as a "peace activist," but it's worth noting that the bulk of his time was not spent jousting with war and weapons. He was far from being a full-time activist. In one letter to me he remarked that many "good people are overworked and underjoyed." When available, he enjoyed a glass or two of wine at the end of the day. His daily walks were a major part of his spiritual life, as were his occasional quiet weeks in the hermitage that William Stringfellow and Tony Towne set up for him on Block Island. I cannot recall Dan ever being in a hurry.

Playing with Cait in Alkmaar.
Jim Forest

"Unless you're coming from somewhere, you're not going anywhere," he said from time to time. The "somewhere" Dan was coming from is not easily described, but silence and sacrament were essential elements and helped keep him from being underjoyed.

So were the works of mercy, most of all visiting the sick. A great deal of Dan's life was spent caring for the gravely ill. He became "a listener of last resort."

One of Dan's great talents was friendship. He was a delight to be with, loved to have guests and to cook for them, often enjoyed company on his daily walk, listened closely and remembered what others had said, and never saw Mass as a solitary event but as a seed of community. When a friend was in need, Dan often found ways to help. On one occasion, aware I badly needed money to fix up my decrepit, uninsulated apartment, he signed over to me a check big enough to cover all the basic expenses of making it more weatherproof. I was astonished—still am.

"What I best remember was Dan's loyalty and friendship over many years," Robert Ellsberg said in a recent letter, "the many kindnesses and acts of thoughtfulness, his gentle encouragement. I am reminded of the disciples who ventured to ask Jesus, 'Where he was staying,' and he said, 'Come and see.' What does it mean to be a disciple? What does it mean to be a peacemaker? Dan didn't issue demands or conditions—he just said, 'Come and see.' He invited people to accompany him and see what the Gospel looks and feels like in action."[328]

I have known many people who lived what one might call Jesus-shaped lives, Dorothy Day and Thomas Merton among them. Dan was another. Such people remind those who encounter them of the Gospels. These are people who, in ways large and small, lay down their lives for their neighbor, including the hostile neighbor, the enemy. Apart from the New Testament, one can make no sense of the pivotal choices Dan made in his long life.

In a conversation he and I had one afternoon with a group of students, I recall Dan saying that everyone has a god—that life is impossible without some center point in one's life. One's micro-god might be national identity, an ideology, politics, science, a religious institution, a baseball team, a theory about health and the ideal diet, might be Hollywood, might be just about anything. But, Dan proposed, if you're going to have a god, it might as well *be* God, capital G. Then the big project begins: the lifelong quest of finding who God is and why we exist and why such great hopes have been placed upon us—the love of creation, the care of life.

In contrast to Phil, Dan didn't look like a warrior, but he was a brave man, not only in his many actions in opposing war and militarism but in challenging his friends

Jim Forest

on issues about which they took a militant opposing view. Like many of the early feminists, Dan was an outspoken opponent of abortion. He saw life whole, from womb to deathbed, and tried to inspire protection of life every inch of the way. Parting company with many friends, Dan had the courage to raise his voice on behalf of those tiny humans awaiting birth as well as women who, in various ways, were being pushed toward abortion.

Dan's commitment to the unborn was in part inspired by the gratitude and wonder awakened in him by the Eden-like beauty of children's faces, a beauty so often dulled as we get older and fears deform us—such powerful fears as being out of step with our peer group.

How often children figured in his writing and how easily Dan connected with children . . . I recall how much he enjoyed playing with our own kids during his stays with us after my work brought me to Holland. In one of my favorite photos of him, he is playing catch with our five-year-old daughter, Cait, in the parking lot behind our house.

As a house gift at the end of one visit he left this poem:

The children!
When they grace
our lives
victimhood, innocence
the fresh possible start,
the alternative,
all are present
at the vulnerable center
of flesh and blood
where the bomb lays waste.
If war is about children,
so is peace.
We cannot put things off,
put off peacemaking,
anymore than we can put off
the discomforts

Rachel and Sarah Wildflower-Williams of the Seattle Catholic Worker at the baptism of Sarah in 1984. Bruce Kellman, courtesy John Williams

of a child's hunger or thirst
in favor of our own comfort.

One of the achievements of Dan's life is that somehow he held on to remaining a Jesuit. As this book records, it wasn't always easy. He once sent me, a young man not even thirty at the time, to intercede for him with his provincial at a point when there was a more than even chance that Dan would be "given the Jonah option," that is, thrown overboard. Following the Catonsville action and other less famous crimes and misdemeanors, quite a number of his fellow Jesuits made their distaste for him and what he represented quite clear. It's not only remarkable that he hung on but that he *wanted* to hang on. However searing his criticisms of the Society of Jesus, that society was his chosen family and he clung to it with both hands. Happily, by the time he reached old age, many, perhaps most, of his Jesuit adversaries had come not only to respect Dan but to take pride in his being a Jesuit. In some cases he even changed their minds.

Dan was buried in priestly vestments. Hearing that, I was reminded of the many priests of Dan's generation who gave up their priesthood. Phil was one of them, and his reason was the most usual—release from the imposition of celibacy, for many priests an unbearable and indeed unchristian burden imposed in the Western church since the tenth century. Phil had fallen in love and decided to build a marriage and a family even at the price of no longer being recognized by his church as a functioning priest. Dan had nothing but respect and admiration for Phil and for others who left or were driven out, but one of the surprises of his own life was the determination with which he held on to remaining a celibate priest even when there were many good reasons to give it up.

Dan once explained this to me as simply keeping a promise. As he wrote in his autobiography, "I had come of age in a church that, for all its shortcomings, honored vows and promises. In important matters . . . that

*"Paul says somewhere in one of his letters something very simple about himself. Speaking of that rocky course he was on (which included floggings, and imprisonment, and exile, and all the rest) he says: 'I die daily.' I think that is a wonderfully brief and striking description of the kind of constant rebirth that is required of all of us. And if we are to be born again, we must be prepared to suffer and die."*
—The Geography of Faith

313

touched on life and death and innocence and marriage and the vindication of the poor—in these, at least, Christians were blessed with coherent moral guidance."[329]

There was also the unbreakable bond he had with the Catholic Church despite his frequently expressed criticisms of its many failures, its damaged history, its institutionalism, its careerist clergy.

In a period when celibacy was regarded by many as an indication of mental illness, Dan remained a celibate and even managed to joke about it. I recall an exchange with Dan at a Student Christian Movement conference in Sheffield, England, in 1973. The question was raised, "Father Dan, would you please explain celibacy?" Without missing a beat, Dan replied, "Forgive me, I forgot to bring my celibacy slide show." Much laughter, but that was all the answer the questioner pried out of him. For a time a poster of his artist friend Sister Corita Kent hung in his shower, decorated with a button that said, "Save water—shower with a friend." Given all the red lights that turned green in the sixties and seventies, there must have been those who wondered why *wasn't* Dan showering with a friend?

As I can bear witness, Dan was unjudgmental, even sympathetic, toward those whose sexual lives had gone off the church-sanctioned tracks in various directions, but he clung to celibacy—he once described it as sexual solitude—like a barnacle to a ship's hull.

Though he had great compassion for those, like myself, who had failed in attempts at marriage, he tried to inspire fidelity and perseverance. In a letter I received from him in 1973, Dan reminded me that he was "a priest for whom marriage is sacred, a sacrament, sealed with Christ's love. This is a very deep thing with me; faithful love. I have tried in my own life to take this course, with fits and starts, but at least a clear vision of the summons; to be a sign of this."

At the center of Dan's life was the Mass. Looking back over old journals while writing this book, I found these words of his celebrating bread, every fragment of which is a reminder of the eucharistic bread: "When I hear the sound of bread breaking I see something else. It seems almost as though God never meant us to do anything else. So beautiful a sound. The crust breaks up like manna and falls all over everything and then we eat. Bread gets inside humans."

His greatest gift may have been the path he, as a priest, opened (or in many cases reopened) to eucharistic life and faith for people who had been estranged from almost everything.

In his vocation as priest, Dan was also a helpful witness and adviser if you had sins to confess. The confession with Dan that I remember best happened late in 1965. I was twenty-four, Dan forty-three. It was nearly midnight. Dan and I, pushed along by a cold, damp wind, were walking back toward his then Jesuit residence on East 78th Street after a meeting with college students at a West Side hotel.

Jim Forest with Dan in 1973.
Cornell University, Division of Rare and Manuscript Collections

It must have been a confessional blackness. Perhaps it was simply knowing that Dan was a priest and that one of the things priests do is hear confessions and that I was in need of that sacrament. It wasn't that Dan's clothing announced the fact of his ordination. As Dan had given up wearing a Roman collar, there were no "Hello, Father" greetings from passers-by as we walked along. Yet Dan's priesthood was an unshedable fact.

By the mid-sixties, confession was becoming an unfashionable sacrament. The Aquarian Age was dawning. The argument ran, "God knows, why tell a priest?" Also events in one's private life that had once been seen as morally catastrophic were now seen in a less critical light. There were multiplying assurances that self-accusations were as immobilizing to our potential selves as bricks tied to helium-filled balloons. For many social activists, sin's main surviving validity was chiefly in the public sphere: complicity in war crimes, greedy use of the planet's resources—social sins, sins we commit en masse. But I was unable to shake off a painful awareness that I was also guilty of sins of the old-fashioned variety: my failures as a husband and parent.

Dan listened. Confession can be like giving birth. Births are always hard, my words were coming hard, but Dan was a patient and cheerful midwife. I finished. We walked along in the special silence of Manhattan on a wet night, not a word from either one of us until Dan announced, "Hey, Jimmy, look at this!" We stopped. I discovered that we were in a wealthy zone of the Upper East Side and that Dan was gazing into the window of a store that sold every sort of sleep gear: silk and velvet eye masks, pillows with radios inside, pillows that provide the sounds of rain and water, down-filled pajamas, Swiss-made ear plugs, cashmere slippers, fur-trimmed blankets, silk and satin sheets. Dan was delighted. He pointed from item to item. "Look at that, Jimmy! Mink ear muffs!" I had never been invited to window-shop in a confessional before. Dan said, "This is how the other half sleeps!"

It dawned on me that the sleep-store window tour was Dan's comment on the unexamined life, his way of laughing at the moral sleepwalk I had been owning up to. And it was a celebration. "Look, Jimmy!" Which is to say, "Jimmy, this is where you were, but now you're awake again."

Walking away from the shop, Dan said to me words I had often heard in the tight enclosure of a confessional, "With the authority I have received from the Church, in the name of Jesus Christ, I absolve you from all your sins."

Later we sat in the kitchen in the Jesuit house, laughing in the high-ceilinged space with its faded walls and ancient fixtures, drinking beer and listening to rain battering the windows.

# Daniel Berrigan's Life and Work: A Compact Chronology

Compiled by John Dear and Jim Forest

**1921**

Born on May 9, in Virginia, Minnesota, the fifth of six sons of Frida Fromhart and Thomas Berrigan.

**1926**

Family moves to a farm near Syracuse, New York.

**1926–39**

Attends St. John the Baptist Academy, Syracuse, New York.

**1939–43**

Enters the Society of Jesus on August 14, 1939; St. Andrew-on-Hudson novitiate near Poughkeepsie, New York, until 1941; then classical studies until 1943.

**1943–46**

Studies at Woodstock College, near Baltimore, Maryland.

**1946–49**

Teaches at St. Peter's Prep, Jersey City, New Jersey.

**1949–53**

Studies theology, Weston, Massachusetts.

**1952**

June 19: ordained a priest.

**1953–54**

Jesuit studies and ministerial work in Paray-le-Monial, France.

**1954–57**

Teaches French and philosophy at Brooklyn Prep, Brooklyn, New York.

**1956**

August 15: Final vows as a member of the Society of Jesus on the Feast of the Assumption.

**1957**

First book published, *Time without Number*; wins the Lamont Poetry Award.

**1957–63**

Teaches New Testament and dogmatic theology at Le Moyne College, Syracuse, New York.

**1959**

*The Bride: Essays in the Church*.

**1960**

*Encounters* (poetry).

**1961**

*The Bow in the Clouds: Humanity's Covenant with God*.

**1962**

Author of several plays done for television. *The World for Wedding Ring* (poetry).

**1963–64**

Sabbatical year in France based in Paris; travels to Czechoslovakia and South Africa. Cofounds Catholic Peace Fellowship. Moves to New York City, appointed assistant editor, *Jesuit Missions*. November 1964: Participates in Spiritual Roots of Protest retreat at the Abbey of Gethsemani in Kentucky.

## 1965

March 15: Dan and Phil arrive in Alabama to participate in the Selma march.

Cofounds Clergy and Laity Concerned about Vietnam.

November: Begins four-month exile to Latin America.

## 1966

March: Returns from Latin American exile to New York City.

*They Call Us Dead Men: Reflections on Life and Conscience.*

*No One Walks Waters* (poetry).

## 1967

Teaches in Colorado and California.

September: Joins Cornell United Religious Work at Cornell University, Ithaca, New York.

October: Arrested at antiwar protest at the Pentagon, first priest in US history to be arrested for a protest against war.

November 12: One of the Poets for Peace who read from their work at Town Hall, New York City.

*Consequences: Truth and . . .*

## 1968

February: Travel to Vietnam with Howard Zinn to free imprisoned US pilots.

May 17: Burns draft files with others, including his brother Philip, at Catonsville, Maryland.

October: Catonsville trial.

*Night Flight to Hanoi; Love, Love at the End* (poetry).

## 1969

*No Bars to Manhood.*

*False Gods, Real Men* (poetry).

## 1970

April: Refusing to report for imprisonment, Dan goes underground.

August 11: Arrested on Block Island, Rhode Island.

Sent to Danbury Federal Prison, Connecticut.

*The Trial of the Catonsville Nine* (drama).

*Trial Poems* (poetry).

*The Holy Outlaw* (film).

## 1971

June 9: Dan nearly dies while in prison due to a severe allergic reaction to the injection of Novocain.

*The Geography of Faith: Conversations between Daniel Berrigan and Robert Coles.*

*The Dark Night of Resistance.*

## 1972

February 24: Released from Danbury prison. Teaches at Woodstock, the Jesuit school now located in Manhattan.

Harrisburg trial of Philip and other defendants; trial ends April 5.

May: Travels to France to meet with Thich Nhat Hanh and attend premier of the Catonsville Nine trial film at Cannes Film Festival.

*America Is Hard to Find* (letters, poems, essays).

*Absurd Convictions, Modest Hopes: Conversations after Prison* (with Lee Lockwood).

*Jesus Christ* (poetry).

## 1973

Teaching at the University of Manitoba.

Arrested at the White House for digging a symbolic grave.

Summer: Move to West Side Jesuit Community at 220 West 98th Street, his home for the next thirty-six years.

October: Addresses the Association of Arab University Graduates, Washington, DC.

*Selected and New Poems* (poetry).

*Prison Poems* (poetry).

## 1974

Lives several months with Thich Nhat Hanh in Paris.

May: Trip to Israel, Lebanon, Egypt, and Cyprus.

*Lights On in the House of the Dead: A Prison Diary.*

## 1975

Teaches at the University of Detroit.

March: Arrested at the White House protesting President Ford's amnesty program.
March: Leads a retreat on peacemaking and reconciliation sponsored by the Student Christian Movement at the Glencree Center near Dublin, Ireland.
November 17: Dan and Phil arrested at the White House.
*The Raft Is Not the Shore: Conversations with Thich Nhat Hanh Toward a Buddhist-Christian Awareness.*

**1976**

Arrested at the Pentagon, the United Nations, and various arms manufacturers; teaches, lectures, and leads retreats at universities and churches around the United States, a pattern that will continue for the next thirty years.
December 22: Dan's mother, Frida Berrigan, dies, age ninety-one.
December 28: Participates in demonstration at the Pentagon protesting the arms race.

**1977**

February 24: Arrested for pouring blood at the Pentagon.
May–June 1977: Dan declared "an Undesirable Alien by the Canadian government" for an "incendiary" pro-life speech in Ottawa. Another visit with Thich Nhat Hanh in France.
*A Book of Parables.*

**1978**

June 12: Charged with "disorderly conduct" for protesting the arms race outside the UN during a conference on disarmament.
Begins part-time volunteer work at St. Rose's Home (hospice for indigent people dying of cancer).
December 26: Arrested at the Pentagon on the Feast of the Holy Innocents.
*Uncommon Prayer: A Book of Psalms.*
*Beside the Sea of Glass.*
*The Words Our Savior Gave Us.*

**1979**

Teaching at Yale University and the College of New Rochelle.
*The Discipline of the Mountain: Dante's Purgatorio in a Nuclear World.*

**1980**

January–May: Teaching at the Jesuit School of Theology in Berkeley and Pacific School of Religion at the Graduate Theological Union.
February 20: Ash Wednesday liturgy for peace at Berkeley, drawing attention to Livermore and Los Alamos nuclear labs, resulting in Dan's arrest at a sit-in.
August: In Northern Ireland to visit IRA prisoners.
September 9: Arrested with the Plowshares Eight at GE missile plant, King of Prussia, Pennsylvania.
*We Die before We Live: Talking with the Very Ill.*

**1981**

March: Plowshares Eight–King of Prussia trial.
May: Vigils outside Long Kesh prison in Northern Ireland as Bobby Sands dies.
Participates in filming Emile De Antonio's movie *In the King of Prussia*.
June: Back in Ireland.
*Ten Commandments for the Long Haul.*

**1982**

Lectures in Germany, Ireland, and the Netherlands.
*Portraits—Of Those I Love.*
*The Nightmare of God: The Book of Revelation.*
*In the King of Prussia* (film, with Martin Sheen).

**1984**

Begins service at St. Vincent's Hospital, New York City, ministering to patients with AIDS.
June: Travels in El Salvador and Nicaragua.
August 6: Arrested along with Martin Sheen at Riverside Research Institute in New York City.

**1985**

April–August: Engaged in making a film, *The Mission*, in Latin America.

Visit to Australia.

*Steadfastness of the Saints.*

*Block Island* (poetry).

**1986**

One of the main caregivers for fellow Jesuit Lew Cox in his losing battle with cancer.

*The Mission: A Film Journal.*

**1987**

February–May: Teaches at Berea College, Kentucky.

*To Dwell in Peace: An Autobiography.*

**1988**

Teaches at Yale.

Spring: *60 Minutes* features a profile of and interviews with Dan and Phil.

**1989**

Teaches at Loyola University, New Orleans.

November 17: Arrested at the Federal Building in New Orleans the day after the murder of six Jesuit priests in El Salvador.

*Stations: The Way of the Cross.*

**1990**

April: Sentenced to time served for the Plowshares Eight action.

May: Receives an honorary doctorate from Loyola University, New Orleans.

**1991**

November: Leads a weekend retreat where he and others are arrested one day protesting war at the Seneca Army Depot and the next day at an abortion clinic.

*Whereon to Stand: The Acts of the Apostles and Ourselves.*

*Jubilee* (poetry).

**1992**

January: Protest of UN sanctions against Iraq that caused many child deaths.

January: Teaching at Wooster College, Ohio.

January 30: Trial in Rochester for abortion protest.

March: Takes part in healing service for AIDS victims and caretakers in Hackensack, New Jersey.

*Tulips in the Prison Yard* (poetry).

**1993**

*Homage to Gerard Manley Hopkins* (poetry).

**1994**

Repeatedly visits Phil and John Dear in a North Carolina jail for Plowshares-related action.

June: At New York Catholic Worker for Merton reminiscences.

November: Two weeks in Switzerland.

**1995**

*Minor Prophets, Major Themes.*

**1996**

June: Dan's seventy-fifth birthday party at St. Francis Xavier Church, New York City.

*Isaiah: Spirit of Courage, Gift of Tears.*

**1997**

Spends a week in Portland, Maine, for Phil's Plowshares trial.

August 6: Civil disobedience on board the USS *Intrepid*, New York City.

December: Visits Belfast with John Dear to attend public reception with Mairead Corrigan Maguire, who nominates Dan and Phil for the Nobel Peace Prize.

*Ezekiel; Visions in the Dust.*

**1998**

Appointed poet-in-residence at Fordham, a post that was Dan's for about ten years.

April: Received the Edmund Campion Award from *America* magazine for literary-spiritual excellence.

*Daniel: Under the Siege of the Divine.*

**1999**

Teaching at Fordham's Lincoln Center campus.

June: Dan in Italy.

*Jeremiah: The Word, The Wound of God.*

**2000**

*The Bride: Images of the Church* (with icons by William Hart McNichols).

**2001**

June: Dan's eightieth birthday party at St. Paul's Church in New York City.

Throughout the fall of 2001 and early 2002, Dan attends a weekly peace vigil in Union Square with Kairos and the Catholic Worker protesting the US war in Afghanistan.

*Job: And Death No Dominion.*

**2002**

December 6: Phil dies at Jonah House.

*Lamentations: From New York to Kabul and Beyond.*

**2003**

October 4: Dan speaks at a memorial for Phil in New York City.

*Testimony: The Word Made Fresh.*

**2005**

*Genesis: Fair Beginnings, Then Foul.*

**2006**

June: Dan's eighty-fifth birthday party at St. Francis Xavier Church, New York City.

**2007**

*Prayer for the Morning Headlines: On the Sanctity of Life and Death.*

**2008**

*Exodus: Let My People Go.*

*The Kings and Their Gods: The Pathology of Power.*

**2009**

98th Street Jesuit Community closes in March; Dan becomes part of a smaller Jesuit community on Thompson Street in Manhattan's Soho area.

*No Gods but One.*

*Daniel Berrigan: Essential Writings* (ed. John Dear).

**2011**

April 2: Last arrest, on board the USS *Intrepid* war museum.

October 5: Last demonstration, supporting Occupy Wall Street.

**2012**

Dan moves to the Jesuit infirmary at Murray-Weigel Hall at Fordham.

**2014**

*A Sunday in Hell: Fables & Poems.*

**2015**

July 26: Jerry Berrigan, Dan's older brother, dies at ninety-five.

**2016**

April 30: Dan dies peacefully at noon at Murray-Weigel Hall at Fordham in the Bronx, New York.

May 6: Dan's funeral at St. Francis Xavier Church on West 16th St. in Manhattan.

# Bookshelf and Title Abbreviations

**AIHF**   *America Is Hard to Find* (New York: Doubleday, 1972).

**AOP**   *Apostle of Peace: Essays in Honor of Daniel Berrigan*, **ed.** John Dear (Maryknoll, NY: Orbis Books, 1996).

**ARB**   *And the Risen Bread: Selected Poems, 1957–1997*, ed. John Dear (New York: Fordham University Press, 1998).

**BL**   *The Berrigan Letters*, ed. Daniel Cosacchi and Eric Martin (Maryknoll, NY: Orbis Books, 2016).

**CT**   *Consequences: Truth and . . .* (New York: Macmillan, 1967).

**CW**   *Cloud of Witnesses*, ed. Jim Wallis and Joyce Hollyday (Maryknoll, NY: Orbis Books, 1991); see "Daniel Berrigan: The Push of Conscience."

**DB**   *Daniel Berrigan: Poetry, Drama, Prose*, **ed. Michael True** (Maryknoll, NY: Orbis Books, 1988).

**DD**   *Disarmed and Dangerous: The Radical Lives and Times of Daniel and Philip Berrigan*, **by** Murray Polner and Jim O'Grady (New York: Basic Books, 1997).

**DNR**   *The Dark Night of Resistance* (Eugene, OR: Wipf and Stock, 2007).

**DUSG**   *Daniel: Under the Siege of God* (Eugene, OR: Wipf and Stock, 2009).

**EVID**   *Ezekiel: Visions in the Dust* (Maryknoll, NY: Orbis Books, 1997).

**EW**   *Daniel Berrigan: Essential Writings*, ed. John Dear (Maryknoll, NY: Orbis Books, 2009).

**FLW**   **Philip Berrigan,** *Fighting the Lamb's War* (n.p.: iUniverse, 2011).

**GFB**   *Genesis: Fair Beginnings, Then Foul* (New York: Rowman and Littlefield, 2006).

**JADND**   *Job: And Death No Dominion* (Franklin, WI: Sheed & Ward, 2000).

**JTW**   *Jeremiah: The World, the Wound of God* (Minneapolis: Fortress Press, 1999).

**KTG**   *The Kings and Their Gods* (Grand Rapids: Eerdmans, 2008).

**LO**   *Lights On in the House of the Dead* (New York: Doubleday, 1974).

**MP**   *Minor Prophets, Major Themes* (Eugene, OR: Wipf and Stock, 2009).

**NBM**   *No Bars to Manhood* (Eugene, OR: Wipf and Stock, 2007).

**NFH**   *Night Flight to Hanoi* (New York: Macmillan, 1968).

**POTIL**   *Portraits of Those I Love* (Eugene, OR: Wipf and Stock, 2007).

**SBAB**   *Sorrow Built a Bridge: Friendship and AIDS* (Baltimore: Fortkamp, 1989).

| | |
|---|---|
| SS | *Steadfastness of the Saints* (Maryknoll, NY: Orbis Books, 1985). |
| ST | *Suspect Tenderness: The Ethics of the Berrigan Witness*, by William Stringfellow and Anthony Towne (Eugene, OR: Wipf and Stock, 2006). |
| STW | *Stations: The Way of the Cross*, poems by Daniel Berrigan, art by Margaret Parker (San Francisco: Harper & Row, 1989). |
| TB | *The Bride: Essays in the Church* (New York: Macmillan, 1959). |
| TBIC | *The Bride: Images of the Church*, with icons by William Hart McNichols (Maryknoll, NY: Orbis Books, 2003). |
| TC | *Ten Commandments for the Long Haul* (Nashville: Abingdon, 1981). |
| TCN | *The Trial of the Catonsville Nine* (New York: Fordham University Press, 2004). |
| TDIP | *To Dwell in Peace* (Eugene, OR: Wipf and Stock, 2007). |
| THGL | *The Hidden Ground of Love: Letters of Thomas Merton* (New York: Farrar Strauss Giroux, 1985); letters to Dan Berrigan, 70–101. |
| TM | *The Mission* (New York: Harper & Row, 1986). |
| TNG | *The Nightmare of God* (Eugene, OR: Wipf & Stock, 2009). |
| TR | *The Raft Is Not the Shore*, by Dan Berrigan and Thich Nhat Hanh (Boston: Beacon, 1975; Maryknoll, NY: Orbis Books, 2001). |
| TWMF | *Testimony: The Word Made Fresh*, ed. John Dear (Maryknoll, NY: Orbis Books, 2003). |
| WB | *Witness of the Berrigans*, ed. Stephen Halpert and Tom Murray (New York: Doubleday, 1972); "Sermon from the Underground," by Daniel Berrigan, 140–43. |
| WS | *Whereon to Stand: The Acts of the Apostles and Ourselves* (Eugene, OR: Wipf and Stock, 2009). |

# Notes

1  *And the Risen Bread: Selected Poems of Daniel Berrigan, 1957–1997*, ed. John Dear (New York: Fordham University Press, 1998), 100. Hereafter referred to as ARB.

2  Murray Polner and Jim O'Grady, *Disarmed and Dangerous: The Radical Lives and Times of Daniel and Philip Berrigan* (New York: Basic Books, 1997). Hereafter referred to as DD.

3  Instructions for making napalm from soap chips and kerosene had been found in a Green Beret manual in the military section of the Georgetown University Library.

4  Shawn Francis Peters, *The Catonsville Nine: A Story of Faith and Resistance in the Vietnam Era* (New York: Oxford University Press, 2012), 4.

5  *Daniel Berrigan: Essential Writings,* edited by John Dear (Maryknoll, NY: Orbis Books, 2009), 105–6. Hereafter referred to as EW.

6  *The Berrigan Letters*, edited by Daniel Cosacchi and Eric Martin (Maryknoll, NY: Orbis Books, 2016), 328. Dan was pleased to learn O'Connell "was resolutely nonviolent *vis a vis* the bigoted British and won important concessions without bloodshed." Hereafter referred to as BL.

7  Daniel Berrigan, *To Dwell in Peace* (Eugene, OR: Wipf and Stock, 2007), 73. Hereafter referred to as TDIP.

8  DD, 23.

9  TDIP, 73.

10  "To My Father," *Prison Poems* (Greensboro, NC: Unicorn Press, 1973), 47.

11  BL, 193–94.

12  DD, 80.

13  Daniel Berrigan, *Lights On in the House of the Dead* (New York: Doubleday, 1974), 14. Hereafter referred to as LO.

14  Daniel Berrigan, *Portraits of Those I Love* (New York: Crossroad, 1982), 102. Hereafter referred to as POTIL.

15  TDIP, 5.

16  DD, 47.

17  TDIP, 13.

18  Ibid., 53.

19  Ibid., 55.

20  *Daniel Berrigan: Poetry, Drama, Prose*, ed. Michael True (Maryknoll, NY: Orbis Books, 1988), 32. Hereafter referred to as DB.

21  TDIP, 16.

22  Ibid., 88.

23  There are also Jesuit lay brothers.

24  DB, 6.

25  BL, October 12, 1942.

26  DD, 71.

27  BL, 1–2.

28  DB, 6.

29  BL, 46.

30  Philip Berrigan, *Fighting the Lamb's War* (n.p.: iUniverse, 2011), 13–14.

31  *America*, October 23, 1943.

32  Jim Forest, *The Root of War Is Fear: Thomas Merton's Advice to Peacemakers* (Maryknoll, NY: Orbis Books, 2016).

33  BL, letter dated September 15, 1943.

34  DB, 6–7. Woodstock College was a Jesuit seminary originally located in Woodstock, Maryland, that existed from 1869 to 1974, after which it moved to New York City, where it operated in cooperation with the Union Theological Seminary and the Jewish Theological Seminary. The school closed in 1974 but is survived

by the Woodstock Theological Center at Georgetown University in Washington, DC.

35   TDIP, 101, 105.

36   FLW, 16–17.

37   DD, 78.

38   BL, 7–8.

39   TDIP, 106.

40   DB, 7.

41   TDIP, 107.

42   Ronald Knox, *God and the Atom* (New York: Sheed & Ward, 1945).

43   TDIP, 107–8.

44   Ibid., 109.

45   DD, 79.

46   TDIP, 112.

47   Ibid., 114.

48   Later popes—John Paul II, Benedict XVI, and Francis—have written approvingly of Teilhard's ideas. In July 2009 Vatican spokesman Federico Lombardi said, "By now, no one would dream of saying that [Teilhard de Chardin] is a heterodox author who shouldn't be studied."

49   TDIP, 116–17.

50   The script for Daniel Berrigan, *The Trial of the Catonsville Nine*, is available at http://ada.evergreen.edu/~arunc/texts/catonsville.pdf. Quote appears on p. 2.

51   TDIP, 118.

52   His essay became the seed of Dan's first theological book, *The Bride: Essays in the Church*, published by Macmillan in 1959.

53   TDIP, 114.

54   DB, 7–8.

55   TDIP, 118.

56   DB, 7–8.

57   Albert Camus, *Between Hell and Reason* (Middletown, CT: Wesleyan University Press, 1991), 97–98.

58   Cardinal Suhard had been appointed archbishop of Paris in May 1940. The following year he appealed to Hitler in an effort to save hostages in Nantes and Châteaubriant. In July 1942 he made a public protest against the deportation of the Jews of Paris and condemned Vichy collaboration in Nazi racial policies. He was subsequently confined to his residence by German troops.

59   DB, 8.

60   TDIP, 137.

61   I was fortunate, while seeking early discharge from the Navy as a conscientious objector in 1961, to have a chaplain who, though somewhat bewildered by my stand, wrote a letter of support.

62   Robert McClory, "Why Yves Congar Is Relevant Today," *National Catholic Reporter*, June 6, 2013, www.ncronline.org.

63   BL, 11.

64   DB, 7–8.

65   Chris Hedges, "Daniel Berrigan: Forty Years after Catonsville," *The Nation*, May 20, 2008, www.thenation.com.

66   DD, 93.

67   Joseph Roccasalvo, *As It Were* (n.p.: Xlibris, 2010), 67–69.

68   TDIP, 139.

69   BL, 12–15.

70   TDIP, 96.

71   John Smestad Jr., "The Role of Archbishop Joseph F. Rummel in the Desegregation of Catholic Schools in New Orleans," *Student Historical Journal* 25 (1993–1994), www.loyno.edu.

72   DD, 97–98; FLW, 49.

73   ARB, 3. The occasional joining together of words—as with "largehandedly" and "riverandsea"—was a trademark of Dan.

74   DB, 9.

75   Ibid.

76   TDIP, 145.

77   In letters Dan sent to Karl Meyer in that period, he repeatedly urged Meyer to avoid extremes, not to use the word "pacifism," and to act prudently. In a letter sent to Meyer in April 1959, Dan writes, "It is crucial that in your life you distinguish essentials from 'fringe' activity . . . in broad outline . . . to give witness of Christian pacifism (perhaps it would be less odious to use the term 'Christian worker for peace'). . . ."

78   DD, 99.

79   Miller was the first man convicted under a 1965 law that made it a felony to "knowingly destroy or mutilate" one's draft card; he was jailed for twenty-two months in a federal prison. See the Wikipedia entry for draft-card burning.

80   See Jim Forest, *The Root of War Is Fear: Thomas Merton's Advice to Peacemakers* (Maryknoll, NY: Orbis Books, 2016), 18–21.

81   Thomas Merton, *The Hidden Ground of Love*, ed. William Shannon (New York: Farrar, Straus and Giroux, 1985), 70–71. Thirty pages of Merton's letters to Dan Berrigan are included in this seven-hundred-page volume. Hereafter referred to as THGL.

82   *Turning toward the World: The Journals of Thomas Merton* (San Francisco: HarperSanFrancisco, 1996), 238.

83    TDIP, 147–48.

84    International House lasted more than forty years, finally closing in 2004.

85    DD, 100.

86    THGL, 76–79; letter from June 25, 1963.

87    A sodality is, in Roman Catholic usage, an association whose members make commitments that may include a more intense spiritual life, more frequent communion, voluntary service, etc.

88    TDIP, 146.

89    Ibid., 150–51.

90    Ibid., 151.

91    HGL, 79.

92    DB, 10.

93    TDIP, 155.

94    Ibid., 157.

95    It was John Heidbrink who, in the days that followed, wrote to Merton, Dan, Phil, and myself suggesting the creation of the Catholic Peace Fellowship (CPF). He also inspired the four of us to join the Fellowship of Reconciliation. For a more detailed account of the CPF's origins, see my book *The Root of War Is Fear: Thomas Merton's Advice to Peacemakers* (Maryknoll, NY: Orbis Books, 2016), 97–111.

96    DB, 11.

97    For an hour-by-hour account of the retreat, see Gordon Oyer, *Pursuing the Spiritual Roots of Protest* (Eugene, OR: Cascade Books, 2014).

98    Mark 10:51.

99    See Jim Forest, *Loving Our Enemies: Reflections on the Hardest Commandment* (Maryknoll, NY: Orbis Books, 2015).

100    See *Franz Jägerstätter: Letters and Writings from Prison*, ed. Erna Putz, intro. Jim Forest (Maryknoll, NY: Orbis Books, 2009).

101    From an unpublished lecture Gordon Oyer presented January 28, 2017, at Corpus Christi Church in Manhattan.

102    This led to the publication of a widely distributed CFP booklet titled *Catholics and Conscientious Objection* (Catholic Peace Fellowship, 1966).

103    A photo of Dan using Brother Thomas's chalice at a Catholic Worker Mass appears in *A Spectacle unto the World*, text by Bob Coles, photos by Jon Erikson (New York: Viking Press, 1973). See p. 19 of the photo section.

104    BL, 66.

105    EW, 55.

106    Ibid., 57.

107    Cornell lost his case and was sentenced to federal prison for six months.

108    TDIP, 180.

109    Ibid.

110    "Death Does Not Get the Last Word," EW, 65–73.

111    Rodger Van Allen, "What Really Happened? Revisiting the 1965 Exiling to Latin America of Daniel Berrigan, S.J.," *American Catholic Studies* 117, no. 2 (2006): 33–60.

112    THGL, 88. In a letter Merton sent Dan three months later he wrote, "I have never managed to get awful sorry for you going to Latin America: it is where everything is going to happen . . ." (THGL, 89).

113    DD, 13.

114    TDIP, 183–84.

115    *Jesuit Mission*, September 1966, 16.

116    THGL, 89.

117    Arrupe was a Hiroshima survivor. Thanks to medical training earlier in his life, Arrupe was able to assist Hiroshima's wounded and dying. The Jesuit novitiate was converted into a makeshift hospital. "Our half destroyed chapel," he wrote, "was overflowing with the wounded, who were lying on the floor very near to one another, suffering terribly, twisted with pain."

118    One member of the community, Elizabeth McAlister, later married Phil Berrigan.

119    John Dear, letter to the author, November 7, 2016; and Amy Goodman, interview with Dan Berrigan, "Holy Outlaw: Lifelong Peace Activist Father Daniel Berrigan Turns 85," *Democracy Now!* June 8, 2006, www.democracynow.org.

120    Daniel Berrigan, *The Discipline of the Mountain: Dante's Purgatorio in a Nuclear World* (New York: Seabury, 1979), 101–2; DD, 156.

121    Jim Forest, "Catholics and Conscientious Objection" (Catholic Peace Fellowship, April 1966), https://jimandnancyforest.com.

122    Dan was unaware that Phil had briefly considered the possibility of placing an explosive device in the US Customs House in Baltimore as a means of destroying thousands of draft records in a single blast, but he abandoned the idea when he realized there was no way to do this without endangering human life (DD, 172). A letter Phil sent to Dan shortly before the Customs House action apologized for not having made his plans clearer: "No, I would never do anything that would harm people physically—but the property that is part of these bloody gearboxes, [that's] another thing" (BL, 37).

123  Unpublished letter dated October 6, 1967, in the archives of the Thomas Merton Center, Bellarmine University, Louisville, Kentucky.

124  Letter from Merton to Dan, October 10, 1967; HGL, 98.

125  TDIP, 210–11.

126  Romans 12:20.

127  A mortal sin, in Catholic theology, is a gravely wrongful act that can lead to eternal damnation if a person is not absolved of the sin before death. A sin is considered to be "mortal" when its quality is such that it leads to a separation of that person from God's saving grace.

128  TDIP, 212.

129  Howard Zinn, "Just and Unjust War," in *Howard Zinn on War* (New York: Seven Stories Press, 2000), www.thirdworldtraveler.com.

130  TDIP, 213.

131  EW, 98–99.

132  Howard Zinn, "The Prisoners," in *The Witness of the Berrigans*, ed. Stephen Halpert and Tom Murray (New York: Doubleday, 1972), 9–10.

133  EW, 101–2.

134  DD, 208–9.

135  Ibid., 211.

136  Ibid., 127.

137  Philip Berrigan, "Napalming Draft Files," *Liberation,* July–August 1968.

138  See, for example, "On Pilgrimage" column, *Catholic Worker*, June 1970, www.catholicworker.org.

139  Dorothy Day, "On Pilgrimage" column, *Catholic Worker*, October 1968, www.catholicworker.org.

140  Letter to Mary Lanahan, June 24, 1968, HGL, 118.

141  *Ave Maria*, June 8, 1968.

142  A booklet on Camus's novel, *The Plague*, was dedicated to Dan.

143  Letter dated September 30, 1968, HGL, 101.

144  TDIP, 220–21; EW, 119.

145  A concise account of the Milwaukee 14's draft board raid can be found in DD, 233–39. Also see Jim Forest, "Looking Back on the Milwaukee 14," http://jimandnancyforest.com.

146  Gray's detailed account of the trial and the surrounding events is included in her book *Divine Disobedience* (New York: Knopf, 1970), 165–228. Daniel Berrigan's play *The Trial of the Catonsville Nine* (Boston: Beacon Press, 1970) provides a compact version of the twelve-hundred-page transcript. Also see Shawn Francis Peter's *The Catonsville Nine* (New York:

Oxford University Press, 2012), 202–39.

147  BL, 268.

148  *No Bars to Manhood* (New York: Doubleday, 1969), 57–85. Hereafter referred to as NBM. Also EW, 109–14.

149  BL, 95.

150  *False Gods, Real Men* (New York: Macmillan, 1969), 3.

151  Howard Zinn, *Disobedience and Democracy: Nine Fallacies on Law and Order* (New York: Random House, 1968), "fallacy two."

152  Daniel Berrigan, *America Is Hard to Find: Notes from the Underground and Letters from Danbury Prison* (New York: Doubleday, 1972), 16. Hereafter referred to as AIHF.

153  Peters, *Catonsville Nine*, 271.

154  Philip Nobile, "The Priest Who Stayed Out in the Cold," *New York Times Magazine*, June 28, 1970, 38.

155  "Sermon from the Underground," in *Witness of the Berrigans*, ed. Stephen Halpert and Tom Murray (New York: Doubleday, 1972), 140–43. Hereafter referred to as WB.

156  Between the Catonsville action and midsummer 1970, when this meeting occurred, these raids included the Milwaukee 14, the Boston Two, the DC Nine, the Pasadena Three, the Silver Springs Three, the Chicago Fifteen, Women against Daddy Warbucks (also known as the Manhattan Five), the New York Eight, the Cleveland Two, the Boston Eight, the Akron Two, the East Coast Conspiracy to Save Lives, We the People, the Rhode Island Political Offensive for Freedom, the Minnesota Conspiracy to Save Lives, and the Pontiac Four. Not only were draft files destroyed but also files and equipment of the Dow Chemical Company, manufacturers of napalm.

157  Daniel Berrigan and Robert Coles, *The Geography of Faith* (Boston: Beacon Press, 1973), 22, 24, 26.

158  Ibid., 25.

159  Founded in 1969, the Weather Underground was a group that conducted a campaign of bombings through the early 1970s. The main targets were government buildings and banks. No one was killed in any of the attacks, but three Weather Underground members died in a Greenwich Village townhouse when a bomb they were making exploded.

160  EW, 154–57.

161  *The Dark Night of Resistance* (New York: Doubleday, 1971). Hereafter referred to as DNR.

162  Ibid., 3.

163  Jim Forest, "The Harrisburg Conspiracy: The

Berrigans and the Catholic Left," *WIN*, March 15, 1973, www.jimandnancyforest.com. *WIN* was the journal of the War Resisters' League.

164 Stringfellow saved the slices, consigning them to the freezer. After Dan was released from prison and returned to Block Island, the welcoming meal included a pie baked from those same apples (Daniel Berrigan, *Block Island* [Greensboro, NC: Unicorn Press, 1985], 17).

165 LO, 11; EW, 63.

166 Philip Berrigan, *Widen the Prison Gates: Writings from Jails* (New York: Simon & Schuster, 1973), 89–90.

167 BL, August 20, 1970.

168 From a letter to the author from John Dear: "An Irish priest, Patrick O'Brien, was walking down a side street in Rome in the late 1970s, when he encountered Pedro Arrupe, superior general of the Jesuits. Arrupe asked where he was from, then asked if he knew any Jesuits. 'Only one,' said O'Brien, 'an American.' 'Who?' Arrupe asked. Pat said, 'Dan Berrigan.' Arrupe was stunned and said, 'Dan Berrigan is the greatest Jesuit of the century.'" Along similar lines, Dan received a letter from Vincent O'Keefe of Arrupe's staff in Rome. It concluded with this sentence: "I am sure you know, Dan, that you give hope to a lot of people" (October 5, 1982, on the stationery of the Jesuit's Vatican headquarters).

169 TDIP, 265.

170 Daniel Berrigan and Thich Nhat Hanh, *The Raft Is Not the Shore* (Boston: Beacon, 1975), 53–54. Hereafter referred to as TR.

171 D. Berrigan, *Prison Poems*, 32–37.

172 P. Berrigan, *Widen the Prison Gates*, 136–37.

173 BL, 68–69.

174 Leonard Bernstein, *Mass: A Theatre Piece for Singers, Players, and Dancers*, commissioned by Jacqueline Kennedy Onassis, premiered on September 8, 1971, as part of the opening of the John F. Kennedy Center for the Performing Arts in Washington, DC. The epistle used in *Mass*, probably chosen at Dan's suggestion, included a paragraph from a letter by Linda Henry describing a visit with me in prison after the trial of the Milwaukee 14. The FBI kept a file on Bernstein. In the summer of 1971, the bureau warned the Nixon White House that the text of the *Mass* might contain antiwar messages, which could cause embarrassment to Nixon should he attend the premiere. Nixon did not attend.

175 The original Jesuit college at Woodstock, Maryland, had been closed.

176 The church's construction was backed by the industrialist, financier, and philanthropist John D. Rockefeller Jr.

177 Letter to the author, December 3, 2016.

178 Daniel Berrigan, *Uncommon Prayer: A Book of Psalms* (New York: Seabury, 1978), 122.

179 Much of the material in this chapter is drawn from my essay "The Harrisburg Conspiracy: The Berrigans and the Catholic Left."

180 Over a period of thirteen seconds on May 4, 1970, soldiers of the Ohio National Guard fired sixty-seven rounds at students protesting the expansion of the Vietnam War into Cambodia, killing four and wounding nine others.

181 DD, 281.

182 In 1973, when I was writing "The Harrisburg Conspiracy: The Berrigans and the Catholic Left," Joe Wenderoth told me how terrified he was of the direction Phil was going at the time and how powerless he felt to oppose him. "To say I was relieved when the FBI arrested Phil in that Manhattan rectory is to put it mildly," Joe told me. "His arrest put an end to the tunnels project."

183 It would have been the Harrisburg Eight, but Ted Glick opted to defend himself and was to be tried separately. In fact, the case against Glick never went to trial.

184 An engaging day-by-day account of the trial, *The Harrisburg Seven and the New Catholic Left* by William O'Rourke, was reissued in 2012 with a new Afterword (South Bend, IN: University of Notre Dame Press).

185 Daniel Berrigan, *Testimony: The Word Made Fresh* (Maryknoll, NY: Orbis Books, 2004), 146.

186 The only charge the jurors were agreed upon was that Elizabeth McAlister and Philip Berrigan had engaged in unauthorized correspondence in violation of prison rules.

187 DD, 284.

188 Daniel Berrigan, *Ten Commandments for the Long Haul* (Nashville: Abingdon, 1981), 24. Hereafter referred to as TC.

189 Unpublished letter to the author, October 28, 1973.

190 All quotations from the lecture are taken from *The Great Berrigan Debate*, ed. Alan Solomonow (Nyack, NY: Committee on New Alternatives in the Middle East, 1974). The complete text of Dan's lecture is available at http://mondoweiss.net/2016/09/berrigans-prophecy-becoming/.

191 TDIP, 281.

192 *The Great Berrigan Debate*, 9.

193 Heschel had died of a heart attack December 27, 1972. One of his last actions had been to be among those greeting Phil Berrigan when he was released from prison.

194 The conversation was broadcast by WNET in January 1974 and the transcript published in *The Great Berrigan Debate*.

195 Abraham Joshua Heschel, *The Prophets* (New York: Harper & Row, 1962), 4.

196 DD, 319.

197 The Ma'alot massacre occurred in mid-May 1974 and involved a two-day hostage-taking of 115 Israelis. It began when three armed members of the Democratic Front for the Liberation of Palestine entered Israel from Lebanon. After killing two Israeli Arab women and a Jewish couple and their four-year-old son, they headed for the Netiv Meir School, where they took 105 children, mainly teenagers, hostage. The hostage-takers demanded the release of 23 Palestinian militants from Israeli prisons or else they would kill the students. On the second day of the standoff, an Israeli military unit stormed the building. During the attack, the hostage-takers killed 25 hostages, 22 of them children.

198 *Fellowship*, June 1974, 12. *Fellowship* was the journal of the FOR.

199 *Thich Nhat Hanh: Essential Writings,* ed. Robert Ellsberg (Maryknoll, NY: Orbis Books, 2001), 145–46.

200 ARB, 45.

201 Some of my memories of living and traveling with Thich Nhat Hanh are available at http://jimand nancyforest.com/2014/01/nhat-hanh-2/.

202 *Vietnam: Lotus in a Sea of Fire* (New York: Hill & Wang, 1967). Merton's introduction was reprinted in his book *Faith and Violence* (South Bend, IN: University of Notre Dame Press, 1968).

203 TC, 28.

204 TR, 5.

205 Ibid., 7.

206 Ibid., 9.

207 Ibid., 23.

208 Ibid., 110–11.

209 Ibid., 45–46.

210 Ibid., 51–52.

211 Matthew 25:40.

212 In an Afterword to a new edition of *The Raft Is Not the Shore*, Dan addressed an affectionate message to Nhat Hanh: "Dear Nhat Hanh, indeed the raft is not the shore, nor are suffering and death the final word. Your steadfast life has testified to that. I thank you with a full heart. Your friendship has brought the raft, not ashore to be sure, but closer. . . . We are closer. Our eyes discern the shore, the gentle green lineaments of the Promise. Soon we shall be home" (TR, 253).

213 TC, 37–41.

214 The Provisional Irish Republican Army was an Irish paramilitary organization that sought to remove Northern Ireland from the United Kingdom and to bring about an independent republic encompassing all of Ireland. It was the biggest and most active republican paramilitary group during the late twentieth century. It saw itself as successor to the original IRA and called itself simply the Irish Republican Army.

215 TC, 37–41.

216 Letter to the author, May 30, 1981.

217 From an undated 1981 letter to the author.

218 A *U.S. Catholic* interview, "Is Anyone Listening to the Prophets Anymore?" *U.S. Catholic*, August 1996, www.uscatholic.org.

219 *Fellowship*, June 1975, 8–11.

220 Jim Forest, "Vietnam: Unification without Reconciliation," *Fellowship*, October 1976, 20–21.

221 Jim Finn, "Fighting among the Doves," *Worldview*, April 1977, provides a good account of the controversy, https://jimandnancyforest.com.

222 Letter from August 11, 1978. Dan sent me a copy.

223 Daniel Berrigan, "Killing for the Love of the Kingdom," *National Catholic Reporter*, May 5, 1978.

224 *Steadfastness of the Saints* (Maryknoll, NY: Orbis Books, 1985), 78–81. Hereafter referred to as SS.

225 Ibid., 21.

226 Philip Berrigan, *Fighting the Lamb's War* (n.p.: iUniverse, 2011), 155–56.

227 After serving thirty-eight months in prison, Phil was released on parole December 20, 1972.

228 In 1996 Jonah House relocated to a building on the grounds of St. Peter's Cemetery, where the community cares for the cemetery and also maintains a vegetable and fruit garden. In 2016 Liz McAlister left the community and moved to New York City.

229 BL, 153–54.

230 The Shroud of Turin is a length of linen cloth bearing the image of a crucified man. It is believed by many to have been the burial shroud of Jesus.

231 TC, 53–54.

232 "First strike" is a preemptive surprise attack employing overwhelming force. First-strike capability

is a country's ability to defeat another nuclear power by destroying its arsenal to the point where the attacking country can survive the weakened retaliation while the opposing side is left unable to continue war.

233   Isaiah 2:9–10.

234   Unpublished letter, September 1980.

235   Letter in the author's Daniel Berrigan archive.

236   Letter to the author, July 28, 1981.

237   EW, 182–83.

238   Ibid., 187.

239   Ibid., 189.

240   The film is available on YouTube.

241   DD, 349.

242   Jim Dwyer, "Remembering Daniel Berrigan: A Penniless, Powerful Voice for Peace," *New York Times*, May 5, 2016.

243   Frida Berrigan, *It Runs in the Family* (New York: OR Books, 2015), Kindle edition, location 254–63; Elizabeth McAlister, *The Time's Discipline: The Eight Beatitudes and Nuclear Resistance* (Baltimore: Fortkamp, 1989).

244   Letter to the author, December 23, 2016.

245   Daniel Berrigan, *Testimony: The Word Made Fresh*, ed. John Dear (Maryknoll, NY: Orbis Books), 23–26. Hereafter referred to as TWMF.

246   For a gripping account of the Y-12 action, its background, and its consequences, see Dan Zak, *Almighty: Courage, Resistance, and Existential Peril in the Nuclear Age* (New York: Blue Rider Press, 2016). Zak also offers the reader one of the best accounts of the development of nuclear weapons.

247   John LaForge, "In Sentencing Radical Pacifists, Judge Miles Lord Assailed 'Worship of the Bomb,'" CounterPunch, December 21, 2016, www.counterpunch.org.

248   Letter from the author to Dan, July 23, 1985.

249   Letter from the author to Dan, March 8, 1978.

250   Jim Forest, "Some Reservations about Plowshare Actions," February 12, 1993, http://jimandnancyforest.com.

251   Letter to the author, March 7, 1985. We had to work out our disagreement by mail, since I was teaching at the Ecumenical Institute at Tantur, near Jerusalem, at the time.

252   BL, 225–26.

253   Ibid., 245–46.

254   Ibid., 246–48.

255   Ibid., April 3, 1990.

256   Daniel Berrigan, *We Die before We Live: Talking with the Very Ill* (New York: Seabury, 1980), 1.

257   Letters to the author, one from June 1977; another May 5, 1978; another "May into June" 1979.

258   DD, 337.

259   Ibid.

260   Berrigan, *We Die before We Live*, 1–2.

261   Ibid., 6–7.

262   Letter to the author.

263   BL, 214.

264   *Apostle of Peace: Essays in Honor of Daniel Berrigan,* ed. John Dear (Maryknoll, NY: Orbis Books, 1996), 103–4. Hereafter referred to as AOP.

265   Carl Siciliano, "Remembering Daniel Berrigan, a Forgotten AIDS Hero," Huffington Post, May 20, 2016, www.huffingtonpost.com.

266   Daniel Berrigan, *Sorrow Built a Bridge: Friendship and AIDS* (Baltimore: Fortkamp, 1989), 3. Hereafter referred to as SBAB.

267   Ibid., 1–14.

268   Letter to the author, January 26, 2017.

269   This and the quotations that follow come from Moore's essay in AOP, "Life in Community with Dan," 139–43.

270   Ibid., 146.

271   BL, 259.

272   *Stations: The Way of the Cross*, poems by Daniel Berrigan, art by Margaret Parker (San Francisco: Harper & Row, 1989). Hereafter referred to as STW.

273   Under pressure from Europe's colonial powers, Pope Clement XIV suppressed the Society of Jesus in 1773. It was restored by Pope Pius VII in 1814.

274   Daniel Berrigan, *The Mission* (New York: Harper & Row, 1986). Hereafter referred to as TM.

275   Ibid., 96.

276   Ibid., 129.

277   Ibid., 126.

278   Ibid., 20.

279   Ibid., 50–51.

280   Ibid., 130.

281   After the film's triumph at Cannes, there was a premiere in New York City, a fundraiser in support of Plowshares actions.

282   TM, 125.

283   Postcard from Argentina, August 6, 1985.

284   Letter to the author, July 24, 1985.

285   Eric Stoner, "How Friends and Family Remember Daniel Berrigan," Waging Nonviolence, May 5, 2016, http://wagingnonviolence.org.

286   Memo to the author, February 4, 2017.

287   Amy Goodman, interview with Martin Sheen, "'It Was the Happiest Day of My Life': Martin Sheen

Recalls His Arrest Alongside Father Dan Berrigan," *Democracy Now!* May 2, 2016, www.democracynow.org.

288    Letter to the author, December 23, 2016.

289    Letter to the author, February 8, 2017.

290    With thanks to John Dear for providing this previously unpublished poem.

291    Stoner, "How Friends and Family Remember Daniel Berrigan."

292    The Occupy movement was an international movement against social inequality and lack of real democracy around the world, its primary goal being to advance social and economic justice and new forms of democracy. A prime concern is how large corporations and the global financial system control the world in ways that disproportionately benefit a minority, undermine democracy, and generate instability. The first Occupy protest was Occupy Wall Street in New York City's Zuccotti Park, which began on September 17, 2011. By October 9, Occupy protests had taken place or were ongoing in 951 cities across 82 countries, and over 600 communities in the United States.

293    Letter to the author, February 2, 2017.

294    Letter to the author, December 23, 2016.

295    Memo sent to the author, February 4, 2017.

296    TWMF, 224–25; EW, 281. John Dear notes that this comes from a talk Dan gave to six hundred Jesuits at Fordham in June 1982. "The New York Province had a one-day forum for Jesuits featuring a just war theologian, a general, and Dan. The best one could say about response to Dan's talk was that, in contrast to the other two, it was muted. The lecture was published in *National Jesuit News* in September 1982."

297    BL, September 26, 2002.

298    Ibid., October 7, 2002.

299    Frida Berrigan, *It Runs in the Family*, Kindle edition, location 161–84.

300    Letter to the author, January 18, 2017.

301    Frida Berrigan, *It Runs in the Family*, Kindle edition, location 179–86.

302    TWMF, 145.

303    "Kate and Frida's Eulogy," Jonah House, www .jonahhouse.org.

304    Letter to the author, January 18, 2017.

305    *Jeremiah: The World, the Wound of God* (Minneapolis: Fortress Press, 1999), xi–xii, 1–5; EW, 245.

306    Unpublished letter, November 21, 2004.

307    EW, 31.

308    This and other quotations that follow come from a *U.S. Catholic* interview, "Is Anyone Listening to the Prophets Anymore?"

309    Luke 4:14–21.

310    Ezekiel 37:1–14.

311    EW, 252.

312    *Daniel: Under the Siege of God* (Eugene, OR: Wipf and Stock, 2009).

313    Ibid., 53; EW, 253–54.

314    EW, 30.

315    Jim Forest, *Saint George and the Dragon* (Yonkers, NY: St. Vladimir's Seminary Press, 2011).

316    Michael Baxter saw this paragraph in draft and wrote: "I remember that night with great fondness, one of the memorable nights of my life. I was struck by how Carmen and I listened while you and Tom reminisced about the early years of the Catholic Peace Fellowship. I recall asking about Archbishop Thomas Roberts and you guys telling stories about him and his role at Vatican II in making known the Franz Jägerstätter witness. I recall Carmen and I looking at each other, sharing, I think, in the experience that leads one to think and feel, 'It is good for us to be here.'"

317    Later some watercolors by Liz McAlister were added.

318    Memo to the author from John Dear, December 23, 2016. John is now a priest of the diocese of Monterey, California.

319    Letter to the author, February 13, 2017.

320    Letter to the author, January 18, 2017.

321    Letter to the author, February 3, 2017.

322    From Maureen McCafferty, "Dan Berrigan, Friend" (unpublished manuscript).

323    For the interview with Frida Berrigan, see Dwyer, "Remembering Daniel Berrigan."

324    A two-part video of Dan's funeral Mass is available on YouTube.

325    John 11:1–45.

326    NBM, 26. My thanks to Steve Kelly for providing the text of his homily.

327    Hedges, "Daniel Berrigan: Forty Years after Catonsville."

328    Robert Ellsberg, "Memories of Daniel Berrigan" (unpublished), sent to the author, January 19, 2017.

329    DD, 226.

# Index